CW01096116

The Gilt and the Gingerbread

The Gilt and the Gingerbread

An Autobiography

ANITA LESLIE

Hutchinson

London Melbourne Sydney Auckland Johannesburg

Hutchinson & Co. (Publishers) Ltd

An imprint of the Hutchinson Publishing Group

17–21 Conway Street, London W1P 5HL

Hutchinson Group (Australia) Pty Ltd
30–32 Cremorne Street, Richmond South, Victoria 3121
PO Box 151, Broadway, New South Wales 2007

Hutchinson Group (NZ) Ltd
32–34 View Road, PO Box 40-086, Glenfield, Auckland 10

Hutchinson Group (SA) (Pty) Ltd
PO Box 337, Bergvlei 2012, South Africa

First published 1981

Set in Linotron Sabon by Input Typesetting Ltd

Printed in Great Britain by The Anchor Press Ltd,
and bound by Wm Brendon & Son Ltd,
both of Tiptree, Essex

British Library Cataloguing in Publication Data

Leslie, Anita
  The Gilt and the Gingerbread
  1. Leslie, Anita   2. Great Britain – Nobility
  – Biography
  1. Title
  305.5'2   HT653.G7

ISBN 0 09 145630 4

For Fleur and Rebecca

Contents

Illustrations

1

Awakening

A bar of early sunlight slipped through the curtains as we woke, my brother and I, to wonder at a strange, cawing sound outside. We were sitting up in bed, staring at our grandfather's old rocking horse, when the door opened and in came the young, pink-faced housemaid Annie, carrying our breakfast. She walked across the nursery and pulled back the curtains. 'Look at the rooks waking,' she said in a dialect which rang strangely on our American ears.

We darted to the bay window which revealed a world we had never seen before. White mists were rising over a silvery lake and from the woods, black wings beating against a golden sunrise, flew thousands of rooks.

'They sleep in the big trees all winter time,' said Annie. 'In summer they do be scattered.'

We stood in our bare feet and gaped. Our new life had begun.

Having gobbled porridge, we crept forth to explore the corridors stretching from our nursery door in various directions. We found bedrooms which had not been used for years, and a cobwebby box-room lined with enormous hanging cupboards designed to hold dresses of the last century. The servants lived in a separate wing with its own stone staircase, at the bottom of which there was a row of bells beneath which were written 'Sir John', 'Study', 'Blue dressing room', 'Red room', etc. Miss Meade, the housekeeper, who had her own room somewhere on the stone stairs so that she could know who passed up or down, issued forth and ordered us back to what she called our proper quarters. Later on we would discover that young housemaids slept in rooms which could only be reached through that of the head housemaid, who was always over forty. Men servants inhabited a suite of their own with a separate staircase.

Impressed by Miss Meade's indignation at our appearance, we scuttled back to where we belonged. Only on the top floor might we roam around. One room frightened us. It had been that of our Uncle Norman, who had been killed five years previously, and it was kept just as he had left it. We tiptoed to the bed and timorously stroked the coverlet. A bunch of withered flowers lay on the pillow.

'Your grandmother likes to leave flowers,' said Annie. 'Her ladyship often sits alone here.'

The room had a strange sad atmosphere. In one corner stood a polo stick and Jack touched it.

'Don't,' I begged, 'don't touch. *He* might not like it.'

We scurried away.

Our grandparents and parents inhabited the big bedrooms on the floor beneath. Jack and I would be allotted the nursery-schoolroom premises, with whoever happened to be our keeper. At the moment this was a pleasant trained nurse, Miss Shinzell, who had crossed the Atlantic with us so that my brother's ear dressing could be changed professionally. She appeared in the nursery to help us dress while we crouched shivering in front of a smoky wood fire. We had been accustomed to steam heat, but no Irish houses had central-heated bedrooms. It was considered unhealthy. Our great-grandfather, who had pulled down the original Castle Leslie to build this enormous rambling house, had disapprovingly permitted the innovation of radiators in the drawing rooms, and these became tepid when two gardeners pushed wet wood into a basement furnace each afternoon. Children on the top floor were not supposed to feel the cold.

Excitement kept us warm that first morning. There was so much to take in. Arriving sleepy on the previous night, we had hardly noticed the dimly lit portico of our home, although, as we ascended the wide staircase, we had grown aware of servants' smiling faces.

I cannot remember the going to bed, only the waking up. We had returned with our parents to this Irish house because war had ended. I had been here before as a baby, but this was the first time that Jackie had been seen by retainers and staff. They gazed with tenderness and curiosity at the poor little 'heir' with his bandaged head.

Outside, in a big walled garden, we were introduced to the head gardener, Mr Bryce. He led us through locked doors in red brick walls, showed us sheds of apples and greenhouses of flowering plants (much warmer here than in our nursery), and old men stopped digging to shake us by the hand.

'Welcome,' they said in vibrant, strangely accented voices.

Then we discovered other realms – that of Jimmie Vogan, the red-bearded gamekeeper, living in his mysterious little house deep in the woods, and that of old Weir, the retired coachman, now approaching ninety, who had worked for our family since he was a boy of twelve. The sight of us evoked, however, merely tears, for Coachman Weir, in his dotage, spoke only of 'the grand old days'. This meant the forty-odd years during which he had been in charge of the horses and carriages which all travelled to London for the summer season. The disciplines which Weir had endured as a boy had duly been inflicted, in turn, on his own minions. 'If a lad left a patch of unbrushed mud on a horse's leg,' he told us, 'he would go supperless.'

Weir had always sailed the Irish Sea in charge of the horses. The under-coachman travelled a day later with the carriages. We listened to Weir's stories, but instead of relishing our presence, as did the other retainers, old Weir gazed gloomily out of the window. His house lay within the Georgian stable building, specially designed to give the head coachman a view of the whole yard.

'I mind the day,' he lamented, 'when not a weed could be seen growing in yon cobbles,' and tears began to flow. We retreated to view the remaining carriages – a brougham with exquisite ivory fittings and the sidecar on which we were promised summer outings. 'But not Miss Anita . . .' for already I had begun to sneeze.

On this first day at Castle Leslie beside the grey-green lake, we started to approve our new kingdom. We realized (because the grown-ups said so) that the rambling Victorian edifice was a disaster. Our great-grandparents had proudly carved '1878' over the coat of arms in hideous red sandstone by the front door, without realizing it was about the most shame-making date in which any house could have been constructed. But we did not care. The beautiful lake and the forests atoned for dank cold, and the five miles of wall encompassing the demesne imparted a magic secrecy. Gradually over the years I would learn the story of the human beings who had made their home on this patch of the world's surface.

The Irish Leslies started with a Scottish bishop. 'The Fighting Bishop', as he was called, devised a prayer before battle which has become famous. Imploring the Almighty to drop impartiality, he would kneel at the roadside reminding Heaven that 'though we be sinners they are not saints'.

The Fighting Bishop lived a hundred years. Married at the age of seventy, he fathered nine children. In 1665 he built the grey stone church beside the lake and his son, who also became a bishop, had printed his own sermons in booklets entitled *A Short Way with the Jews* and *A Short Way with the Catholics*. These diatribes of tedious length were intended not to encourage massacre but to demolish theological views of which he did not approve.

The Fighting Bishop's son and grandsons built around the old lakeside fortress until a rather nice Georgian house resulted. This was torn down at the insistence of our great-grandmother, the Lady Constance Dawson-Damer. Married at the age of twenty-one to John Leslie, a handsome Life Guard officer, dilettante artist and gentleman rider, who had in the same year won the Grand Military steeplechase and had a picture hung in the Royal Academy, Constance had expected to live in London, where her cronies were Landseer, Watts, Millais, Dickens and Thackeray. To her annoyance, when his elder brother died, John Leslie inherited a vast, forested, lonely Irish estate. She had, according to her husband's diaries, always shown temperament – rushing to the nearest balcony if he did not immediately do her bidding, and threatening to throw herself over.

Constance's tantrums, balcony-hanging and fainting fits became so alarming that her amenable husband agreed to pull down old Castle Leslie and build a new one. This gave her a chance to escape from the wilds of County Monaghan for two years while she and her husband travelled through Italy buying four-poster beds, Roman columns, early Italian pictures and a marble fountain adorned with cherubs to set up in front of their new abode.

Lynn was the architect chosen and although John Leslie designed the interior with that sense of proportion which he had learned during Italian travels, the Scottish baronial style of the massive exterior would cause future generations to groan.

By luck, some early Leslie had added a library and billiard room to the side of the old house, and these were retained by my great-grandfather when he embarked on his demolitions. Being an admirer of Michelangelo, he decided to link this billiard room and library to the new building by a replica of Michelangelo's colonnades around Santa Maria degli Angeli in Rome. This whimsy resulted in a very long corridor with rooms built into angles. There was even a 'chemistry room' for experiments – the walls of which had become mottled by explosions.

When Lady Constance returned to her new home, she insisted that all the eighteenth-century furniture be painted white, and a large glass conservatory had to be attached to Sir John's bewildering, but from some angles attractive, conglomeration of colonnades. According to eye-witness accounts it was in this conservatory, beneath the Venetian Madonna by Giacomo del Campagna,* that Lady Constance was wont to faint with temper when gardeners misunderstood her bidding.

Despite the fantasies of our Victorian forebears, a veil of Irish moss soon made improvements. Set amidst dreamlike forests beside that silvery lake, with the cry of wild fowl coming from mysterious swampy islands, the new limestone house donned a charm of its own. Within, Tudor and Georgian fireplaces had been salvaged and placed in fresh settings, fine plaster work covered the ceilings, marble columns were set up as in Italian palazzos, one bedroom was completely furnished with dark carved oak from a demolished Perugia *castello*, and the drawing room was embellished by a unique fireplace made by the Della Robbia brothers for the sacristy of Santa Maria Novella in Florence. (Noticing that the fifteenth-century sacristy was being pulled down, my great-grandfather had added its contents to his crates going to Ireland.)

On the drawing-room walls hung pictures by early Italian masters collected during the tours. The dark dining-room walls carried only family portraits. There were the Leslie brothers – staunch Jacobites, who accompanied the Stuart king to St Germain and had been painted there by Belle in their periwigs. And Robin and Harry Leslie, friends of Dean Swift, whom he satirized in verse – one brother being thoughtfully stingy and one carelessly generous. Swift ends the portrayal crudely:

> Old Robin all his youth a sloven
> At fifty-two when he grew loving,
> Clad in coat of Podesway,
> A flaxen wig and waist-coat gay
> Powdered from shoulder down to flank
> In country style addresses Franck.
> Twice ten years older than his wife
> Is doomed to be a Beau for life;
> Supplying those defects by dress
> Which I must leave the world to guess.

* Now in the Victoria and Albert Museum.

And there hung another Leslie whom Dr Johnson called 'a reasoner not to be reasoned with' (what a bore *he* must have been!). There also sat paunchy Charles Leslie, Member of Parliament, who fought so hard against the 1800 Union of Ireland and England. The portrait was painted by Gilbert Stuart before that artist departed to America where he produced George Washington's famous portrait.

Lady Constance bore four daughters and one boy, who was, according to the new Victorian fashion, sent to a private boarding school at the age of eight in preparation for Eton. My grandfather never recovered from the misery of those years under a sadistic headmaster. The small boy had no contact with his mother (painted lilylike by Watts), or his father engrossed in artistic projects. The headmaster must have been very kinky, for after thrashing the boys he would insist on slobbery goodnight kisses.

The four Leslie daughters, our great-aunts, did not go to school. They were all educated by the same elderly governess. They were taught nothing except how to read – but read they did. On rainy days at Castle Leslie the girls raced up and down the long corridor leading to the library and fetched what books they pleased. The old governess had no idea that handsomely bound volumes of *Tom Jones* might be improper.

Free to drive over the countryside by dog-cart, the girls made friends with country people and learned to talk that beautiful Irish dialect with its vast vocabulary translated from the Gaelic. When one of our great-aunts escorted by a groom visited a distant cottage, he allowed the horse to run away while she sat talking by the fire. The dog-cart overturned and slid down into a bog, trapping the groom underneath, while the horse lay kicking on its side.

'Are ye killed?' called cottagers who hurried to the scene.

There came a long silence while the groom constructed the correct reply. 'I'm not killed – just spaachless.'

The lessons to be learned from such pithy exactitude made it easier for girls to converse when they were 'brought out' into London society. At seventeen the daughters of the aristocracy suddenly had their hair pinned up, were laced into white evening dresses and ordered to converse with ambassadors and politicians. Girls reared in Ireland suffered less than those who had learned their social graces in the more reticent stableyards of England.

Our grandfather, known as 'Pink Jack', so rosily did his cheeks flush beneath his surprised blue eyes, left Eton to enter the Grenadier Guards.

When he met the American Miss Leonie Jerome in the Dublin house of her elder sister, Jennie Churchill, he fell immediately in love but it took him several years to get her.

My father was the eldest of their four sons and Leonie taught them all to walk on a drawing-room sofa above which hung a splendid Poussin, *The Marriage of Thetis and Peleus,* in which debauched cherubs are lowering a red canopy over the amorous couple while sunburned satyrs carry off white-thighed Baccantes with obvious intent. Meanwhile a large-bottomed infant Bacchus leers drunkenly on the riverbank. Each of Leonie's children in turn peered up at this scene, asking, 'But what are they all doing?'

My grandmother could think of no better reply than, 'Having a lovely picnic, dear.' *

Stories such as these were woven into the fabric of the house which had now become our home. Each room in turn, however forbidden or haunted, was gradually examined by us. Our mother and grandmother always expected a morning visit while they lay breakfasting in bed, fussily asking maids to hand them this or that. Gentlemen ate downstairs in the dining room, helping themselves from a marble sideboard.

Our American grandfather, to whom we had said goodbye in Vermont, had always seemed fond of us, but this Irish one appraised us coolly before asking if we would like to see the heronry. As we obviously did not know what a heronry was, Papa Jack, as the old gentleman instructed us to address him, then suggested a visit to 'the biggest badgery in Ulster'.

'And will we see badgers?' I asked.

'No,' said the new grandfather. 'You'd have to wait up all night. . . . But you can see their earth.'

Well, an earth was better than nothing, and we stared up the big holes hoping to glimpse a striped face.

'Can I wait up tonight?' asked my brother.

But Papa Jack had tired of our company. He returned us to the house and as we climbed upstairs to the nursery floor he called out, 'By the way . . . is there a rocking horse up there?'

'Yes,' we chorused — Jack guiltily, for he had pulled out its tail in order to insert some marbles which now rattled irretrievably in its wooden inside.

---

* This picture, bought by our great-grandfather in Lord Spenser's sale, was sold to Sir Hugh Lane. It now hangs in the Dublin National Gallery.

'That was *my* rocking horse when I was a child in the old house,' said our grandfather.

He had been born in 1855.

2
The American
Connection

Exactly how had we reached this mysterious house beside the silent lake and the old forest? And who were we? Jack had been born in America only two and a half years before, but I had arrived on the scene in London just before the outbreak of the 1914 war and had been greatly praised for doing so.

I was the first child of Marjorie Ide, American belle, bred of pioneer stock, and of Shane Leslie, Anglo-Irish man of letters from County Monaghan. How had they ever come together, those ill-assorted parents? Two more disparate beings could hardly be imagined.

They had met at a dinner party on Long Island and within a fortnight they became engaged. Why my father proposed marriage I shall never know. Perhaps he didn't. Perhaps he just wrote a poem that sounded like a proposal, and my mother accepted because, in her own words, 'All Long Island was agog.'

She had been born and bred in Vermont. Her father, Henry Clay Ide, had been born in 1844, eleven years before my Leslie grandfather, but he came of utterly different stock and from another world. The sixth child of a strict Puritan miller, he had to walk three miles to school and three miles back, enjoying perhaps the most beautiful scenery on earth, but, snow or sleet, he had to trudge. And when the time came he had worked his way, American fashion, through college.

Later on we would learn how these two grandfathers disapproved of each other, and how opposite were their standards. John Leslie had suffered the misery of Victorian boarding school in England but this was followed by Eton where the boys might be beaten but all regarded themselves as rather special young gentlemen. As an only son he knew himself heir to wide acres and considerable fortune. It never entered his head that a person of his caste might strive to raise himself in the world. Feeling no bent for politics he simply became an officer in the Grenadier Guards and marked time according to the dictates of London society.

He was amusing. He was a womanizer. He told stories well. He never contemplated doing a stroke of work. In fact the cleverest thing John Leslie did in his whole life was to marry the lively Leonie Jerome, younger sister of Lady Randolph Churchill.

The childhood of the two grandfathers had been harsh in different ways. I recall one story about the Vermont Ides. Little Henry tended to become overexcited as Christmas approached. He could not stop talking about the presents he hoped to get. His parents thought such expectancy should be curbed, and when he ran to his stocking on Christmas morning it contained only a stick to punish him with. 'But didn't he get *anything else*?' I would ask my mother and she never knew quite what to answer. Puritan parents were like that – they thought it their duty to crush a child for its own good.

Henry Ide knew the deep urges of a self-made man. He had a good brain and during holidays from college he taught in summer school. While boarding with a farmer by the glinting stretch of water called Shadow Lake, he fell in love with the daughter of the house. He had returned to college when her parents wrote to say that she had died suddenly of tuberculosis. Beneath her pillow they found her most precious possession – a gold watch that had hung on a chain around her neck. Beside it lay a note: 'Give this to Henry.'

So she loved him too. Henry Ide, shattered, worked harder than ever and after graduating it looked as if he might never care for another girl.

By 1869 he had become a promising lawyer. Then in 1871 he married a diminutive beauty, a blue-stocking who had also graduated at college. Her own tragic story matched his. Two years earlier Mary Melcher had been engaged to marry and she was sewing her wedding gown a few nights before the wedding when she heard knocking on the door. She put down the dress – only one sleeve remained to be stitched in – and hurried down. There she learned there had been a train disaster. A railway bridge had collapsed and her bridegroom was dead.

I remember another Ide story dating from the early days of Henry's marriage to Mary. She had bought a new bonnet and she could not resist trying to extract a compliment from her husband. This way and that she turned her head, asking what he thought of it, hoping for a little praise. But my grandfather, who adored her and thought her the most beautiful creature in existence, did not allow himself to tell the truth lest it make her vain. However much she hinted, he feigned indifference. Years later, long after she had died, he told my mother this story and added, 'If only I had not felt it wrong to give her a compliment. If only I could have that hour back.'

Those raised in the Puritan tradition could not escape it. One grandfather considered infidelity to a wife unthinkable. The other had been taught that all gentlemen kept mistresses and that it was slightly comic to be faithful to a spouse.

How could they like each other – the self-made man who cherished one woman only and the gentlemanly gallivanter? From these extremes of contrasting beliefs came Jack and I.

Mary Ide died young, leaving Henry heartsore and lonely, with three daughters on his hands. Now a judge of the Vermont Supreme Court, he accepted the post of Chief Justice of Samoa and crossed the Pacific to arbitrate over the islands in the name of the three nations who shared sovereignty at that time – Great Britain, Germany and the United States. With him went his three motherless daughters.

From the age of twelve to sixteen Mama lived among flower-garlanded, canoe-paddling Polynesians and while her elder sisters obtained a certain amount of education from a fascinating neighbour – Robert Louis Stevenson – she chose to study *nothing* and ensured that her crate of lesson books ordered from America was sent immediately in-error-on-purpose to the island's leper colony.

Robert Louis Stevenson's amusingly worded joke certificate of Adelaide's progress in French, which he gave her when she departed for the University of Chicago, stresses charm more than grammatical ability, but during her short life Adelaide remained proud of his words. The certificate survives. So does a deed that R. L. S. made out in mock legal language establishing a new birthday for Anne, who complained bitterly of having been born on Christmas Day. But Marjorie, the youngest, received no word or mention from the great man before he died and was buried on his hilltop overlooking the Pacific.

From Samoa, Judge Ide became Governor General of the Philippines and during his four years of office Marjorie acted as her father's hostess. Adelaide, the eldest sister, who had been so eager to improve her mind and had diligently obtained a university degree in Chicago, died of typhoid, and Anne, too delicate for life in the tropics, married a brilliant older man – a politician named Bourke Cockran, who had befriended the young Winston Churchill. In fact he had taught Winston his art as an orator.*

During the years in which her father remained Governor General and worked out a legal code for the Philippines, Marjorie Ide* – or Mama as I may as well call her – put in time with champagne picnics and the listing of marriage proposals. She scored one hundred names in a notebook and this was good going even when the fleets of three nations were there to help out.

But pleasure-loving Marjorie left two great memorials. One day she saw the wonderful old walls of Manila being torn down and created such a furore that their demolition was halted. Today Manila can thank Miss Ide for those old walls which are the city's pride. And animals can thank her for starting a society to combat the cruelty with which Spaniard and Filipino treated four-legged creatures. It took someone of her imperious temperament to impose such alien views.

In 1908 Judge Ide went to Madrid as ambassador and Mama discovered a certain delight in the picturesque formalities of the Spanish court, but she fretted at the restrictions. She could never go out alone, and her Irish maid Clara would shake an angry fist at Spaniards who ogled them during walks. And Mama hated bullfights. Early in 1912 she returned to America to stay with her married sister Anne. The Bourke Cockrans lived magnificently at their Long Island home, The Cedars, and among their guests happened to be an outstandingly handsome twenty-seven-year-old poet.

Marjorie had heard a certain amount about him from Bourke. The son of Sir John Leslie and Leonie Jerome, he had been brought up in the usual aristocratic British mould and then stunned his class by taking to Roman Catholicism and Irish Nationalism. Marjorie had not expected to find Shane so good-looking or so witty. It was by candlelight, entranced by the quick repartee with which he enjoyed keeping a dinner table spellbound, that she decided to cast her lasso. And after all that practice in the Pacific she knew how to go about it. Shane,

* Adlai Stevenson told the author that when he asked Winston on whom he had modelled his style in oratory Winston answered, 'It was my mother's great friend Bourke Cockran who taught me how to pull out the emotional stops – like playing an organ.'

who to date had rather scorned women, may not have realized he had become the quarry, but within a fortnight she had landed him. Snowy weather helped speed the process. Bourke's car taking them for a drive conveniently skidded and overturned into a snowdrift. By the time the chauffeur had dragged the couple out Shane and Marjorie were engaged! The announcement was made the next day. None too soon, for Marjorie's maid informed her that a long golden hair had been found on Mr Leslie's dinner jacket and 'the footmen were talking'.

Mama travelled back to Madrid to explain the romance to her father, who listened thoughtfully. He did not like the idea. He wanted her to marry an American.

On the return voyage to New York in the Cunard liner *Oceanic* Marjorie had an extraordinary experience. It was 15 May, just a month after the *Titanic* had sunk and 200 miles south of the spot where it had hit the iceberg. Marjorie was playing shuffleboard on deck when suddenly the liner swerved off course and the engines came to a halt. Running to the rail the passengers saw a lifeboat bobbing up and down on the calm sunlit sea. Mama has written her own account:

'It was only when a wave from the wash of our ship went gently over the whaleboat and the people in it didn't stir that I had my first premonition. We lowered a boat and as the first officer and the ship's doctor climbed in I asked, "Is it the *Titanic*?" "Oh, no," they said, "every boat was accounted for." They rowed over and looked at the lifebelts while our ship's engines and passengers remained in silence. Then our captain's voice from the bridge called out, "What line is it?" and the answer came, "White Star, sir."

'In silence they rowed back to the liner for a prayer book and the weighted flags and canvas for a burial at sea.

'Standing by my rail and looking down into the boat, I could see the occupants, whose hair had been bleached fair by the salt water and sun. One man was in evening dress with an overcoat with a fur collar. He was lying in the stern, with his legs over one seat and feet under another as if for purchase. Beside him in the same position lay a stoker, while in the bow in navy-blue jersey and trousers was a young seaman.

'Our boat returned to them, and the doctor read the burial service. Then the bodies were lifted and placed in the canvases. But as they took hold of the young seaman's arms to lift him, one long white arm pulled completely out of the blue sleeve.

'When lifted aboard to be taken back to New York the lifeboat was proved to be the *Titanic*'s Number Fifteen. In the bottom of it were women's wedding rings, side-combs, a man's walking stick and a baby's comforter. As our engines restarted, the stewards went around the decks beating gongs for a long-delayed lunch. But only the children aboard could swallow.'

In the following month, June 1912, Marjorie and Shane were married in the Bourke Cockrans' flower-filled conservatory on Long Island. As Marjorie had never been baptized, and this omission complicated the service, my mother had the unusual experience of being baptized on her wedding day in her white satin wedding gown.

The honeymoon couple sailed back across the Atlantic to stay at the American embassy in Madrid. King Alphonse and Queen Ena asked Marjorie to bring her spouse to tea. Handsome Shane might be, but his crest of dark hair stood up untidily and Marjorie surreptitiously pinned it down with one of her hair slides. Busy scribbling, he never noticed and they left for the palace. When in the middle of polite conversation an object landed plop into a cup of tea, the King and Queen gazed apprehensively at the ceiling. Bombs and assassination gadgets were only too prevalent, and no one could imagine how this object could fall out of a chandelier. Marjorie did not dare confess for twenty years.

In the autumn my parents settled in London. They lived near to Shane's aunt, Jennie Churchill, in a small house in Bayswater. Here, at 10 Talbot Square, I came into the world. No one then went to hospital to have babies. Doctors wearing tailcoats drove to the house and nurses flounced in frilled caps while the housemaids threw hysterics.

Apparently my arrival was fraught with difficulties and Pa 'carried on no-how'. Eventually he fell into exhausted sleep on a sofa and when my weeping Aunt Anne ascended to the drawing room to await news a curious sight met her eyes. In the doorway stood Clara, my mother's Irish maid, shaking her fist at the unconscious figure. Logical reaction to a male! Just as everyone reached their wits' end I arrived. Aunt Jennie donated two of Winston's white cambric dresses, but these had been made for a plump one-year-old, so Aunt Anne hastened to order a hand-embroidered layette in Paris.

My mother thought that the act of reproduction conferred on her the right to talk of nothing else. This idiosyncrasy exasperated London society where money, servants, illness and children were considered conversational anathema. The great hostesses of Mayfair could hardly be expected to appreciate the fact that ebullient Marjorie, who had spent ten years in the Pacific, had little time for conventions. When introduced by those star turns of the Edwardian ballrooms, her mother-in-law Leonie Leslie and her aunt-in-law Jennie Churchill, Marjorie held forth on what interested her at the moment. And for the first six months after she became a mother, the subject happened to be *me*.

While a uniformed nurse pushed my pram in Hyde Park, Mama became her graceful self for that last London season which ran into Armageddon. It was, according to all accounts, the hottest summer in memory and the number of balls seemed to increase each night. With interesting invitations pouring in, Marjorie Ide felt that she had married not only a strangely attractive man but one who brought her to the world's hub.

When July ended and the houses began to close down, she took me over to Ireland where it was usual for 'family' to rest in a 'family home' till the next social round began. She was there in Castle Leslie while the newspapers grew ominous and Leonie fussed over her daily post – for friends were writing their opinions from every capital in Europe. Our grandfather and his son Shane seldom spoke to each other, but now they went for long walks around the estate and the farm men and gardeners and foresters kept asking, 'Might it mean war?'

It was during this summer that my father, who boasted that he had as an undergraduate walked fifty-six miles in a day from Cambridge to Berkhamsted, broke his own record by walking sixty miles between dawn and sunset – from Dublin to Gorey. He broke eggs in his boots to prevent blisters. This kind of activity maddened Mama, who did not consider such behaviour husbandly or poetical.

A curious situation had occurred in the Leslie family. When the eldest son, my father, had become a Roman Catholic he signed away his inheritance. So violent were his religious inclinations that at twenty-one he declared he never wanted to own *anything*, nor had he any intention of marriage. He wished to devote his life to Ireland, untrammelled by possessions. Taking up politics and encouraged by Winston, who favoured Home Rule, he had stood for Londonderry as an Irish Nationalist and been defeated. Then, feeling he could do more by writing poetry and charming America into some understanding of the complex Irish–English situation, he had crossed the Atlantic to visit Bourke Cockran. We know the rest.

When Shane outraged the Protestant ascendancy of Ulster, the entail on the Leslie estates was broken so that the inheritance passed to his brother Norman – delightful, intelligent, sporting. conventional Norman, famed polo-player, and captain in the Rifle Brigade. The legal transaction was expensive and irrevocable. When Shane explained to Marjorie that Castle Leslie would not be his, she did not mind. The place struck her as 'moody'. When she produced me – a girl child who could not inherit anyway – she felt only relief that Shane had chucked his inheritance. 1914 was to change all that. Within a few months Norman would be killed and within a few years Castle Leslie would lie within a new country – the Irish Free State which became the Republic of Ireland.

My mother and father were together at Glaslough during that autumn when the first staggering losses of the war began. The Leslie boys had grown up intimate with the red-bearded gamekeeper, Jimmie Vogan. Jimmie had taught them to shoot and to fish and the name of every wild bird. One evening Jimmie Vogan looked in at the basement kitchen of Castle Leslie to tell the servants, 'Captain Norman is home. I saw him on the path outside and he in uniform.' That night, my mother (who was not psychic) awoke in the carved Italian four-poster of the red room where she and my father slept. To her surprise she saw Norman walking through the room smiling. In the half-light she woke my father. 'Norman is back,' she said sleepily, and he puzzled. No one was there. It would be strange indeed if his brother should enter without knocking.

The following afternoon a yellow envelope arrived for my grandfather. He tore it open, threw it on the floor and went up to his room without speaking. Norman had been his favourite son. He was everyone's favourite really, a laughing, happy man. Even Shane, who did not care for many people, adored him. Leonie never got over the loss.

The mode of Norman's death was typical of those early days before the battering of trench warfare had begun. An attack had been ordered and, being an officer, Norman walked ahead waving his men on with his cane. A sniper got him and he died instantly. The engraved sword given him by Prince Arthur, Duke of Connaught, must have been by his side for it was found long afterwards in the mud by a farmer's wife and returned to HRH who placed it in Norman's mother's hands.

After Norman's death the women of the family yearned to *do something*. Leonie volunteered to serve mugs of tea at Victoria Station, and my mother travelled back to London, with me and the nurse, to join a bandage-rolling class in someone's drawing room. The cold gloom of that winter in London filled her with despair. As the casualty lists rolled in and newspapers printed the names of slain thousands, Marjorie saw the England into which she had married disintegrating. Was it possible that only last summer she had been dancing with these men who were now dying in England's volunteer armies?

Shane, unhinged by the loss of his brother, hurried over to France to find Norman's body and lay it in a grave near Armentières. Then he enlisted with the nearest unit and found himself used as an interpreter, but after a few days' training he was suddenly made an ambulance driver on roads that were slithery and mud-covered. Brakes and accelerator remained indistinguishable to the heart-stricken poet; and wounded soldiers complained when he landed them in ditches. Pa was sent back to England to join a mule-transport unit preparing to go to the Dardanelles. Winston was still First Lord of the Admiralty. All the cousins were fighting. Hugh Frewen and Jack Churchill, officers in Gallipoli, were sending eye-witness accounts of the horrors there. The only girl to be produced by the Jerome sisters, Clare Sheridan, was soon to lose her husband in the Battle of Loos.

Marjorie booked passage for herself, her baby, her lady's maid Clara and my nanny to cross the Atlantic and leave all this misery. Before sailing she wrote a short cable to Anne and Bourke Cockran: 'Gosh. I'm coming.' She took it to Paddington post office. Standing at the head of the queue, she began to wish she had worded it differently. When the post office clerk read her message aloud and said, 'What does GOSH mean? You are not allowed to use code words,' my mother felt herself blushing. For the unsmiling queue could overhear.

Mama let her house to Lady Gwendeline Churchill, Winston's sister-in-law, who was my godmother, and set sail with many trunks for New York. Pa's mule unit had already left England. He was badly kicked before even reaching Marseilles. Mules, however, were better suited to his handling than motor cars.

During the next three years we lived with the Bourke Cockrans at their lovely house on Long Island, or in Vermont with my American Grandpa Ide. My English nurse had an insatiable desire for me to wear lace frocks and she saw that Aunt Anne, rich and childless and herself exquisitely gowned, could be cajoled into endless extravagance. Eventually my mother insisted that my dresses be counted. There were eighty-two!

I can remember right back into my third year. Every day I would be changed at teatime into one of these dresses and taken downstairs.

My mother's greatest friend, Alice Longworth, the daughter of President Theodore Roosevelt, often came to tea in Bourke's Washington house. When I raced around she said how awful I was. Mama flared up. 'Better than toad-eyed Roosevelts.' Alice understood injured maternal pride and next day a tiny silver teaset arrived from her – the kind to be placed in a glass case, not the toy box.

Despite the petting of Mama's friends, my childhood remained unpleasurable. Not only was I overdressed, I was also overfed and this resulted in agonizing nights of asthma for which no petting could compensate. None of my aunt's expensive doctors could diagnose the cause.

To start with, my favourite man was my mother's father. He would give me horse rides on his button-booted foot and lead me through the snow around his Vermont house to watch the maple trees being tapped for syrup. But eventually he hurt me grievously.

I had been taken to some crowded place wearing a white gaberdine coat trimmed with beaver and a beaver bonnet with matching muff. Suddenly I found myself hemmed in by the crowd, lost and overwhelmed by fear. The memory surges back – the primeval terror of a baby-thing left by the tribe alone on the desolate face of the earth. A woman pointed at me. Strangers stared sympathetically. Muff in hand, damn beaver bonnet over one eye, I opened my mouth and bawled. Then suddenly I saw Grandpa Ide just behind me. He was shaking with laughter at my anguish and I never quite forgave him.

Around my third birthday I had to endure a painful blow. My English nurse was sent away because she talked so much that it annoyed my mother. She had been my whole world – and suddenly she vanished. When after a few weeks she returned for nursery tea, joy flooded my being for I thought she had come back for good. When she left I screamed until my mother grumbled, 'This is what comes of having her back to see the child – she mustn't come again.' I have never seen that nanny since, and never forgotten my loneliness without her.

For a time in Washington I had a black nurse called Lucinda, whose mother had been a slave. When she pulled me on a sledge downhill, the sledge kept hurting her heels and I laughed. 'It sure is not nice to laugh when people get hurt,' Lucinda reproved me. And I still feel the shame.

Then, for some reason, I was put in the charge of a trained nurse. A strange shadow was approaching. Grown-ups whispered and pushed me away when they talked. My lack of security increased. One evening, tiptoeing down the corridor, I entered the forbidden room which held something to do with whatever threatened to displace me. I saw a wickerwork bassinet on wooden wheels with a frill inside the hood. Climbing onto a table I lowered myself into it. The door burst open and a grown-up hurtled in. I don't suppose I was actually carried away by the scruff of the neck, but that is what it felt like.

I recall nothing more until after my brother Jack had been born. His poor little jaw had been pulled open by the cord which got wound around him in the womb, resulting in an inability to close his mouth for months. I watched surreptitiously and as he received a great deal of attention I too started drooling. This maddened my mother and I was slapped and scolded. Mingled emotions filled me – jealousy, frustration and resentment.

Where was my father during all this? I can only remember seeing him once. Kicked by mules and fevered by mosquitoes, he had been sent to a military hospital at Malta and there his mother Leonie travelled out to nurse him. (Families were encouraged to undertake such junketings during that war.) When eventually the authorities sent him back to England he was implored to abandon his military activities. Instead he worked in Washington with the British ambassador, Sir Cecil Spring-Rice, who was striving to bring America into the war. As an Irish Nationalist, a cousin of Winston Churchill and a brother-in-law of Bourke Cockran, my father seemed to be in touch with all factions – with John Redmond, who had brought his Irish Nationalists into the war, and with the anti-British Irish Americans. My mother only saw her husband on brief visits and the unhappy Shane of those days was very different from the entertaining young man she had married.

However, Jack arrived and as Norman had been killed and the entail turned topsy-turvy, our Leslie grandfather decided to make this baby his heir. I heard that Grandmother Leonie in Ireland had driven around the estate giving tea packets to tenants and that bonfires were lit to celebrate Jack's birth – all because he was a *boy*! Puzzling, when girls were so much nicer.

The urge to own certain objects reveals an ugly streak in my nature. I desired things with passion. One day a boy showed me his toy watch bought at the five-and-ten-cent store. It had hands that could be wound round and round all day. How I coveted that watch on its elastic metal snappable bracelet! When kind Uncle Bourke asked what I would like as a present, I immediately chirruped: 'A REAL GOLD WATCH.' He must have been puzzled at such early rapacity, but next week he placed a box in my hands and I tore open the paper. *What a disappointment*! There lay a wristwatch on a black ribbon, in no wise resembling that from the ten-cent store, and when I began non-stop winding some grown-up snatched it away.

Truth? I found it difficult to understand exactly what truth meant. I always told lies if they were what people wanted to hear. It had become my habit on summer evenings at The Cedars to creep down to the dining room before dinner parties and partake of the pink and white peppermints which lay in silver dishes on the table. One night Mama swooped into the dining room and found me.

'Have you been stealing peppermints?' she asked.

'No,' I answered firmly.

'Blow,' said my mother.

Innocently I puffed in her face.

'You have been eating peppermints. You told a *lie*.'

I wanted to slink away and let her forget about it but this was not allowed. My mother kept me with her until all the guests were seated at dinner. Then the story was repeated aloud and while I nearly died of shame, every person in turn, while trying to restrain laughter, pulled a long face and made some remark about telling the truth. The worst moment of all came when Uncle Bourke, whom I worshipped, turned his blazing blue eye on me and asked outright, 'Did you really tell a lie?'

How I longed to lie again, to say, 'No, I didn't!' But I was trapped and now my hanging head and scarlet cheeks evoked yet more laughter. It took me years to realize how my mother knew I had been eating peppermints when she said, 'Blow.' However I lied more carefully henceforth.

But then came an incident when truth seemed immensely important and no one took my side. A footman enjoyed baiting me. Usually my mealtime bibs were pink, but on this occasion I had wandered onto the verandah wearing a blue one.

'Ha, ha – a blue bib – you must be a boy.'

'I'm not, I'm a girl.'

'You can't be if the bib is blue – you're a boy.'

'But I'm not. . . .'

The argument continued. A sense of outrage filled me. The footman went on teasing while I spluttered and wept. Sammy, the black boy who cut logs and made ice-cream in a tub, came by and listened. He laughed too.

'A boy – '

'No, I'm a girl.'

I stamped my feet and they laughed louder than ever. The injustice of it – the denial of *truth*! I knew I was a girl and the blue bib could not change it. I ran to the cook for confirmation but even she laughed.

All through these years, as far back as I can remember, the grown-ups were talking about the war. I often dreamed of it and strangely enough in those childhood dreams I saw exactly what Flanders fields must have looked like – muddy desolation under a grey sky – and I knew the sense of fear and danger. I also used to dream that I got up in the night and flew out of the window. So vivid were these dreams that I had to learn not to tell the grown-ups or they started that chant: 'But you weren't really flying. You were asleep.' I *was* flying. I could remember it.

On the whole I must have talked too much. On a train journey Mama offered me ten cents to keep quiet. I thought it over and then said, 'Thanks, but I'd rather talk.'

There came one morning in Central Park which I never had to describe. The describing was done by my mother. Grandpa Ide had taken a New York apartment for us at the corner of 59th Street and Fifth Avenue, and one morning Mama was putting on her hat and looking out of her bedroom window to watch our new nurse pushing Jack in his pram beside which I walked. Then she noticed the nurse running with her load to a rustic summerhouse while I appeared to be dragged along by one hand. A low chain bordered the path and beside this, four or five feet from us, something that looked like an enormous sheep dog was keeping pace. Mama hurried out and met policemen, who told her that a grizzly bear had escaped from the zoo and mauled two soldiers who tried to capture him. Mama screamed that she must rescue her children but the policemen held her back until troops arrived with a net and caught the poor animal. Meanwhile in the summerhouse we suffered from our nurse's infectious fear, until soldiers waved us to come out. During the chase the park zoo-keeper had died of heart failure. He was lying just inside the gate with newspaper under his head. A grizzly bear *and* a dead grown-up made a splendid morning!

Later on I was sent to kindergarten and here I learned the agonies

31

of the untalented. We sat at wooden tables in a big room, and teachers distributed modelling clay. The class was told to make *nails*. The teacher, whom I hoped to impress, came around and said, 'Yours looks like a carrot.' Tears filled my eyes. Henceforth I *hated* kindergarten.

We were in Vermont when the Armistice came. My brother and I marched out to see the parade down Main Street in St Johnsbury. Jackie had a drum which I coveted and I was given a bugle I didn't want. A man dressed up as the Kaiser went by on a cart, trying to be funny but we could not see the joke. Jackie banged his drum for days. Then it was taken away and he bellowed. The end of the war disappointed us both.

When we returned to New York, my parents both came down with that Spanish flu which killed millions. My poor little brother, too, had had Spanish flu, followed in his case by pneumonia and then by an operation on his ear for a mastoid. I remember driving across Central Park with the nurse of the moment, who kept whispering to her companion about the likelihood of my being left alone in the world. Without quite understanding the word orphan I felt chills down my spine.

Eventually one of my mother's more unlikable friends took me to stay with her own little boy. When she took us walking in Central Park and told me not to suck 'germ-covered icicles' I disobediently continued to lick. She then took me home and put me to bed in the middle of the day as a punishment. The room where I lay was large and cold. After a time she grew anxious and entered to lay a fur coat over me. I hated the tickle and tried chewing the collar. Later that evening there were cries of 'My mink coat will never be the same again,' followed by smacks with a hairbrush. Hairbrushes were much in my life by now. The next 'trained nurse' used to pounce when I crept out of bed at night to see what was going on. She would drag me back – while belabouring me in my nightgown. Mummy and Daddy were obviously having their Spanish flu elsewhere, for my screams would have wakened the dead.

Then I was sent on a farewell visit to Grandpa Ide in Vermont. It must have been in the February of 1919 for the country was snow-covered. I went around solemnly explaining that we were off to Europe *for ever*. I did not know about England or Ireland – only about Europe where they made war. Grandpa Ide gave me a big box for the voyage. In it there was a surprise present for every day at sea – seven presents.

And then we congregated at the New York docks with cries of 'All aboard', which filled me with such excitement I began an asthma attack. My mother's Vuiton trunks, covered with the maker's initials, were being stowed in a luggage room. There were siren blasts and the noise of rattling chains. Gasping for breath, I pressed my nose against a porthole and watched America disappear. When the liner got out into the Atlantic, my wheezing subsided but the special non-allergic mattress would not fit my bunk. I opened the first of Grandpa Ide's seven presents. It was a red celluloid heart on a red chain – an object most glamorous to childish eyes.

My mother was given special treatment on the Cunarder. She never travelled anywhere without special tables, special attention and special friends. She and our father graced the captain's table. Jackie and I and Miss Shinzell, our nurse, sat in ordinary places. My early desire to become the cynosure of all eyes had been replaced by sneakiness, but at three years Jack still wanted to show off. When taken to the dining saloon, his head swathed in bandages, he aroused a fair amount of comment, but he wished to make an indelible impression, and in this he succeeded. Having sat down, napkin around throat, he assessed his audience. Then when a plateful of spinach was placed before him he lifted up the whole green mess in his hands and washed his face in it. The expressions of consternation down that long table made up for the mortification of nice Miss Shinzell, who hurried her charge away with his blue eyes gleaming through a green mask.

My brother must have been in a traumatic state after his painful mastoid operation. Reading the baby book proudly kept by our mother, it seems amazing that after Spanish flu and pneumonia and a mastoid, followed by vaccination *and* tonsil removal, he managed to survive at all. Mama and the delicate Aunt Anne had become keen on doctoring and Uncle Bourke was dangerously rich. Specialists were given *carte blanche* when they talked about the dangers of taking children to Europe unvaccinated and complete with tonsils.

My mother, her maid Clara, Miss Shinzell, my bandaged brother Jack – these are the people I remember all through that journey, but not my father. That attractive man, whom I heard so much about, was on board the liner, but he never spoke to us or came near us. I cannot even remember his good looks. Later, I would learn that he had just published a book of reminiscences, *The End of a Chapter*. He had scribbled out his own memories while in hospital in Malta. Then, in

America, he threw the pages into a wastepaper basket. My mother found them and took them to her friend Charles Scribner, the publisher. Looking through an old edition I am struck by the final paragraph which so perfectly described the world which was melting around us and which we would see a little of in the years to come. Pa wrote: 'I had witnessed the suicide of a civilization called Christian and the travail of a new era to which no gods have been as yet rash enough to give their name.'

Our grandmother – that legendary Leonie Leslie – whom we had heard talked about ever since we could remember – had travelled to Liverpool to meet us and, strong as a horse herself, she gazed with horror at the grandson who toddled off the boat, his head swathed in bandages. She did not yet know that he had been rendered stone deaf in one ear. She expressed more dismay when a large canvas roll was manhandled down the gangway and my mother explained that owing to asthma I could only sleep on a special flock mattress!

From Liverpool we travelled to Belfast, and from there a sixty-mile train journey ended at the little station called Glaslough. We tumbled out onto the platform and the stationmaster and porter bade us welcome. How well we would come to know and love those Victorian-Gothic station buildings which our great-grandfather had designed when he permitted the railway to be laid across his land. He had also insisted that the station be built where it suited his convenience – four miles from Tynan in County Armagh and seven miles from the town of Monaghan. As yet, in that spring of 1919, no Border had been designated and the Six Counties had not been carved out of the ancient nine-county kingdom of Ulster.

As it was dark when we arrived we hardly registered the welcoming voices. A horse-drawn vehicle of some sort took us through the rainy night, past lodge gates, and eventually we reached a big front door that stood open with light streaming out. The servants and retainers thronged the stone-floored hall. 'Miss Anita' they called me – a mode of address new to my ears – and I heard them remarking with sympathy on the bandaged head of 'Master Jack, him that will live here in time to come.' They were all around – these people who seemed to know and like us. Spoilt and sickly as we were, we became aware of wondrous kindness even as they carried us upstairs.

3
Irish Childhood

Our light-hearted days at Castle Leslie continued for a month or so while Miss Shinzell was still needed to change Jack's ear dressings. Poor little fellow, he was always in trouble. Soon after our arrival he bounced with such exuberance on his pot that it broke and the pieces cut his behind. As there was no telephone, a boy had to bicycle off to summon the doctor, for stitches were necessary. I peeked through a chintz screen and watched Mama, tearful and in evening dress, cramming chocolates down his roaring throat while the doctor plied a needle. After that dressings had to be applied fore and aft. But eventually Miss Shinzell departed and a grim nursery governess arrived from Belgium.

Miss Butler was dressed in black bombazine. Fanatically religious, she had been chosen with an idea of giving us good French accents. Grandmother Leonie was distressed at our strident American voices – she kept begging me not to call the farm cock a rooster – so, although we had never even heard of a French language, Miss Butler, who had been with the same Belgian family for twenty years, was engaged to impart culture to the nursery. What a bigoted old brute she was! And how she disliked the Leslies! We were incarcerated with her on the nursery floor and I have wondered since what Mama would have thought if she had known Miss Butler's ideas on religious education. Unfortunately for me, I had attained five years of age and an ordeal called 'lessons' now began. Miss Butler was supposed to teach me to read and write. She did not seem to know that it might be as well to teach the alphabet first. I can see now the primer she used – the dismal black and white picture with DOG written beneath and the following page with CAT. Frightened and frozen, I began to memorize whole

35

words as if they were hieroglyphics and, as I had a good memory, when anyone read me a printed page I could soon recite it, catching wildly at one look of the top line. I was all alone with this odious woman and she never thought of explaining that letters represent sounds. Sums puzzled me as much as letters. I had a slow, methodical little mind and wanted to know exactly how things fitted together. Miss Butler never explained – merely rapped my knuckles and made me cry with bewilderment.

This was nothing, however, to the religious horrors she unfolded. Obviously she suffered at finding herself in a Protestant family in which only my father and more lately my mother were Catholic converts. In those days parents seldom visited the schoolroom. My mother would have swooned had she seen the illustrated catechism into which Miss Butler thrust my terrified nose. There were full plates of Limbo, Purgatory and Hell. Limbo was macabre, but Purgatory warmed up, and Hell was shown with demons busy at every sort of torture. To date I had been rather keen on Baby Jesus. Now, baby no longer, but a bearded surveyor of demons, pitchforks and flames, Jesus frightened me. The things I could not help doing became 'sins' – mortal sin or venial sin – how difficult to tell the difference! And if you dropped dead without repenting of a mortal sin you got burned in fire *for ever*. Now was it a mortal sin to steal those ginger biscuits? And had I repented *enough*?

These dilemmas cast a lurid aspect over the nursery floor. Our only respites occurred outside with the country people, or in the drawing room at teatime when we went down to meet my grandmother's guests. For a brief interval a playmate arrived for me. This was Peter Scott,* tough son of the explorer who had lost his life at the South Pole. Peter was older and bigger and immensely strong. I admired him while sizzling with jealousy. Peter's mother, determined that her son should grow up hardy, would not allow him to wear ordinary clothes. In the coldest weather he was clad in loose canvas short trousers and a tunic embroidered by her in wool. I begged my mother to allow me the same garb – I was sick of leather gaiters and mufflers – but Mama refused. 'Do you want to be covered with long golden hair like Peter – just look at his arms and legs?' Yes, that was just what I did want.

We enjoyed the routine of luncheon in the grown-up dining room, although sitting at a separate table. The room impressed us with its

---

* Now Sir Peter Scott, head of Wild Life International.

dark green walls hung with family portraits. In fact it looked then as it does now – the same old mirrors, the same marble fireplace, the same green velvet curtains. Over one door was an oil painting of a lady in a satin gown which I heard my father discussing with guests. 'And this,' he was saying, 'is my grandmother's grandmother painted by herself – she wasn't a bad artist.' I stared up at the portrait. My father continued, 'She became Lady Portarlington. Her sisters raked in two other peers but they couldn't be sure of the catch. One can tell that by what their grandmother wrote.' * Their grandmother was the famous Lady Mary Wortley Montagu, who had stringent ideas concerning the education of girls.

I have since looked up the letters he used to read aloud and quote Lady Mary Wortley Montagu's actual phrase in a letter to her daughter, who had married Prime Minister Lord Bute: 'I look upon my granddaughters as sort of lay nuns; destiny may have laid up other things for them, but they have no reason to expect to pass their time otherwise than their aunts do at present, and I know by experience it is in the power of study not only to make solitude tolerable but agreeable. . . . The ultimate end of *your* education was to make you a good wife (and I have the comfort to hear that you are one). Hers ought to be to make her happy in a virgin state.' The words were beyond me but not the laughter. I realized it was important to be learned. Then you did not have to depend on what that distant ancestress called 'the lottery'.

Lady Mary Wortley Montagu continued, 'The same characters are formed by the same lessons, which inclines me to think (if I dare say it) that nature has not placed us in an inferior rank to men, no more than the females of other animals.'

If I dare say it? I would say it. *I* would disdain 'the lottery' and learn to read and write. No gentlemen would wonder if they deigned to consider *me*. I would be quite 'as good as the females of other animals'. Resolving thus, I took a deep, if wheezy, breath.

That summer of 1919, while Europe was licking her wounds after the terrible war, passed peacefully enough at Glaslough, although we heard much talk about gun-running. On our daily walks Miss Butler warned us not to run on ahead for the woods were 'full of men hiding'. This frightened us pleasurably.

* Eventually these ugly ducklings managed to become Countess Macartney, Duchess of Manchester, and Countess of Portarlington.

More disturbing was Miss Butler's insistence on the mode in which we should contemplate death. I was only five years old when I picked up a dead rook on the grass and ran proudly showing it. 'Throw it away – it is dead and full of worms, as you will be.' Excitement turned to disgust as I flung the bird down. Full of worms? *And* being burned on hot coals? Death, which had seemed an adventure on the lines of those flying dreams, changed its aspect. Beneath her high-piled hair and big felt hat held on by long pins, Miss Butler watched my discomfiture with sadistic triumph.

I longed for a dog and eventually we were allowed to bring one of the keepers' labradors into the house. He seemed gratified by his new quarters. Every day we walked him with Billy, a sealyham, who had been left in the charge of the housekeeper, Miss Meade, by our absent Uncle Seymour. Billy was inclined to take small-dog liberties and snap at the labrador. One afternoon Miss Butler remarked, 'What a nice shiny coat that labrador has!' As if he understood her remark, the sealyham snapped offensively, and suddenly the big dog turned and carried him yapping into flood water. There in full view of us all he deliberately held Billy down until he drowned. It was a shattering experience for children and I have never heard of such a thing since. When I ran screaming to the house, Mama came out on the stairs, anxiously asking, 'What on earth is the matter?'

'He's dead, he's dead,' was all I could gasp.

Mama began to tremble, 'Who is dead? Jackie?'

'No,' I choked out, 'Billy is dead. Drowned.'

At this Miss Meade, the housekeeper, who had been listening over the bannisters, proceeded to have hysterics. While Mama collapsed with relief, Miss Meade wept and moaned. 'Mr Seymour will never come back to the place.' Poor dear, she worshipped dogs, but Seymour had forgotten Billy's existence. Miss Butler appeared with a tear-stained Jackie to corroborate the extraordinary story. The labrador returned in disgrace to the kennels and our nursery remained dogless henceforth.

In the autumn came new battalions of rooks to argue noisily over winter quarters. In the Great Wood, as we called that primeval patch which was all that remained of the Forest of Truagh, lay the biggest rookery in Ireland. Throughout September and October, thousands of black cawing birds would swirl in, interspersed with jackdaws who added a curiously different note. All turned together as if on a word of command. We would watch them dipping and circling over the lake during sunset. After half an hour of racket suddenly they would settle.

Later, in the gloaming, one or two tired birds always arrived, separately and silently, to find a perch. 'Look, the last rook,' we would call as dark descended. 'No, another one – the last rook of all.' Then night fell and no sound came from the lake except the occasional startled cry of waterfowl.

A new aunt arrived for Christmas and the whole house vibrated with her personality. Aunt Jennie was our grandmother's sister. Although she had a jolly husband known as Colonel Montagu Porch, the servants called her Lady Randolph, and Miss Butler was full of derisory insinuations. We loved Aunt Jennie – age meant nothing to us if people were over twelve. In our eyes this gorgeous apparition with her shining eyes was no older than the dapper 'Porchy', twenty years younger than herself. He took us out to watch the planting of special trees and she coaxed my brother to sing in his little true-toned treble. This he would do shyly hiding under a table but the notes never wavered. When Aunt Jennie and Granny Leonie sat side by side at the Bechstein piano and sought to develop our ear, we sat spellbound.

Convalescent from asthma, I was allowed to lie on a sofa by the fire in my mother's red bedroom and there Aunt Jennie and she would gossip about gentlemen. I listened intently and later on tried artlessly to join the grown-up conversation downstairs. 'And was he a good lover?' I once asked. Jaws dropped. Stony silence. The innocence of a five-year-old made it impossible to remonstrate *or* to continue talking. 'Take the brat away,' said someone. Only Aunt Jennie's lips twitched.

And then came the debâcle with Miss Butler. Our mother had, since her girlhood in Samoa, admired beautiful human bodies. She thought her children looked adorable naked. It was too cold in Ireland to run around the lawns in this state, but she decided Jack and I should have our bath together. Five and three? Well, maybe we *were* getting rather old – certainly Miss Butler thought so. Thunderous of countenance, she would obey orders and scurry us along the corridor to the mahogany-encased bath tub of the nursery floor. But she could not let well alone. While we splashed in pristine innocence she kept telling Jack *not to look down*. Curiosity caused him to bend over, staring between his legs. What was there to see? I could not fathom what she was hinting at, but eventually the little boy twigged, and with a naughty smile pointed to himself. The reaction was just as he had hoped. Miss Butler slapped his hand and threatened retribution. So it was that when

Mama brought Aunt Jennie to see the darlings being soaped, Jack stood up and gleefully *pointed* between his little legs. 'Well, what is there so interesting?' asked Mama. Miss Butler stood back rolling her eyes, while Aunt Jennie, who had been examining through lorgnettes a lifesize photograph of herself on the wall outside the nursery bathroom, came in to view this scene with her humorous smile. We were aware of Mama and Miss Butler at odds with each other and of Aunt Jennie's sympathy. What was said I shall never know, but Miss Butler won. That was the last time we were allowed a bath together.

Occasionally we were driven to play with seven-year-old Oriel Scudamore at Castle Shane, a Victorian-Gothic house lying deep in its forest, five miles away. One morning at nursery breakfast the news reached us that Castle Shane was burning down. The grown-ups hurried around looking grim and in the afternoon we went to see the smoking ruin. Oriel's tear-streaked mother was directing firemen and police to search for her jewellery in the ashes. Charles II's prayer book had been burned with other precious volumes in the library and a pet Pekinese had succumbed. We watched the activities unmoved. The burning happened to suit our book, for Oriel and her governess came to stay with us at Castle Leslie and she was dressed in my clothes until her mother could purchase more.

When Oriel departed we were left with a variety of childless neighbours – Lord Caledon three miles away, Sir James Stronge four. Perhaps the jolliest outing was to Rossmore Castle near Monaghan town. This vast Victorian edifice had developed dry rot. Mushrooms grew on the drawing-room ceiling and when we left we had to wipe our feet on a mat impregnated with disinfectant so as not to spread the culture to other houses! Cheerful Lord Rossmore would welcome us and show where his father, a famed if eccentric sportsman, had held a midnight steeplechase by full moon.

Once Granny Leonie drove me a whole thirty miles to Enniskillen and there we had tea with Lord Belmore and his five unmarried sisters all over sixty. I have never forgotten the outing because the Ladies Lowry-Corry talked with a curious hissing intake of breath and on the way home my grandmother told me that was how genteel people spoke in early Victorian times. She added, 'Did you see them walk out of the room in precedence, according to age?' Of course I hadn't, nor had I taken much notice of Castle Coole,* the most austerely beautiful Pal-

* Castle Coole is now owned by the National Trust and open to the public.

ladian house in Ireland. I did register the flock of resident greylag geese unique in the British Isles, but for the rest I could but observe Lady Violet spooning honey onto my toast with peculiar hisses.

The Earl and Countess of Belmore, parents of this strange brood, had married in 1861, to produce three sons and seven daughters. None of them married, except one girl who ran away with the colonel of the regiment stationed nearby, a gentleman they considered 'below her station', so she was never spoken to again. The present Lord Belmore, fifth Earl, of elephantine proportions, lived in the graceful dreamlike house with six remaining sisters, whom he bullied. Each girl had been given one London season and when she found no suitor of equal rank returned to the Irish demesne for ever.

The bachelor brothers, who were also of vast stature, hung around the place. Nothing ever happened. Nothing could happen. One of the six sisters drowned herself in the lake and when the butler announced the news at breakfast, her brother, Lord Belmore, reportedly said, 'Well, don't stand there, man. Bring in the porridge.'

In the summer of 1920 my mother found the forests of Monaghan overpowering so she took me away for sea air. For the first time in her life Mama travelled without a lady's maid. We climbed into a train at Glaslough and changed twice to reach Bundoran, the Donegal resort seventy miles away, which had a big hotel and a famous golf course. My mother enjoyed golf – but not on this occasion. When the sidecar delivered us at the hotel, no maids or waiters remained and over the entrance had been painted a black hand – the Sinn Fein warning to 'Get Out'. A manager of some sort warily led us to our bedroom overlooking the Atlantic. The same manager served us bacon and eggs for dinner, and next morning he carried more bacon and eggs into the dining room for breakfast. There had been explosions during the night – when the railway station was blown up. The other guests in the dining room complained they did not know how to get away. Instead of a trip to the beach, Mama marched me into the town. She was looking for a post office from which to dispatch telegrams. But the post office, like all the shops, remained closed. Then she looked for a chemist. This also was closed and had a bullet hole through the plate-glass window. Mama recoiled. There were no trains running and no method of sending a message. Happily the hotel could replenish the supply of eggs and bacon. Several nights passed and I enjoyed the drama. There were no other children around but the constant whisperings and twitterings of the grown-ups, the bangs in the night and the atmosphere of vague danger seemed delicious.

On our last night came more explosions and we could see a house in flames in the town. Someone knocked at our door. 'It's the Sinn Feiners,' whispered Mama and hid her rings in the soap dish. But it was just a nice old colonel (who had, like my mother, come there to play golf), telling her not to be afraid. We went back to bed and Mama pulled a mattress from a spare bed over the window, 'to stop stray bullets', she said.

Next morning the manager produced a man who offered to drive us forty miles to a shooting box we owned in the village of Pettigo in County Donegal. After fixing the price we set off over the bumpy roads. Frightened or resentful, the driver never spoke all the way. When we reached our house in Pettigo village, he flung out our suitcases and the smart American golf clubs, pocketed his fee and drove away without a word.

Knowing a caretaker lived there, Mama tapped at the front door. The door opened an inch and out came the barrel of a shotgun.

'What do you want?' asked my grandfather's voice.

'Papa Jack, it's Marjorie!'

'Good God, what are you doing here?'

We went in and recounted our adventures. It may seem extraordinary that at the beginning of a civil war my mother should be trying to play golf and my grandfather trying to catch trout – but so it was.

Soon after this, Mama reckoned she'd had enough of Ireland and we travelled back to her London house in Talbot Square. Aunt Jennie lived five minutes away in Westbourne Street, and when the detested Miss Butler took us walking in Kensington Gardens we passed her door, and often, though not often enough, looked in for tea. How can one describe the magnetism of Jennie's personality? What was it that made her so different from other human beings? Originally she had held men captive by her beauty, but at this stage she had reached her late sixties. The beauty must have gone, but we children – primitive creatures – felt the fire and the charm.

Over Aunt Jennie's doorstep lay another world. Even the doorknobs, made from the backs of old watches, were gloriously sensuous to the touch, and she kept the electric light bulbs painted yellow. 'One must always pretend the sun is shining even when it isn't,' she said. There were many treasures that children could play with, and a piano on which she could always win our attention. Above all, there was the excitement of her presence.

Walks in the park seemed boring after the Irish countryside, but they were alleviated by stops at No. 8 Westbourne Street. Miss Butler collected a clique of dismal governess friends in the park. I heard her discussing the length of my mother's skirts. They were, she thought, too short. A real lady, she said, wore long skirts and low heels. Mama's skirts were getting shorter and shorter as her slim American legs evoked increasing compliments.

In the hot June of 1921 things in our house began to go wrong. We heard that Aunt Jennie had broken her ankle, and then one day, on returning from the park, we learned that Grandpa Ide had died in America. Children accept death lightly and we had not seen him for two years. We rushed into our mother's bedroom where she and her sister Anne were weeping and our voices caused them distress. 'You cannot realize what's happened or you would not have a face like that,' exclaimed my mother, and I felt ashamed. She had recently become unapproachable and a week later she vanished. The servants hinted that there might soon be 'a little sister for Miss Anita'. But on the morning that the whistle rang in our nursery and a maid snatched at the speaking tube, it was to relay different news. 'A brother for Master Jackie.' I went into a sulk.

An hour later the whistle rang again. 'Lady Randolph is dead. . . .' That afternoon we passed her door. People were going in and out – Winston, his brother Jack, and Granny Leonie in tears with Auntie Clara, her other sister. Papa brushed by us looking distraught. We did not immediately grasp that we would never enter that house again.

For a few days the grown-ups appeared to be out of their minds. Bourke Cockran took us to Harrods and bought a lot of expensive toys but that did not compensate for the emotional turmoil. Our mother had been shattered by her father's death a week before her own caesarian operation. And her sister Anne over in London for the occasion suffered grievously at having left him alone in Vermont. Grandpa Ide's last words in the pains of angina had been, 'Don't tell Marjorie about me.'

Granny Leonie had been at the hospital holding her son's hand during the caesarian when *her* sister died unexpectedly. Beloved, brave Jennie had suffered septicaemia and amputation after breaking her ankle. She had been getting better and Winston had just cabled Porchy that the danger was over when, handing her breakfast tray back to the nurse, Jennie said, 'Mrs Leslie's operation is just over. I wonder what the baby is.' Then she added, 'The hot-water bottle has burst. . . ,' lay back and closed her eyes. An artery had given way.

Our visit to the Hospital of St John and St Elizabeth, where the new arrival lay in a cot, could hardly have been less entertaining. We were shown a baby yellow with jaundice and horribly grimacing, and allowed to enter our mother's room but not approach her bed. Then we saw our father – he who never spoke to us – having a black armband removed by Granny Leonie in the corridor. 'Don't let her know about Jennie. Her own father is enough.'

In those days children were not told how babies came and we never caught on. Seeing an empty cardboard box which had carried flowers, we thought that baby brother had arrived in that.

Bourke Cockran rented a country house for the rest of the summer and there we all trooped with two nurses added to the retinue – a nanny to look after the baby and a trained nurse to care for Mama, who recovered her elegance but not her energy.

When autumn came it was decided to winter on the Riviera. Mama, her maid, and baby brother with his nanny would travel out to San Remo by train. Miss Butler departed and a new governess arrived on the scene. My grandmother engaged this not very prepossessing person because she was young. The story she told of the governess she did *not* employ wrings one's heart. This woman had been with the children of the great singer Chaliapin. At the interview Granny Leonie thought her too old for a winter in Ireland and made excuses. The governess burst into tears. 'It's because I'm too old – I'll never get another job!' Compassionately my grandmother pressed a fiver into her hand but did not relent. The story reveals the heart-rending situation of elderly governesses in those days. Jackie went off to Ireland with his new Miss, and because San Remo was supposed to benefit asthma I joined that frolic.

The dagger of mortification has carved one episode of this journey deep in my memory. Nanny travelled, of course, with a battery of baby-feeding and washing accoutrements and I, aged seven by now, had not only my own anti-asthma mattress but, as Mama did not allow her children to use train lavatories, my own pot. I was seated thereon in our sleeping compartment when the ticket-collector came along. Hysterical with embarrassment, I leaped up, but Mama let the man in and my modesty was deeply affronted. Mama scolded me. 'Don't be silly,' she said. 'He's got rows and rows of little girls of his own at home all sitting on pots.' Those were her actual words. The vision has remained with me all through the years.

During that winter at San Remo no one noticed that I still had not learned to read. My visual memory enabled me to recite certain books by heart – *Alice in Wonderland* among them – and now I was supposed to be learning Italian. To this end I walked every day to a convent where I was the sole pupil. The nuns wore white habits with red wimples and black veils. They let me play with rabbits in their garden and at the end of four months I knew the Italian for 'bunny' and one or two other words. I was at the same time being prepared for my first communion. In Italian I recited the answer to catechism questions without having any idea of the meaning, but this did not trouble those sweet-faced nuns.

Christmas Eve proved as exciting as first communion. I was again clad in white to carry Baby Jesus in at midnight mass and lay the little effigy in a manger. This necessitated sleeping in the convent spare room hung with red brocade and reserved for bishops. I went to bed early to be woken towards midnight. Mama appeared to dress me for the service. I was extremely sleepy and she had never dressed a child in her life. I reached the chapel in a state of curious discomfort – my white dress and veil were in place, but Mama had put my two legs into one leg of my panties, so that I could only walk with tiny steps. The organ began playing and the nuns' pure voices rose in song. Baby Jesus was placed in my arms and I started up the aisle horribly aware of being the cynosure of all eyes. What an embarrassingly long time that walk took! No matter how quick my steps, I advanced at snail's pace. I saw nuns signalling and panic filled me. At last I reached the manger, laid down the plaster babe and knelt on a special prie-dieu, trying to find out what was constraining me under my dress without too much wriggling. How cross Mama became when she undressed me and discovered her mistake.

My father came to San Remo briefly. But he never spoke to me. Mimosa bloomed and my asthma continued unabated, and, despite the Riviera climate, just before we were due to return to England I developed pneumonia – a most painful disease in those days. Mama and her maid and Nanny with baby Desmond had to depart, leaving me to the charge of a trained nurse (we'd known a battalion of them by now).

We were back in London, in between governesses, when it was discovered that I could not read. At first my mother thought I was pretending stupidity. Over and over again I had read *Alice in Wonderland* out loud – I knew it by heart and could recite all the words which went with and between the illustrations, but when given *Alice Through the Looking Glass* not one syllable could I decipher.

For a time Mama rejected the unpalatable truth. Reading sessions generally occurred while she was getting dressed for dinner and when I hesitated over this new *Alice* she snatched away the book and gave me instead her box of hair combs. There must have been thirty or more jewelled combs which she stuck in her tresses. My favourite occupation lay in arranging these in order and placing a few in my own hair. But eventually she had to accept the hard fact. Her daughter, this prize child approaching eight, could not read *at all*. I had learned to memorize and to observe, but the printed page meant no more to me than hieroglyphics did to Egyptologists before the discovery of the Rosetta stone!

4
The Twenties

We could not know that we had entered a decade unique in human history. During the twenties the whole world believed that there would never be another war. No rumour of Germany's desperate troubles reached us, not even when Clare Sheridan appeared from the Baltic wearing a Cossack hat and Russian boots. Mama did not greatly like her. She resented Clare's imperious ways and said that after lending her the Talbot Square house there had 'never been a thank-you'. Actually, Clare had been too busy for thank-yous; she was plotting with my father how to run away to Soviet Russia without letting Winston know. Cousin Winston as Minister for War had been anxious to bring down the Reds and instal a moderate government in Moscow. Naturally he was furious when his glamorous cousin Clare nipped off to the Kremlin to sculpt Lenin and Trotsky. 'Fiends,' Mama called them, causing us to visualize devils with pitchforks as per the catechism.

Civil war in Ireland now rendered our Monaghan home 'dangerous for children'. My grandfather did not care; he lived on at Castle Leslie, a Protestant landlord of the old school, liked and respected by all. And my father, that passionate Nationalist – of opposite religious and political persuasion – often stayed with him during this heart-searing period. They never fell out. Father and son could argue opposing views while my grandmother – American born, intensely English in allegiance, but always sympathetic to Ireland's demand for Home Rule – would drop an occasional caustic comment. Although she regarded it as her duty to run the family home, she was bored stiff in the country and lived for political news from the capitals of Europe. She spoke French and German perfectly, and her education had equipped her for the role of ambassadress rather than the wife of a country gentleman whose estates lay too far from London to make possible the entertaining of important politicians. We children disliked sooty London and longed for the glamorous dangers of those dripping woods surrounding our home. For Castle Leslie was home – our London house merely a perch.

During 1921–22 we scarcely ever glimpsed our father, yet he must have been in and out of the house quite often, for at this time he was involved in the Anglo-Irish peace talks taking place in the studio of Sir John Lavery, the artist. Lady Lavery, a beauty whose wistful oval face would enhance Irish banknotes for fifty years, was admired both by Michael Collins and Lord Birkenhead. They met secretly under her aegis. My father attended these meetings with relish but his habit of shoving love poems to Hazel Lavery under doors, where servants invariably found them, enraged Collins, Birkenhead *and* John Lavery. Pa's heart had been given long before, not to any woman, but to Anglo-Irish understanding. When the treaty of January 1922 was about to be signed, Birkenhead remarked thoughtfully, 'This is my political death warrant.' Collins capped him: 'It is my own true death warrant I am signing.' And he was right. In the civil war which followed Michael Collins paid with his life for agreeing to terms which ardent Republicans deemed intolerable.

Clare Sheridan came to see us on her way back from Dublin, having made her name there as a journalist as well as a sculptor, by writing vivid accounts of the civil war for the American press. She alone had interviewed both Michael Collins and his opponent Rory O'Connor, the leaders who were to die in the conflict.

Incidentally, when Clare was talking about the blowing up of the Four Courts and the destruction of Ireland's historical documents, Winston made one of his typical comments – 'Well a State without archives is better than archives without a State.'

Mama was shocked by Clare, who was so obviously excited by the fighting she had witnessed.

'Don't you care about anything except getting material for your articles?' she asked.

Clare angrily answered, 'No!'

Meanwhile Granny Leonie remained at Castle Leslie 'sticking it out'. None of the servants left. 'Sure it wouldn't be fair to Sir John.' Life in the big house continued as if nothing was happening outside the demesne wall.

It was around this time that we moved to a larger London house.

Number 10 Talbot Square, in which I had been born, proved too small when a third child arrived entailing a nanny and extra nursemaid. Mama bought a mansion around the corner, 12 Westbourne Terrace, built in the 1840s, when Mayfair sneaked out along the edges of Hyde Park towards Kensington Palace. Architecturally praiseworthy, from the practical point of view these houses must have been hellish to run. The kitchen lay below ground and the servants' hall where they ate and gossiped overlooked a cavern known as 'the area' out of which ran a coal cellar under the pavement.* The men servants slept in the basement and their silver-polishing room overlooked the area steps. At least they could jeer at housemaids setting forth on days off. A windowless boxroom and sky-lighted kitchen pantries stretched out at the back and here elaborate meals were prepared. Ground level consisted of the dining room, the 'gentlemen's wash place' for after-dinner use, and a sewing room or the lady's maids' quarters. Lady's maids were different to housemaids; often French, and *always* over child-bearing age, they did not have to be kept out of the range of men servants.

We were never allowed down the dark stairway which led to the basement. From this darkness we were chased up to 'where we belonged'. I doubt if my mother went down to the kitchen more than twice in her fifteen years in this house. But although deeming such places better left unvisited, she copied Aunt Jennie and ordered the entire sunless basement to be painted 'sun yellow'.

Mrs Young, the cook, whose art became well known in London, would every morning climb four flights of stairs to stand by Mama's bedside discussing the day's meals. Food had to be taken seriously. The L-shaped drawing room occupied an entire floor as in most London houses, and in this rather magnificent room Mama placed her Murillo and the old Spanish furniture she had collected. A crystal chandelier hung from the ceiling and yellow brocade curtains framed the long french windows opening onto a balcony. There were smaller rooms called 'boudoirs' on the landings, and lavatories and housemaids' cupboards had been inserted into the back of the house. The master bedrooms lay on the next floor with a bathroom which must have been installed long after the house was built. Prior to that, hot water had to be carried up from the basement. The next flight of stairs led to the nurseries and as our schoolroom lay directly over Mama's

---

* These houses have all been smartly converted and the 'areas', now called 'patios', are full of trellis and potted plants.

bedroom, everyone, including sour-faced governesses, had to wear felt slippers until 9.30 a.m. so as not to wake her.

From the children's floor the stairs, getting meaner and narrower, went up to the maids' bedrooms and their bathroom under the slate roof. All bedrooms as well as the drawing room and dining room were heated by coal fires only. It is unlikely that the servants felt like carrying scuttles of coal up to their own sleeping quarters, so presumably over the last ninety years these rooms never knew any heating whatsoever.

This was the general layout of all London houses. Many were bigger than ours but, large or small, they must have been equally difficult for staff. Maid servants always slept at the top of the house and their meals were served in the basement. Food deliveries had to be made down the area steps and then carried to the kitchen. The men servants never ascended higher than the dining room except on rare occasions such as when preparing drawing-room tea. This meant folding tables being unfolded and a silver hot-water urn set alight.

Coal, arriving on carts pulled by dray horses, was dropped through a circular iron trap in the pavement. Thence human hands had to transport it to every fireplace. Once a week a man was employed to carry sacks of coal on his shoulders up the stairs to our nursery floor, where he poured it into a coal cupboard. I can see him now, sweating and panting as he slowly ascended. He had a nice smile and my mother said he was very poor and needed to make a few extra shillings in the evenings. So he must have volunteered for this labour after his regular day's work. Coal for the drawing room and dining room was carried by the under-housemaids in brass scuttles. Men servants did not descend to such menial work. Naturally the 'servant class' disappeared with alacrity when other methods of earning a living appeared.

Out of our sight but not out of our ken lay the problem of 'the poor'. Having spent eight years in the Pacific and four years in Spain, Mama frequently exclaimed at the horrors of poverty in a bleak climate. At Christmas time she asked a priest near Paddington to give us the name of a poor family to visit with gifts. Laden with food and toys, we arrived at dank lodgings and ascended wooden stairs to the room where an unemployed man lived with his wife and children. I suppose they were grateful. I remember the man's eyes, the deep animal distress and the terrible sour smell of that room. Told to hand presents to the children, I did so, while the misery of it all froze my heart. For a moment, an expression of wild hope flickered across the wife's face and shy smiles lit the children's as they reached out for toys.

Our mother regarded poverty as something of a disgrace. She fussed about the unfortunate while maintaining a firm American belief that such straits could be struggled out of. Somehow she reconciled this attitude with frequent comments on the nobility of Samoans. When Christian charities were explained to them, Samoans simply asked, 'How could anyone see a man hungry and not feed him?'

In that London of the twenties old soldiers were selling matches in the streets. Unemployment was the reward for ex-servicemen who had spent years in sodden trenches. There were many old sad warriors in that London of the twenties when peasoup fogs closed down and lamp-lighters shuffled by with long sticks to reach up to each gas-fed lamp post and the muffin man's bell rang in the winter dusk. For us children, servants were the real human beings. Their pleasures and sorrows became understandable, likewise their rages and faults. The remote alien world on the floors immediately beneath the nursery-schoolroom habitat had a different flavour. There lived 'the grown-ups', our parents and their friends. Mama seldom ascended the nursery stairs but we went to her bedroom or to the drawing room at teatime. We always saw her looking lovely, arrayed in velvet or chiffon tea-gowns, soignée of head and hand and foot. She tried to cheer up her French lady's maid, who found London 'tellement triste', and she enjoyed our admiration of her adornments, especially of her evening shoes of gold or silver kid with diamanté buckles over the straps which held them securely for dancing. In the evening Mama's feet shimmered ready for the Embassy Club, which was, I suppose, London's first smart night club, much frequented by the Prince of Wales and Mama's American women friends and considered 'fast' by our grandmother's generation.

Soon after we had moved house, there came a momentous event. Mama bobbed her hair! Until then her dark gold tresses had been worn in braided coils over each ear. After shearing she arrived up in our nursery – a rare event – took off her hat and said, 'Look – I've done it.'

We stared. 'Where is your hair?'

'Being made up into pieces to pin on later.'

She was afraid of breaking the news to our father – and with reason. Later on that evening we heard him wailing angrily, 'But I married you for your wonderful hair.' When they went out for dinner, with Mama tossing her head, our father sulked and would not speak.

Soon, however, many ladies began to arrive with Eton crops. They preened in the hall mirror before going up to the drawing room. Pa continued to lament his wife's tresses, but I noticed him running his fingers along feminine necks and making shingled visitors laugh with his sly remarks.

For a time after the move to Westbourne Terrace no governesses appeared. We attended school in the morning, and exercised with jolly servant girls in the afternoon. Sometimes flirtatious soldiers in uniform walked with us. Having never been to school before, we greatly enjoyed entering the Convent of the Holy Child in Cavendish Square.* Here Jack disported himself in kindergarten and I struggled manfully in my first classroom. As I still could not read and my only idea of arithmetic was to copy other girls' sum books, they teased me.

'Copycat!' my neighbours exclaimed as I peered anxiously over their shoulders. No one ever *explained* the simplest mathematical formula to me.

The convent atmosphere, when lessons did not need to be floundered through, proved a delight. We went to a chapel smelling of incense and flowers and we had end-of-term junketing when parents came to see their darlings presented with prizes. Even I got one.

In the following year we were not returned to this convent. Jack went to a boy's school off Portman Square, and a hysterical new governess, Miss Crouch, arrived to blacken my horizon. Without any training she took on the onerous task of instructing *me*, the dunce of all time. For three lugubrious hours every morning we sat in the schoolroom and I stared weepily at the yellow walls and blue linoleum while she grew crosser and crosser. But Miss Crouch had heard of an institute called the PNEU whereby children could be coached at home using excellent textbooks and copybooks grandly emblazoned PNEU in silver. I slowly managed to learn to read – haltingly because I still did not understand letters. Teaching me to write proved very heavy going because the old habit of memorizing the pattern of each page, coupled with inability to grasp the sound of letters, remained. I hated lessons. It was like trying to build a city without tools. I wanted to lay each brick neatly in place. And I couldn't.

The curriculum of the PNEU included history and geography. The latter subject pleasantly revealed how important and how safe we were, for in every atlas the enormous British Empire appeared coloured red.

* The superb Madonna by Epstein, placed over the portal, merits a moment's pause to this day.

England ran the British Empire and the people who ran England came to dinner – or so the servants said. With satisfaction I dabbed red on my paint brush and drew maps of the wide spaces that were *ours*.

Euphoria reigned. When humans, having survived a war, really believe that their species are never going to kill again – what do they do? We saw them at close range. They shake cocktails and they dance – dance the rumba, dance the black bottom, dance as darkies do. The English may not be talented at letting their flanks go, but they try hard. I remember Mama repeating the French ambassador's remark while watching a bejewelled peeress jazzing in a ballroom. 'Le derrière si gai – mais le visage tellement triste.'

Once a week Jack and I attended dancing class, but this in no way resembled a grown-up 'do'. The girls wore muslin dresses and bronze slippers, the boys black velvet trousers and frilly shirts. We waltzed and circled and did back bends. This was our sole training for the social world into which the servants assured us we would one day step.

Although we were confined to our nursery floor, hints of exciting goings-on – criticized by governesses – drifted into our ken. Each evening, to shrieks of laughter, Mama would be shaking cocktails in the drawing room. And her skirts grew shorter and shorter, revealing those spun-glass legs and narrow feet peculiar to American women. Our father was, we heard, the best conversationalist in England, but he never looked at us. We knew that he wrote books, that he was 'brilliant at the dinner table' and that he had been 'fierce for Home Rule in Ireland'.

To one of our merry Irish maids I dared put the question, 'Has Ireland got Home Rule now and is that why we have to stay in London?' The light went out of her round blue eyes. 'Sure, there's our own government now in Dublin but all the North is out of it.' I could not know that a body called the Border Commission was drawing lines around the very walls of our estate. What they were thinking about is today hard to surmise. But the British Government of the time did not appear to notice that its Commission was devising an unpatrollable 300-mile-long squiggly border around six counties which contained 40 per cent of indignant Catholic Celts. Winston innocently believed that what he called the 'rebel Protestant counties' would soon wish to join up with a united Ireland governed from Dublin, and then all would be cosy.

Winston remained a friend of Bourke Cockran and although he did not agree with Bourke's Irish philosophy, he inhaled through him the emotions of that other island, so different to England, although so ready to rally to her armed forces. When Anne and Bourke came to England they often spent the day at Winston's country home, Chartwell. After one of these excursions my aunt came back deploring the failure to arouse any form of conversation with her luncheon companion, Lawrence of Arabia. He had sat beside her with downcast eyes and never spoken a word beyond a mumbled yes or no. She tried hard but Lawrence hated feminine women, especially when they dressed in Paris. Maybe if she had been barefoot and untidy communication might have become possible.

My brother soon rose to fame in his boys' school. Unlike me Jack showed scholastic ability. Very soon he could read and with admirable curiosity he perused the instructions on a fire-extinguisher on the school stairs: 'Remove from bracket and drop on floor.' Surrounded by admiring friends, Jack managed to do exactly that. Fountains of foam gushed relentlessly from the nozzle. Masters appeared and struggled with the apparatus in vain. A nice bill for damages reached Mama.

Natural history with living demonstrations became Jack's favourite subject at this establishment. One day when we went to tea with Grandmother Leonie he took his jar of tadpoles to show her.

A very talkative lady sat in the drawing room commiserating on our father's conversion to Roman Catholicism.

'Come and say how do you do to Lady Astor,' said Grandma, and I curtseyed as I had been taught when shaking a grown-up hand.

Nancy Astor made a fuss of Jack and the fuss must have gone to his head. Anyway he showed her the tadpole jar and whispered the offer he usually reserved for other boys: 'If you give me sixpence I will swallow one.'

Lady Astor's smile froze. She did not seem able to find suitable words for an answer. Odd for one never at a loss in the House of Commons.

5
High Jinks

We could not fail to be impressed by the high jinks taking place downstairs. Our parents gave dinner parties or dined out every night of the London season. They went to the great balls which a remnant of prominent hostesses were re-imposing on a shattered world; they also attended parties where people slid downstairs on teatrays, and got mentioned in the papers. 'Shocking,' muttered Miss Crouch when Mama told us about the fun she was having. 'Children ought not to hear of such things. It puts *ideas* in their heads.'

Ideas? What sort of ideas? *We* slid down the bannisters but would not have dreamed of using a teatray. That was for grown-ups.

Fearful as she was of stimulating our imaginations, when the Tutankamen exhibition came to London Miss Crouch did not hesitate to take us to see unwrapped mummies. We had heard talk of the retribution falling on the invaders of Tutankamen's tomb and the sight of withered dead faces frightened the wits out of us. For years we woke screaming in the dark.

During these formative years we were never taken to concerts, although Granny Leonie taught us to pick out Wagner's themes on the piano and with slow unmusical fingers I tried to copy her renderings of Chopin.

Then Mama took us to our first movie. It was *Little Lord Fauntleroy* in which Mary Pickford played Dearest as well as the Little Lord. After this came a 'mistake'. Mama thought she had found a film suitable for children – no such thing as A or X in those days – but it concerned vamps and opium-smoking. We sat puzzled until a Chinaman carried an opium bowl to the heroine. Then Jack shrilled out, 'Is she going to be sick?' The audience turned their heads and Mama forced us to leave.

Charlie Chaplin's films were considered suitable, but not when Clare Sheridan was around. There was some mystery about this. We over-heard governesses' gossip. Clare had apparently been loved by Charlie *and* by Mussolini *and* by Ataturk. Winston was sore displeased at all three. Our heads spun.

Maybe my stupidity at lessons helped me to grow observant. I perceived people's emotions and my memory became sharp. One ear was always listening in on the grown-ups, the other ear recording what the servants said about them. On the sensitive untouched negative of my mind many beings engraved their personalities deeply. I can see now the woman who sold balloons at the gate of Kensington Gardens; she wore a little black bonnet and her nut-brown face would light up with a smile for every child. There would always be a moment of happy contact when she took the pennies from one's hand. 'And which colour would you like today?' She let us hesitate and choose slowly, and smilingly she exchanged the balloon when power of decision failed. The balloons did not last very long so we bought them quite often – they were not the expensive gas-filled kind that floated up in the air if you let go the string. Those were kept for indoors where footmen with long sticks could retrieve them from the ceiling.

Sometimes we were all dressed up and taken to children's parties. The ones I remember most clearly were those given by General Sir Ian Hamilton* and his gentle elderly wife, who had adopted a son and daughter. They lived in an enormous house, quite four times larger than ours, in Hyde Park Gardens. It is now the Royal Society of Literature and when occasionally I enter those august portals I remem-ber in particular one Easter party when we searched for eggs wrapped in tinsel. Mama arrived late and asked where Jack was. I did not know. Leaving the other girls twirling in their muslin frocks I accompanied her into a big empty library. There was silence in this room but at the far end she spied her small velvet-trousered son. He too was silent, and with reason. On approaching we saw that he had tried to cram a solid chocolate egg into his mouth and it had stuck. There he stood jaws wedged open, somewhat resembling a boa constrictor who has mis-judged! Mama drew the egg out with her fingers, threw it into the fire and wiped his face with her handkerchief. Jack had been rather fright-ened by the danger of this gorge and returned reluctantly to play Nuts-in-May with the others. He felt the episode might have ended in

* Commander of the land forces at Gallipoli.

death and by this time we knew only too well what happens to gluttons in hell.

Sometimes, instead of a party, one just went out to tea. This meant sugared cakes and the inevitable snob talk of nurses and governesses. We had some very grand cousins whose house was nearly as large as Sir Ian Hamilton's, and Miss Crouch took a particular pleasure in accompanying us there to chat with the grim old French governess whose sadistic domination of the schoolroom was never revealed to her parents by the chief sufferer, Kitty, who was my age. She was the daughter of Lord and Lady Kerry and they lived at 20 Mansfield Street. Elsie Kerry, the family beauty, was my father's first cousin and even I could see that her heart-shaped face and large brown eyes were unusually lovely. She had spent many happy childhood months at Castle Leslie and, although herself very conventional, I think she understood the tempestuous oddities of my father's nature. Lord Kerry, a quiet gentleman, was the heir of Lord Lansdowne, one of the great politicians of the old Tory school.*

I only saw the intimidating old man once and that was at an unfortunate moment. With incredible dexterity Jack had just broken a clock encased in a Boer War shell which stood on the grand staircase. In some way my small brother had managed to pry open the back of this shell. As the whole thing began to wobble and Kitty whispered, 'We'd better own up,' Lord Lansdowne appeared with his daughter-in-law, Lady Kerry.

'Your little cousin,' he said, 'has managed to *smash that clock*!' Our keepers had to be called and we slunk away in disgrace.

I had heard much grown-up gossip about this old man. My parents said how brave he had been to favour peace instead of forcing Germany to her knees. Kitty was the eldest of Lord Lansdowne's grandchildren. Then came Maurice, the important first boy, heir to splendid Bowood and all that went with a great name.† Dark lively Charlie followed and, finally, baby Ned who still sat roaring on his nanny's knee. Mademoiselle taught Kitty all her lessons as well as French and sketching. With envy I viewed her watercolours and the old sense of hopelessness

* Fifth Marquess of Lansdowne. Conservative leader in the House of Lords, Viceroy of India and Foreign Secretary. In 1917 he had wanted to negotiate peace without fighting to a finish. Lansdowne had lost a son in battle and he was accused of weakening because of this personal tragedy. He did not live to see two grandsons killed in 1944.
† Maurice died in an accident in 1936.

swept over me. Why when the world was so beautiful could I not sing, paint, or write poetry?

In March 1923 a cable arrived from Washington to say that Bourke Cockran had died. No trans-Atlantic telephone existed but Mama sent daily cables to her distraught sister. Bourke had been speaking in Congress that very afternoon. Anne had given him a sixty-ninth birth-day dinner inviting their oldest friends – Alice Roosevelt Longworth and her witty husband Nick, Teuila, the step-daughter of Robert Louis Stevenson, who had remained a friend since Samoan days, and a certain lawyer whose casual comment had caused Bourke (who was an Irish-man, don't forget) to give up drinking brandy thirty years before. After the celebration, Bourke complained of a headache and, turning to open a window, fell dead.

When Mama broke the news I shiveringly recalled the last summer Uncle Bourke had spent with us in London. His flashing blue eye and tremendous personality appealed to children (as to the crowds he could so brilliantly harangue), and as the giver of expensive toys he had held a special place in our estimation. But there was more to it. We had had time to grow to love him. On his last visit there had been a terrible complication. Bourke was a devout Catholic and he had rejoiced to see us, the scions of a Protestant Ulster family, brought up in what he called The Faith. One evening in London when I had been to confession and was to take Holy Communion on the morrow, he came to kiss me goodnight. As he did so he asked, 'And did you pray for me?'

'Yes,' I lied.

I had not thought about him at all, but this tendency to return the soft answer in order not to hurt a person's feelings stopped me giving the truthful reply. Now was it a mortal sin to tell that lie or only a venial sin? I was in no fit state to receive the sacrament if in a state of mortal sin. If I did so and was run over on the way home, it would be Hell for ever. Despairingly I crept out of bed and tried to discover from the governess of the moment if such a fib might be considered venial (one couldn't at midnight go to church and start confessing all over again). But she happened to be a Protestant. In dismay she listened to my story. 'I don't know about your religion,' was all she could say. I slept ill and, because I could not face explaining to grown-ups the abyss in which I had landed myself, went to Communion next day. I never dared to tell Uncle Bourke I had lied to him, and the priest at my next confession did not seem particularly interested. Now it was all over. I had risked Hell by not returning a churlish answer. Years would pass before I realized how Bourke would have regretted his own thoughtlessness in putting such a question to a child.

I was in fact, during all these years, tormented by fear. I was afraid of asthma and very much afraid of ghosts. Jack and I had been taken to see what was called 'the Bone House' in Lord Caledon's deerpark and someone told us that this ornamental summerhouse was built of human bones. We believed the myth, and when in Ireland we goaded each other to creep out and climb the demesne wall to see the Bone House by *moonlight*. The terror of this expedition which never actually took place became as bad as if it *had* taken place. In the end we believed that we *had* paid midnight visits and that human skulls were included. We lay sweating in the dark.

I was also afraid of despair. I wondered if God existed and then in a panic wondered if God knew my doubt and was going to send me to Hell because of it. Hell played a very big part in my mind – to go or not to go depended entirely on myself.

Then, at about nine years old, I had an extraordinary experience. I was kneeling in a dim little London church, in one of my black moods, when suddenly everything cleared and I became aware of myself in eternity. The revelation of a universe which had meaning came in a flash. It was impossible to retain the momentary elation but the vision remained. Unreasonable depression never assailed me again. I have always known that a sudden feeling of melancholy merely means that I am about to get flu. When later on I read of that black arid desert described by mystics as the area from which they rose to a sudden clarification of truth, I knew what they were talking about. Without having any urge to become mystic or saint, I have been glad to understand their aspirations and since that curious moment of mental release in the dark church I have accepted the existence of worlds beyond my ken.

During the summer of 1923 we did not return to Ireland. Mama rented a house in Sussex near Rye. It came, as houses did in those days, with a specified staff and this group included Myers, a chauffeur. Mama had sent to America for the Packard car inherited from her father. This dark green limousine with its let-down step for passengers looked enormous, but Mama was nothing if not game and she had decided to learn to drive. As a chauffeur came with the house it seemed the perfect opportunity. But even we children, who enjoyed bouncing, soon regarded these jaunts with apprehension. Every morning Myers would drive us to the sea for swimming and Mama, under his guidance, drove home. The noises, grindings, roars of acceleration and, above all, our mother's expression of wild-eyed horror as the Packard bounded along caused us to clutch the seats. No one was allowed to speak while she was at the wheel. Myers sat respectfully beside his Madam, occasionally grabbing at the brake. She always avoided Winchelsea, where pedestrians were considered likely to give any driver a brainstorm, but at the final unavoidable hill with its narrow twisting road called Dumb Woman's Lane, Mama would grit her teeth and the engine explosions as she changed gear grew shattering. Occasionally the car came to a jolting halt blocking the entire lane. Then Mama would cry out, 'I can't bear it. You take over.' And she would change seats with her instructor. The summer was nearly over when she returned from some teaparty triumphantly exclaiming, 'I've learned about neutral! Myers never told me!'

But eventually Mama sold her father's Packard. She said, 'I feel it wants to kill someone – it has the instinct of a man-eating tiger.'

When in Sussex we often went to stay with another set of cousins, very different from the offspring of Lady Kerry. These were the Frewens of Brede Place, whose grandmother was Clara Jerome, sister of Aunt Jennie and Granny Leonie. Their home near Hastings had been called by the architect Edwin Lutyens 'the most interesting inhabited house in England'. The walls had been built in 1350, and apart from Tudor 'improvements' two hundred years later, which included a porch around the main door with a mews where visiting gentlemen could park their hawks, no alterations had ever been made. The main Frewen home, Brickwall, an Elizabethan manor, stood in a deerpark seven miles away and Brede Place had lain intact and untouched on Frewen land for centuries. It took the American Clara Jerome to recognize its potential. She had married a younger son, Moreton Frewen, and from the moment she set eyes on this magical house inhabited by one gamekeeper, she yearned to make it her own. Procuring Brede Place, with a few hundred acres, Great-Aunt Clara proceeded to do it up. As the great beamed rooms were completely unfurnished, she frequented local auctions to acquire oak tables and four-poster beds.

The huge fourteenth-century timbers of the top floor she left revealed. Neither electricity nor plumbing was yet installed. At night we tiptoed, candle in hand, to a panelled room in the middle of which stood an earth closet. This was for ladies and children. Gentlemen were expected to walk out to the medieval jakes which overhung a steep bank leading down to the vegetable garden! We washed in basins and hip baths. Cookie and the other servants who came from the village talked in a matter-of-fact way about the ghosts which they took for granted. Returning to the empty house on a summer evening, we would hear footsteps. 'Owls,' muttered the grown-ups nervously – but we knew better.

Great-Aunt Clara's grown-up offspring – Hugh, Oswald and the fabulous cousin Clare – were coming and going. Hugh's two sons and Clare's son and daughter slept in a vast beamed bedroom with us. We were all under ten years of age. Two children would be relegated to a four-poster, and the others lay on sofas. Hugh's eldest son Roger would one day own the house. The second boy, Jerome, called Romey, was red-headed and tough. He led us into the chapel in the evenings by candlelight and, rolling his eyes, he would quote my father like a professional guide. 'Look at the traceried window. How did it survive the Tudors?' And Margaret, Clare's dark-eyed daughter, would put her arm around the little fellow. We were a very close band, hemmed in by adored and adoring servants, intimate ghosts and the strange atmosphere which Brede Place had accrued through undisturbed centuries.

Mothers, but not fathers, were around a great deal during that hot summer of 1923. Roger's Italian mother, Memy, daughter of the Duke of Mignano, would rush up trying to protect her delicate son when, brutes that we were, we knocked him down and punched his kidneys which we had been told were weak. Margaret and Dick Sheridan were able to recount blood-curdling stories of their romantic mother Clare, and we sometimes lured Oswald – Clare's bachelor brother – to play with us. A bounding naval officer, he hurled us down the steep grassy garden banks until we were bruised and breathless.

But then autumn came and the threads of our young lives, so happily plaited together, were in the grown-ups' heartless fashion torn apart. Margaret and Dick departed with their mother towards Turkey, and Roger departed with his to Italy. Romey was left alone with his old grandparents until summoned to Australia by his father.* Jack and I were taken to Paris.

---

* We never saw Jerome Frewen again for he grew up in Australia and became a bomber pilot in the Australian Air Force during the Second World War. He survived, only to be blown up when piloting for an Indian prince in 1947. I was in Brede Place when the news arrived. Unaccountably a blackbird had been trying to get into the house for three days.

This was the start of a new era. Miss Crouch left, and we realized with surprise that she had become fond of us for tears shone in her eyes when she said goodbye. The prelude to her departure haunts. A short time before we left England, Miss Crouch met a 'fellow' who asked her to marry him. She had always been the hysterical type and this event rendered her delirious. We only saw the fiancé once when he accompanied us during a walk in the park. Mama was displeased and said he looked 'common' because he wore a black and white check cap. No matter; he was a man, and he had come Miss Crouch's way. Did it really matter if governess class married working class? But what then happened mattered very much indeed.

She was Catholic, he was Protestant. It was possible to obtain a dispensation for a mixed marriage, but the Protestant had to sign an agreement that all children should be brought up Catholic, as laid down by fairly recent Vatican law. This fellow in the checked cap said the girls could be Catholic but any boys must follow his own faith – and he would not budge on this point. The terrible crisis was played out in our schoolroom. Miss Crouch threw herself on the linoleum weeping – that dark blue lino on which I remember my own pools of tears. She screamed, 'Damn the Church! Damn the Pope!' Knowing the intensity of her religious beliefs, we watched with horror. My father came upstairs and pulled Crouchie to her feet. We went to bed unable to swallow supper. We did not pity her. We were frozen.

Poor Miss Crouch! Her fellow did not relent and she never married.

In Paris Mama rented an apartment in the Avenue Kleber, and a jolly American called Major Logan appeared on the scene. We did not realize, for we scarcely ever glimpsed him, that our father had been left in England. Mama had 'had enough'. She was always surrounded by men she called 'beaux' – but now she meant business. Major Logan was very rich and very eager to marry her. All her American friends regularly stormed in and out of the divorce courts gathering fortunes as they did so. Only one thing stood in Mama's way. After marrying my father – some time after for she was never one to slip into the obvious convenient groove – she had become a Roman Catholic. This jaunt to Paris was therefore a time of agonizing indecision for her.

We children were supposed to benefit from our up-rooting by learning French. Actually we were too unhappy to learn anything. A very cross French maid took out 'les petits diables', as she called us, each day, to stand about in the small detestable Parc Monceau where architectural merit was wasted on us, but the emanations of the earth beneath our feet, which had been a charnel pit during the Revolution, penetrated our spirits. Eventually someone's retired French governess was engaged to take us out in the afternoons. She also called us 'les diables', which was probably an accurate description, and sought to enliven our intellect by visits to historic places of overpowering gloom. In the Conciergerie, where the royal family had been imprisoned, I became aware of such feelings of grief that I came home in a shivering fit. Very often when I was young a kind of radio link with past despair would hit my consciousness. I did not have to be told what Marie Antoinette suffered – the atmosphere told me. At ten years of age I did not know how to deal with this suffocating sense of other people's emotions.

Memories of the Paris winter are blurred, except that Jack took all his birthday money to a smart antiquary shop and asked to buy an Egyptian statuette, which much impressed the shopowner, who was not used to small boys with such tastes. New Year's Eve, however, remains clear and memorable. Mama went off to a fancy-dress ball, costumed as the Queen of Sheba in a sparkling sequin gown and golden turban. Jack and I, who shared a room, went to bed soon after she departed. At midnight I awoke gasping with asthma. Struggling for breath I rang the bell pull until a frightened maid arrived in her dressing-gown. Then we saw Jackie moaning with pain. Already deaf in one ear after the mastoid, he remained prone to agonizing ear abscesses. The maid wrung her hands and cried out, 'Mon Dieu, comment trouver le docteur à cette heure. . . ?' Then Mama arrived back from her ball with what she had guessed was an attack of *la grippe*. I do remember through my own acute discomfort the sight of her, still wearing her golden turban, and with the heavy blue eye make-up fashionable at the time running down her cheeks in dark tear streams, while she tried to phone for a doctor. I think one did arrive towards dawn and poor Jack was operated on next morning in the apartment.

Later on he described the horror of the anaesthetic. The doctor forcibly held a rubber mask over his face, but the gadget did not immediately work so no air or chloroform got through and he actually passed out from suffocation. Mama retired to bed for three weeks and I enjoyed one of my periodical bouts of pneumonia – I think it was the third. As we were all ill with different symptoms it was difficult to know how to react to the obsession with germs popular at that time. A trained nurse arrived to put flaming cottonwool in Von-touse jars on my back. I shrieked with terror, but the odd pulling sensation caused by the vacuum did not really hurt although purple bruise rings remained for weeks.

Then came convalescence. I still could not read without hesitation but I sewed neatly. Given pink silk and lace, I made cradles and bedcovers – not for dolls which I hated, they represented the human race – but for my stuffed animals. Someone had given me a toy kangaroo with a baby in its pouch. Removing the baby, I created for it a cradle out of cardboard covered with silk, with tiny lace-edged pillows. The French maids wondered if I was quite all there. During the long period of convalescence Jack and I decided we liked being ill. Once the pain ended we preferred being in bed to out of it. One could think and make things. It was safer.

Meanwhile our mother's moral dilemma continued. Our grandmother Leonie was appalled at the word divorce, not for religious, but for social reasons. She had been reared in an era when the revelation of marital unhappiness was considered disgraceful. Whatever happened, the outer forms must be adhered to for the family's sake. And after a lifetime of careful watching, Granny Leonie had formed the opinion that the most uncongenial temperaments could adjust as soldiers do to enforced companionship. She upheld the old Edwardian principles that within the iron strictness of social demands humans remained human. They must be allowed freedom for disciplined amours that upset no one. Divorce upset everyone. The family was riven. Children knew. Servants gave notice. In fact this deplorable American practice must – like cocktails – be avoided.

Suddenly our father appeared in Paris. Mama was having breakfast in bed when he burst into her room in one of his 'amusing moods'. At the corner of Avenue Kleber stood a seller of faded smelly violets. As he jumped out of the taxi Pa had purchased a small bedraggled bunch. These he offered kneeling on one knee. The contrast to Major Logan's enormous bouquets caught Mama's fancy. She agreed to try again. So the amiable major went out of our ken and once more we saw this handsome dark stranger who was our father entering and departing.

When spring approached Mama rented a larger apartment beside the Bois de Boulogne. And Nanny arrived with little Desmond. There had been a hold-up because after her winter in San Remo Nanny had said she could never bear to leave England again. Eventually she relented.

Now I was sent to a lycée and there I sat dolt-like amidst girls of my

Papa and Mama. Sir Shane Leslie and Marjorie Ide, in a photograph
taken in 1912

The author with her mother, Marjorie Ide

On a tricycle in Central Park,
New York, in 1917

Right: With brother Jack,
London, 1920

Above: Grandfather Henry Clay Ide

Above right: The author's grandmother, Leonie Jerome; a photograph taken in 1895

Right: Leonie Jerome with HRH the Duke of Connaught in the ducal cabin on HMS *Renown*, 1903

Below: Sir John Leslie at Glaslough, *c.* 1925

own age whose neat essays and shrill ability to read made me more conscious than ever of my own ineptitude. But the teachers thought my blank copybooks were caused by lack of French. They could not know that I was equally hopeless in English.

In the afternoons I walked in the Bois de Boulogne with several English nannies and various small boys. It was idyllic. But this contentment was shattered when Jack was sent off to boarding school in Switzerland. Great-Aunt Clara had by now recovered from the loss of her sister Jennie and, forgetting Winston's horrific experiences at a school for small boys, she was on the prowl for places in which to dump her Frewen grandsons. She discovered what was supposed to be a reputable English boys' preparatory school at Glion. Mama thought Switzerland must be 'good for ears', so poor little Jack, aged seven, was taken to the station. He looked so frightened and babyish that Mama burst into tears as the train left. Momentary emotion. I knew in my bones the misery of that small figure plucked out of the nest, and I wept through night after night thinking of him. Yet when he returned for the Easter holidays we still fought with our fists.

Our father had returned to England and Mama went out dancing every night. She loved the night clubs of Montmartre and came home late in taxis which were driven, she said, by Russian princes. Naturally she liked to sleep late. On Easter Sunday Jack and I got up early to examine our eggs. Bells were ringing in churches all over Paris when we began to snatch and punch. The noise woke Mama, who appeared sleepy and furious in what used to be called a negligée, to find her son and daughter, their faces daubed with chocolate and blood, engaged in fisticuffs. Her outrage found utterance on religious lines – how could we behave thus when all French children were praying on their knees? We remained silent and ashamed, aware of our iniquity. Aware of Easter. Aware of the church bells. And with nothing to do.

It was high summer when my Aunt Anne arrived in Paris – exquisitely turned out as usual, ready to cast aside widow's weeds and order new outfits of *demi-deuil* at the great dressmakers. Once or twice I was taken to fashion shows. Bored stiff, I put in time by noting the particular jargon which the elderly *vendeuses* used to address their clientele. When I got home I practised the gait of the mannequins. Mama watched me with amusement and in my nightgown I was called in to show off to dinner guests, who screamed with laughter at my imitation and said I should be an actress. A what? Were actresses just copycats? I thought they had to learn Shakespeare by heart!

Since Bourke's death my aunt had become even more delicate. She believed every doctor she met. At the time a man called Dr Kocher in Berne claimed to cure *everything* by injecting animal glands of some sort into human beings. Unfortunately I was caught up in this medical jamboree. Asthma and recurring pneumonia had rendered me thin and unattractive. Mama thought it would be wonderful if Dr Kocher injected glands that would make me plump and sweet, like her baby of the past. So Auntie Anne agreed to take me with her to Switzerland. On the very afternoon of our departure by train I was taken to a dentist and suddenly had four golden crowns affixed to my back teeth on which wires were hooked. Within an hour the pressure on my teeth became agonizing. I lay sleepless in the train all night with my fingers in my mouth trying to pull at the wires. When we reached Berne next day I was in a fever of pain. We drove to a big hotel and the manager, staring with horror at this woebegone child who had been holding back the wires in her mouth for hours, telephoned a Swiss dentist, who unhooked the contraption and I fell into bed ill from lack of sleep.

Once on my feet, I had to accompany Aunt Anne every morning to Dr Kocher. There, on his white couch, my aunt and I would lie in turn while he injected a hypodermic needle into our respective behinds. Heaven knows what glands he used for Auntie, but my injections were certainly not innocuous. Within the month I had grown two inches and become even less attractive.

After the morning's outing to Dr Kocher, my aunt would take me to little shops where carved wooden animals were sold. She bought me a whole collection of carved bears and these I played with during the long, dull afternoons when we were supposed to be 'resting' in our expensive hotel rooms. So bored was I that I devised a species of gymnastics for these hours. Jumping up and down on the springy mattress, I would finally soar as high as possible and then come down bang on my back. No one could hear the noise although the bed did begin to look rather peculiar.

There was a diversion when Jack arrived from his Glion boarding school. Auntie's personal maid complained of his suitcase full of dirty clothes. As he did not want to 'rest' through the long afternoon any more than I did, we tried to 'do a laundry'. Tiptoeing into my aunt's bathroom we plunged Jack's clothes into a full tub and did our best with scented soap until the rinsing got out of hand. Then I jammed the plug and the shower. As the bath overflowed, the floor became covered with water, which we tried to mop up using bathtowels squeezed down the toilet, but the inflow increased. Auntie's nap was disturbed by strange sounds and suddenly she appeared in the bathroom with the special black eyemask, devised to shut out light during daytime slumbers, pushed up on her forehead. 'Oh, children. . . !' cried our gentle aunt as we gazed up from the flood. Bells were rung and hotel maids appeared cold-eyed. Cold also was the expression of our aunt's personal maid who had grumbled about the suitcase.

When I returned to Paris Mama came to the station eager and expectant. She really thought Dr Kocher's hypodermic needle would have made me prettier. Her face fell.

'But now she's sea-green,' she wailed. 'Why has my daughter turned sea-green?'

Back to England I travelled with Nanny and baby brother. We were to return to our haven in Ireland, and there I could forget the ignominy of being the family failure.

For some reason Mama remained in Paris while closing down her summer apartment in Boulevard Flandrin and she was alone there when Zizi the leopard escaped from the Jardin des Plantes. Great efforts were made to capture him alive. Baited traps were laid throughout the Bois de Boulogne but they remained untouched. On his fifth day of freedom Zizi made his way to our flat and came face to face with the caretaker, who hurled a mug of coffee at him and ran upstairs to shout from a window. His cries brought the soldiers who were searching for the animal. They shot Zizi dead in the tree outside our door. Mama wrote how sad she felt at seeing the beautiful body stretched on the doorstep but she had to laugh at the reason the bait had failed. The autopsy revealed that Zizi's stomach was full of the paws of alley cats.

So it was that we returned to the bliss of Monaghan woods. There I could run for hours amidst the huge trees – the tallest larch in Ireland, my father would boast, the oldest oak, the greatest Douglas – but it was not their size that overwhelmed me. Alone in the woods, I had only to stare up into the leaves to know a sensation of leaving my body. I swept into tree form. Once or twice when autumn had turned our forests to red-gold I came home so exalted by this feeling of transformation, of having roots and waving arms of rustling leaves, that I was unable to speak at the tea table where people were forever pressing scones on one.

'What *no* hot scones! But you must. Whatever will the cook think?'

6
Curious Schooldays

In my parents' view schools performed the same function that kennels did for dogs. They were places where pets could be conveniently deposited while their owners travelled. It did not occur to Mama that inspections might be made or questions asked.

She never let her house but occasionally she loaned it to friends, complete with her servants who were to be 'kept happy by entertaining'. According to my mother, servants needed to be amused by streams of the great and famous. If allowed to hang around with nothing to gossip about they got bored and 'went all to pot'. The luxury of gossip could seldom have been in short supply in our household. The personalities who came to dinner might have been specially picked as fodder for this sport.

My parents' most intimate friends were Lord and Lady Dufferin, who owned an immense family place in Northern Ireland. The expense of keeping up Clandeboye prevented them running a town house, so they would move in to 12 Westbourne Terrace whenever Mama went on a trip. Sometimes Brenda Dufferin and Mama went off together on what they called 'a Paris spree'. They both enjoyed night clubs more than their husbands did. Lord Dufferin and Pa regarded with amused tolerance their wives' delight in dancing. However, I heard my mother saying that 'Brenda's English views on lovers' shocked her. Brenda could not see why married women should not have lovers, whereas Mama deemed only *beaux* permissible. Lovers and beaux? One term was English, one American. The basic gymnastic difference evaded me.

Before my twelfth Christmas Brenda and Mama must have fancied a spree, or maybe they were on one of their economy jags ordering new gowns in Paris because clothes were so much cheaper there than in London! I was, therefore, in the middle of term, sent to my first boarding school. This happened to be the nearest to hand, the Convent of the Assumption in Kensington Square. Mama drove me there by taxi and I was left, terrified and tearful, with a bustling nun, who led me to a dormitory in which I was allotted a bed in a cubicle. When we undressed, white curtains on an iron framework were pulled around each bed. We slept incarcerated in these roofless tents. I presume windows were opened somewhere for air.

Lessons did not worry me at this convent for I was put in a class of children younger than myself and to hold our interest all work was done in different-coloured inks from four pots, violet, green, red and blue. This simple device I understood. The weeks passed in a dream, with frequent trips, white-veiled, to the chapel where the pure clear singing mingled with the perfume of incense and flowers alleviated my first impression of having been deposited in Sing Sing.

And I made a friend. She was a pale little creature with blond hair and intense religious fervour. After a nun's talk about the joy of early death I remarked in goody-goody tones, 'How I hope to die young!' But my friend argued passionately, 'I don't. I want to live so that I can show God how much I love Him.' I felt snubbed, but I knew already that the veil was not for me.

Term ended and the girls went home for Christmas. Only this friend and I were left in the empty convent. I did not mind. There were no lessons, but the pots of ink remained and for hours each day we sat drawing in different colours. We never went out of the convent door but played occasionally in the yard. Existence was very peaceful and did not tax the brain. Suddenly, on Christmas Eve a maid called to escort me to a train, and I found myself staying in the country house of Mr and Mrs Richard Hart-Davis. Mama was already there, confined to bed. She had a special trained nurse in attendance as well as her lady's maid. Her Paris spree had resulted in gastroenteritis – due, she said, to one mouthful of watercress.

Mrs Hart-Davis was the sister of politician Duff Cooper, who had married Lady Diana Manners, the greatest beauty of the age. Sybil's unusual face I can see still, with straight hair cut like Joan of Arc's, the lamplight always glowing, it seemed, just behind her, while my father roared with laughter at her jokes. The Hart-Davises must have accepted their house party with good nature. Maybe troops of servants make good nature easier. As well as Ma and Pa they had to suffer a French lady's maid, a trained nurse and Jack and myself. Their own son and daughter – tall, handsome Rupert and ethereal Deirdre – had reached their late teens, so were beings of a different planet who could not be expected to communicate with children. We watched them, listened to them, but never exchanged a word. For recreation Jack and I baptized their dogs and cats with water, and occasionally held a slap-up funeral for a frozen bird.

It was Mrs Hart-Davis who taught me to sew patchwork squares. She was herself intent on 'making a dressing-gown for Rupert to wear swanking around Oxford'. * She taught me to cut out squares of paper and tack each one with velvet or brocade. When a heap of coloured squares lay ready they could be sewn together. A new creative urge assaulted me. Here was something beautiful I could make with my own hands. In those days every house had a sewing room littered with scraps of silk. I too planned a dressing-gown – or maybe an evening cloak of shimmering patchwork. Sybil Hart-Davis taught me to lay dark velvet squares beside paler satins and golden brocades. Through-out days of wet snow I sat in a haze, visualizing my future wardrobe. But as the rainbow piece increased in size its shape became odder. Not quite square, resembling rather a crooked diamond – it became evident that cutting and shaping would become complicated. Even Sybil suggested that it might be best used as a cushion cover. I could not accept her verdict. Raiding wastebaskets, I determined to work on through the years until a swathe of shimmering colours existed – then it could be cut into any garment I chose, or even just used as a tent.

In the midst of these deliberations we were whisked off again to Paris. Jack was put on the school train for Switzerland and I found myself once more in a rented apartment. I spent only a few nights there, for this abode was quickly pronounced 'too small for children', so a new boarding school had to be found. The trained nurse had disappeared but Mama was still unwell. The onus of finding a dumping ground for me fell to my father, who thought he would inquire of a friend of his, Father Hemmick,† a well-known American priest of private fortune, who owned a house in the Rue Monsieur and entertained in style while taking a particular interest in young male ballet dancers. Pa hurried me to Father Hemmick and to my delight I was asked if I wanted to go to the bathroom. I had heard much of this

* Does Sir Rupert Hart-Davis, the eminent publisher, remember how that glittering robe turned out?
† Later Monsignor Hemmick, Canon of St Peter's.

famous bathroom from Mama, who when dining there had once mistakenly turned a tap which shot a high fountain from the bidet and drenched her evening dress. The walls were of red lacquer, the bath and other objects of merit being encased in panels to match. Carefully avoiding contact with the bidet, I studied the decor with interest and felt it unlikely that any other child had ever entered those portals.

When Pa asked Father Hemmick about schools the immediate response was, 'She must go to my friends, the Mesdemoiselles San Carlos – three Spanish sisters of the nobility, fallen on hard times. They have the nicest school in Paris. Of course they will take her.'

I listened with misgivings while he telephoned to make arrangements, but no means of protest existed. A young man showed us to the door – obviously one of the rescued ballet dancers for he had blue on his flickering eyelids.

'Shall we call a taxi?'

'No,' said my father, 'I like walking.'

So we walked home without speaking, miles it seemed, and Mama learned with relief that I could be removed from her dressing room.

Next morning I departed and never saw that flat again. The Mesdemoiselles San Carlos happened to run a finishing school for young ladies about to step into the world. I was twelve. Father Hemmick did not know that any difference existed between girls of twelve and eighteen.

We reached a large house standing in a garden and the elderly sisters received me with rapture. Le Père Hemmick was one of their dearest friends and he obviously thought that, by recommending *me*, he was doing them a favour. I was led to a pleasantly furnished bedroom where a maid unpacked my clothes, and I was told I must speak to the other girls in French only. This was to prove easy, for over the next three months hardly anyone addressed me at all. At the first *déjeuner* I caused some amusement and was christened *le bébé*. Then, after a little petting, I was thrust from thought. One beautiful Spanish girl, Emmanuella, asked if I liked museums. Museums? Except for the nightmare visit to that exhibition of Egyptian mummies I knew nothing of such places.

The young ladies were exquisitely turned out. They went to the hairdresser and manicured their fingernails. I still wore woollen socks to the knee like a boy. I was an unalluring, somewhat grimy child, yet the ease with which thirty older girls could obliterate me from their consciousness hurt my feelings. Of different nationalities, the young ladies obeyed rules by striving to converse in French, and every morning we sat reading grammars and doing the most horrible *devoirs*.

Because I was so young nothing remarkable was expected of me, but I chaffed with boredom. At midday we were loosed in the garden and several maidens trotted around to improve their figures. I could really run. Round and round the garden I raced, but nobody noticed, no one spoke to me. At lunch I sat silent while the others chattered and giggled and held their heads while thinking how to produce French phrases correctly. Then came the afternoon outing which, being educational, most of them hated. They said that picture galleries made their backs and feet ache. I tagged along listening, until my back and feet began to ache too. The Mesdemoiselles San Carlos commented, 'Such pains are caused by high heels.' The pathetic elderly ladies, hired as chaperons for these outings, looked as if their feet also hurt, but not from the wearing of high heels.

Home we came for tea and a study hour in classrooms. The others changed into silk dresses for dinner, but I, *le bébé*, had a tray brought to my room by a maid. What hours I spent alone in that bedroom and how tired I grew of my French grammar! I still had the patchwork but there were no wastebaskets of glittering remnants in this establishment, and I was not encouraged to sew. Instead I perused in rotation the three English books I had brought with me. These were *The Canterbury Tales*, marvellously illustrated with woodcuts, *Legends of Greece and Rome*, in a green leather binding, and my favourite, *The Wind in the Willows*. Only three books, and they had to last me three months. Of course, in my usual way, I had learned them by heart so I was not really reading at all but turning over the pages and visualizing with an intensity which increased with repetition. I imposed a certain discipline. I never permitted myself the luxury of reading *The Wind in the Willows* twice running – the books had to be kept in order.

The good-natured, amiable Mesdemoiselles San Carlos did not inspect or confiscate our reading matter, at least not mine. They gave me two volumes of that detestable *Bibliothèque Rose*, but *Les Malheures de Sophie* could not compete with the ancient world, and *Memoires d'un An* seemed horribly cruel. In the end I selected my favourite chapters – and the magic episode when Toad and Water Rat meet the great god Pan became more real to me than daily life.

My bitterest disappointment occurred when sweet Emmanuella asked if I would sit with her when they went to the opera. How excited I was! Every week the young ladies were to be taken to what I visualized as a wonderful kind of circus where the music would be that taught me by Granny Leonie in Ireland. And *someone* had asked me to sit beside her! I actually had a friend! Shaking out my navy-blue dress, I wondered if it was good enough for evening. Unfortunately I mentioned this during tea, and Emmanuella was called to the San Carlos' sitting room. She came out with tears in her brown eyes. We always spoke in French for she knew no English and I no Spanish.

'Je suis desolée,' she began. 'J'ai fait une erreur. . . .' The San Carlos trio had scolded her. I was too young for opera. I must remain in my room while the others went off. *I*, who already knew many of the themes and overtures and longed to see the glories of an actual performance! It was no good protesting; I had to sit bleakly before my supper tray hearing the taxis arrive and the laughing voices of those gossamer butterflies as they flitted down the stairs. Even Mr Toad could not hold my attention that night.

The term ended at last and I suppose I had learned a few French phrases. I never saw Emmanuella again but her invitation remains unforgotten. Now the Easter holidays were upon us, and as the apartment was so small, Jack, who had arrived from Switzerland, and I and a Norwegian girl Hedwig, who had attained the extraordinary old age of nineteen, were sent to the Château de Berchère near Chartres which the Mesdemoiselles San Carlos kept for pupils unable to return home. As soon as we arrived Hedwig hired herself a bicycle and vanished on long trips into the countryside, studying medieval churches and improving her French. Jack and I were left with absolutely nothing to do. As we were lively, inventive children, this was bound to result in trouble.

First we got into the farmyard and watched a kid being born, an event which seemed completely natural to us and never caused us to entertain the suspicion that human beings might enter this world in the same way. But Jack whispered to me that the Mesdemoiselles San Carlos, who were in residence, had heard of our presence and scolded the farmer. We wondered why. Then we were given a hutch of white rabbits to play with, presumably not in-bunny, and the naming and taming of these kept us quiet for a while. Finally, as the weather turned warm, we built a hay fort where we could spend the daylight hours imagining ourselves in historic roles. We loved the night, for electricity had not arrived and dusk meant the glow of candles and lamps. Unfortunately Jack found a clock to take to pieces and clocks were always his downfall. He could not resist unscrewing the back to see how it worked, then little wheels got lost and it became impossible to put together again. This clock had stood on the mantelpiece ticking loudly. After Jack's investigations it did not tick at all. The Mesdemoiselles San Carlos were to add a substantial sum for its repair to the bill which eventually reached our mother. Jack was an expensive son.

One day Mama motored down from Paris to see us. She came with an American friend called Mrs Betty Pell, who wore a cloche hat and, like Father Hemmick's ballet dancer, had deep blue on her eyelids. She was a Christian Scientist and a divorcée – very American. None of the English ladies we knew had ventured into either fold. Mrs Pell liked children and she roared with laughter when we kept fetching beetles for her to examine.

'These are Siamese twins,' I exclaimed, 'locked together by their tails.'

Mama grew worried. She felt it was time to tell me something before 'other girls with nasty minds' did so. I listened stonily while she discoursed on the charms of bleating lambs. Yes, I understood all that. Goats and sheep produced their young from inside, but it still did not enter my wooden head that humans might do the same, nor could I connect the beetles with sexual junketings. No matter how often Mama tried to tell me the facts, I never grasped them.*

In the evening, in golden sunshine, Mama and Mrs Pell drove back to Paris. Their car vanished in a cloud of dust. I was now to be allowed to hire a bicycle and could accompany Hedwig. Mama had said I must study Chartres cathedral, whose spires showed in the distance, and write to her about the stained glass.

How empty of traffic the straight white roads were! Hedwig's strong Scandinavian legs pedalled fast while I laboured in the heat. We spent long hours in the great dim cathedral. Hedwig marched around reading the guidebook while I felt overwhelmed by incoherent feeling. The jewelled glory of those windows and the soaring grey arches were almost more than I could bear. I just sat there and let the beauty burn me. What could I possibly write to Mama? What did one say about this sort of place?

When the holiday ended and we returned to London, Mama wished to show the small book she had given me with instructions to 'keep a diary' to Granny Leonie, who had expressed displeasure at my recent schooling. The diary proved a nasty disappointment and Mama sent

---

* So veiled was the language then used concerning sexual subjects that my cousin William Crawshay, after an explanation as to how babies arrived, asked lugubriously, 'And does this happen to gentlemen too?'

for me. She was, as usual, dressing for dinner and I stood dejectedly by the mirror while she explained what a blow it had been to read of my first visit to Chartres, 'the most wonderful cathedral in Europe that people saved up to go to see'. All I had written (in French of course, though I was almost illiterate in both languages) concerned white rabbits and the metres of blue ribbon purchased to tie around their necks. Such entries revealed a shallow mind.

I started a larger diary, but all I could bring myself to record concerned the animals in my life. Those gusts of emotion that swept through me, the urges and elations evoked by cathedrals and forests and the night sky, I could not describe.

Around this time occurred the General Strike. I remember it because my father had remained in Paris and did not immediately return. When he did so, bringing Mama a ring which she did not think much of and which he tactlessly described as a way of ridding himself of unwanted francs, they had tea together in a small room called the boudoir. I was uncomfortably present while Mama delivered sarcastic shafts.

Winston had rung up and asked if Pa could drive a tram. After my father's ambulance efforts during the war this seemed hardly a reasonable request, but Mama insisted that any man worth his salt would at the very least be driving trams. Pa listened with his bored expression, then rushed from the house and did not return for days. He had found some amusing job through one of his lady admirers, a person I had heard much about for she had left her husband and then, to Mama's delight, been left in turn by her lover. Actually I rather liked the wicked Lady X, for she had given me a kitten. Her eyes rolled and sparkled. 'False eyelashes,' said Mama. As it was then smart to paint the lids navy blue this was difficult to disprove.

When the General Strike ended and the workers had been brought to their knees, Pa sided with them. 'Don't all be cock-a-hoop,' he said. 'They've had a go and been beaten. Respect men in defeat.'

But Mama refused to entertain magnanimous thought for the 'Bolshie-minded'. It was part of her American philosophy that men who worked hard would attain their deserts. After all, her father had started in a Vermont farm and become an ambassador. She never assessed the difficulty of struggling out of poverty in England where labourers outnumbered jobs and a boy could not work his way through college. And yet, looking back, I think she reacted with more compassion to the unlucky than any other person I met in that blinkered social world.

7

Grown-Ups

Our great-grandmother, Lady Constance Leslie, died, aged ninety, in her London house in Manchester Square. She had always been amusingly outspoken. When Mama had given her a studio photograph of us children, she looked at it gravely and then handed it back saying, 'Thank you, my dear, but I cannot collect any more rubbish.'

She was descended from that Lady Mary Wortley Montagu who had written so feelingly about the 'virgin state', and just before she died she produced a short memoir which ended, 'In my youth it was not only impossible to go in a hansom cab even with a governess, we were not allowed to drive in one at all. Today life is more interesting for girls.'

Well, yes. We could now take taxis.

As we were back in London a new school had to be found for me. By luck a PNEU establishment functioned around the corner. Miss Faunce and her partner Miss Lambert happened to be teachers of genius. It is not often that great teachers fall from the sky. These two women possessed a flair out of the ordinary and a quality of charm exciting to children. Marched around for an interview, I put on my sulk face. Little did I dream that here, in a day school run for the daughters of London's upper crust, lay my salvation.

The twelve-year-old class into which I was directed contained several girls whose parents happened to be friends of my parents. There were Rosemary Peto, whose mother had been in love with Uncle Norman before he was killed in 1914, and Mary Ormsby Gore, whose father, Lord Harlech, was Minister for the Colonies. And there was Betty Shaughnessy, whose father had been killed in the war and whose step-father, Sir Piers Legh, was now equerry to the Prince of Wales.

When Betty and her brothers invited us to tea in their house which lay five minutes from ours there was always some chance of glimpsing that slim golden-haired young man who would some day be King of England. We could hang out of the nursery windows and pelt him with old toys, which he enjoyed, even if the private detective looked 'unamused'. His Royal Highness would listen patiently to Betty reciting the poems she had learned at Miss Faunce's and admire her copybooks. Royalty are trained never to show boredom and maybe this was not worse than many a banquet speech he had to sit through.

Two other girls in our class saw much more of him. Angela and Penelope Dudley Ward, whose mother was the Prince's greatest friend, could boast of going to evening theatres with their mother and the Prince. With a somewhat studied nonchalance Pempy would yawn, 'I didn't get to bed till midnight, but Uncle David insists we do our homework first.' These late hours made me even more envious than the idea of sitting in a theatre box with the Prince of Wales.

One could hardly not grow aware of 'goings-on' in the grown-up world, and there were now occasions when my father actually spoke to me. Mama and he were back in the world of Bright Young Things. I have a vivid memory of the time they went to a 'Baby Party'. Everyone had to be dressed as babies. Mama wore a romper suit which enticingly revealed those long American legs and my father was arrayed in one of my nightgowns ripped apart and stitched over his shirt and shorts. Blue ribbons were tied on the shoulders and a blue sash bound his waist with devastating effect.

Late that night I was woken by the sound of an ambulance bell. Hanging out of my bedroom window, I saw my father, still in my white nightie, being led into the front door by two men. Always overexuberant he had mimicked a child taking diving lessons, climbed on a table, slipped, and broken his collarbone. Pa, who never touched alcohol, was affected by people and applause as if they were champagne – on this occasion quite literally.

The week following this baby party proved sombre. Pa's collarbone hurt him considerably. He could not put on a jacket or sleep in comfort and when Ma tried to arrange his tie he uttered deep groans of self-pity. She was angered by the occurrence and said he had been showing off to his 'band of alley cats' (the phrase in which Mama always alluded to my father's lady admirers). I will not name them, but a couple of peeresses who were, to put it mildly, fond of the opposite sex headed the throng.

A maid walked me to school each morning – but for some reason it was considered safe for me to walk back alone for lunch. In the afternoons I was returned for tennis or swimming. A bus drove us to special establishments and we sported brown and orange school blazers and panama hats with the PNEU ribbon. I noticed how well-dressed my companions were – especially the Dudley Wards who wore striped cotton dresses with bloomers to match.

For the first time I began to enjoy lessons. We had Century Books in which to paste pictures relating to each year. Overambitious, I produced a watercolour for the year 1918, intending to make a dramatic impact with trenches, barbed wire and a pink dawn out of which flew a dove of peace. The teacher was hardly able to keep her face straight.

We learned a great deal of poetry by heart at Miss Faunce's – and this was easy for me. On the first day I was allotted a poem beginning 'Where the remote Bermudas ride / In the ocean's bosom unespied. . . .' I had no idea what the Bermudas might be – but I became aware of the sensuous delight of words.

Then came the first honey touch of approbation. Miss Faunce herself took the literature class and it was her habit to read out a chapter of Plutarch's *Lives*, commenting as she did so, and then to lay down the book and ask if any girl would stand up to give a resumé of what she had read. On that particular morning the subject was Alcibiades. Miss Faunce read well and I felt a curtain lifting in my mind. Just as I could see and feel the river in *The Wind in the Willows*, so I could see the Athens in which strolled that gorgeous youth. I raised a shy hand. The vision of Alcibiades quivered before me (naturally I did not know his predilections or how rotten he was behind the façade of good looks!). Miss Faunce remained silent while I held forth on the beauty of Alcibiades and his curls. When, dry-throated, I sat down, Miss Faunce remarked kindly, 'I wish some others would give me a paraphrase like that.' A sigh of wonder went up from the class at what a dunce could do.

The next triumph occurred at the end of term, and again I have never forgotten the stunning novelty of praise. We were told to write an essay entitled 'If there were dreams to sell – what would you buy?' This was just down my street. My entire life had become a dream. If there were dreams to sell I'd choose a green valley with a running brook, all the animals I knew would come to drink there, and some that I didn't know – deer and otter. Spring and autumn would sweep over my secret glade and every wild flower show its face in turn. I wrote what I saw in my mind's eye, then copied the pages in my best handwriting into my silver-crested PNEU exercise book.

When the day of assessment came three essays were read aloud to the assembled school. A gasp of amazement arose at my name but Miss Faunce read beautifully and sceptics were stilled. Only when she smilingly handed back my essay did I see in red ink: 'Twenty spelling mistakes – you must learn.'

Unfortunately the eye of the speller eluded me and all my life I would be plagued by the necessity to learn every English word letter by letter. I possessed the opposite of a photographic memory, yet I could on certain wavelengths visualize scenes with absolute clarity, and when I thought quietly about a human being or animal it was as if they were caught in my mind's binoculars. Their emotions entered me and often this became uncomfortable. When I read Maeterlinck's *Life of the Bee* and learned of the range of colours visible to that creature, my heart began to pound. I could half remember colours beyond the ordinary range of the human eye in strange dreams which seemed more real than reality. Such fancies were difficult to transmit but something of my dream world must have gone into the essay which Miss Faunce praised. During the next two years I tried so hard to improve my mind that Mama became irritated. She did not want an idiot for a daughter but neither did she want a bookworm.

How dismal London seemed after our Irish home! Our sole treat consisted of inviting other children to tea and for these occasions Jack and I devised an entertainment which rendered guests ill with excitement. I had discovered that it was possible to climb out of the servants' bathroom window and along a narrow ledge to the next-door roof. While governesses remained chatting in the schoolroom, we would creep up to the top floor and our friends were allowed to fill and pass out jugs of water. Carrying these I crept along the gutter with a sheer drop of forty feet beneath, and then poured the water down smoking chimneys. These pleasurable excursions, which we hoped would result in a sootfall into some unseen fireplace, went on for years. I miscalculated once and poured a jug down one of our own chimneys. On descending we discovered turmoil in Mama's bedroom. After shampooing her golden hair, she had been drying it in front of the bedroom fire when a cloud of soot descended. Maids rushed around clearing up the mess and she was with difficulty washing black dust from her tangles. Innocently we expressed sympathy, and I never risked that line of chimneys again.

By the time I reached thirteen the mere pouring of water grew tame, and to the applause of chums, I began to throw old clothes and rude notes into the open windows of servants' rooms in our neighbours' houses. Splitting our sides with laughter, we composed love letters for me to climb out and deliver.

Eventually the joke went too far. Several times we had dropped missives into the house next door and the maids there became so frightened that they complained to their mistress. I blush to recall the silly lines which caused such consternation. 'Be back soon – Big Bad Bill.' The maids were certain a cat burglar or a maniac was visiting their sleeping quarters and the old lady who owned the house called in private detectives. Imagine my shock one evening when the butler announced, 'The police are in the dining room waiting for a word with Miss Anita!' He added, 'Madam has retired to her room and wishes to see no one.'

Alone I faced two detectives and decided to answer their questions truthfully. Yes – I had climbed along the roof. Yes – I had thrown letters in open windows (I never mentioned the deluging of chimneys). Yes – I had written the note they produced. Could I prove it? No. In vain I tendered specimens of my handwriting and led the two unsmiling men to my desk in the schoolroom where I always snatched paper for our notes. Search as I might, no corresponding sheet could be found. The detectives remained unsatisfied. Such ardent pleading of guilt struck them as fishy. Meanwhile the butler was enjoying every moment. Mama did not laugh. She had been preparing to go out to dinner when the detectives called and the last I heard as she left the house was her cry of 'Why has God given me such children?'

Next morning Miss Faunce and Miss Lambert lifted their eyebrows a little when I answered roll-call. Many years later they told me that the detectives had gone to them and asked what sort of a delinquent I might be. They had been asked to compare the Big Bad Bill note with my copybook writing and had nearly died of laughter.

Our neighbour was not amused; neither would she believe my attestations. A nice old lady, she accused the detectives of bullying me into false confession and wrote to my mother saying she could not believe 'that angel-faced child' could entertain such ideas. Barricades of barbed wire were set up around her servants' windows, which eventually had to be brought down for contravening fire regulations.

Then, by an extraordinary coincidence, a real burglar broke into her basement and stole the silver. She and the maids were certain that Big Bad Bill had indeed returned. She sold the house and moved away. When my father learned this story he looked at me stonily. 'Time you grew up,' he said. I never climbed on the roof again.

Among our cousins, those on the Leslie side remained good friends, admiring us 'daredevils', but on the Jerome side we had the 'clever Churchills' to cope with as well as Clare Sheridan's brood. Randolph and Diana, Winston's oldest children, ignored us when we met. Only Sarah, who was my age, plotted rebellion. I liked Sarah, but Winston's niece Clarissa Churchill filled me with jealousy. Granny Leonie was entranced by this alabaster madonna of a girl and I remember being taken to tea with her mother, Lady Gwendeline Churchill, who was also my godmother and had given me brooches and leather-bound poetry books. On this occasion Clarissa was not to be found until Granny, going to the window and pulling back the curtain, revealed the girl, her lovely contemptuous mouth slightly curled, reading Milton. As I was so often rebuked for frivolity, Granny never let me forget that episode and used to remark how different Clarissa was to *me*.*

By day my mother and father pursued their lives in different strata of London society, but at night they entertained together. Mama belonged to the new American world of jazz and cocktails which had emerged after the First World War, while my father was turning out erudite books as well as volumes of verse in the Irish tradition. He put his hand to a few novels as well – *Doomsland*, about his Irish boyhood, *The Oppidan*, which many deemed the best book ever written about Eton College, and *The Cantab*, covering experiences at Cambridge University. Mama thought it very funny when *The Cantab* was censured by the Bishop of Clifton, but Pa asked his publishers to withdraw the entire edition, whereupon all copies in bookshops went up from five shillings to five pounds in price. I think Pa was upset by this scandal – I remember him saying, 'Don't let Nanny know.' She was, I think, the only person for whose opinion he really cared, but certainly she never read anything more sensational than her knitting magazines.

Years later, out of curiosity, I read *The Cantab* and wondered why it had caused consternation. Maybe bishops disapproved of the heroine's habit of inserting a large sapphire into her navel. I remember

* One day Clarissa would make an harmonious wife for the statesman Anthony Eden.

Lord Dufferin chaffing my father, 'How did she keep it there? Seccotine?'

An Irish childhood does something to one's toes, causing invisible roots to grow into the soil. Every holiday, carrying our parrot in its cage, we took the boat train at Euston, drove across Liverpool in a taxi, marched up a gangplank, and were led by stewardesses in starched caps to cabins where blue lights glowed all night. Travelling as a family party, we usually had at least one big cabin with four berths, where Jack and I fought to climb up the ladders. If Mama was with us a *cabin de luxe* would be booked, but these had what to us were ordinary dull beds.

Never feeling sick, we enjoyed that rough Irish Sea. Poor Nanny, a bad sailor, dreaded every crossing. Mother Sill's seasick pills would reduce her to a coma before the ship started and Desmond had to be handed over to the care of the retinue of servants accompanying us. This was the signal for 'playing up'. We thought it wildly adventurous to clamber out of the bunks and lie on the floor to watch passing feet. We fell asleep to the sound of buffeting waves and woke to the stillness of harbour. Then came the sound of chains and rope-pulling and men's voices shouting. We would eat breakfast in the dining saloon while porters came aboard shouting their numbers and carried off trunks and suitcases. The stewardess would be kind to Nanny, plying her with cups of tea, and there we were in Belfast. Taxis took us to the railway and then came that glorious hour in the train which would deposit us at Glaslough. We knew the name of every station. At Armagh, the ecclesiastical centre of Ireland, whose spires we recognized in a fever pitch of excitement, we were only eighteen miles from home – a stop at Killylea, a stop at Tynan, and then the darling little Gothic fantasy of Glaslough where the stationmaster would be the first of many friends to greet us. From then on we enjoyed a triumphal progress, saluting everyone on the road, into the village, through the lodge gates and to the front door where Miss Meade, the housekeeper, and Wells, the unsmiling English butler, received us more soberly. Three times a year we experienced the joy of return and three times the gloom of departure.

Men servants were invariably English. *Irish* butlers or valets did not seem to exist. Irishmen became labourers, soldiers or politicians; they did not wait on other men. My great-grandmother had once tried it. She imported two Irish footmen for a London season and they celebrated Queen Victoria's Jubilee by getting drunk and running down Oxford Street shouting, 'To hell with your bloody old Queen' – a terrible humiliation for the Leslies, who carried their noses high when driving forth from their Palladian mansion, Stratford House.

By 1923 the island had been divided into the Irish Free State with its green, orange and white flag, and the Six Counties under the Union Jack. A five-mile wall ran U-shaped around our estate. At its open end lay a river and a bog. This was 'The Border'. Beyond the bog lay the walls of Caledon demesne and from our hills one could see the white Nash house which now lay in a different country – different stamps, different food prices, different laws. From the bog which had suddenly become a political boundary came our turf. Over the little 'unauthorized road' one might walk or bicycle or ride a horse but only priests and doctors were permitted to drive cars.

Lord Caledon often walked the three miles between Caledon House and Castle Leslie. His mother, the Dowager Countess, lived on in her grown son's home and ruled him with a rod of iron. Her unmarried sister, Lady Charlotte Graham-Toler, came to stay each summer and they would drive over to tea in a carriage. I don't think the stables at Caledon had ever closed down to make way for that horrible innovation, a mechanical vehicle, and so the new restrictions did not affect them. Lady Caledon's carriage would take her to the station when she departed for London, and I believe she always refused to pay for a railway ticket, explaining to various bewildered ticket collectors that the train ran through Caledon land.

When Lady Caledon and Lady Charlotte visited Granny Leonie with her sister we always hung around, fascinated by their vast hats perched on coils of false hair of variegated colours. One day they were sitting out on the terrace with my grandmother's house guest, Madame Wolkoff, a Russian exile who had been lady-in-waiting to the Czarina. The subject of breakfast in bed arose. Madame Wolkoff grimly pronounced, 'If my daughter asked for breakfast in bed, I would turn her out of the house.' Mama, who had not breakfasted out of bed since the age of fifteen, flared up, 'If I was your daughter, I'd walk out of the house.' The Dowager Lady Rossmore, who was present, shrieked with laughter, but our grandmother felt that a visitor had been affronted.

The estate of Castle Leslie remained our own enchanted kingdom. The four gate lodges, amusingly built in various Victorian-Gothic styles, housed employees. Jimmie Vogan, the red-bearded gamekeeper, had died, but a new keeper took his place in the gingerbread gabled house deep in the woods above Kelvey lake – a still sheet of water, haunted, it was said, by 'the little people'.

Pa revelled in ancient legends and often took guests to a 'fairy fort' where an old storyteller would come out of his cottage and explain in his marvellous version of the English language – as rich and variegated as Shakespeare's – what the fairies liked and disliked. They could not fly over iron railway lines so there were fewer little people here since his boyhood. The fort was one of many hundreds of earth rings built in pre-Christian times for defensive purposes. The great ditch and earth walls must have been surrounded by palisades so that women and cattle could be herded in for protection. Occasionally a glorious golden adornment would be dug up, or a bronze sword found intact in Monaghan bogs. Even more moving would be the occasional discovery of a *sous-terrain* – an underground stone-built hiding place where remnants of a real 'little people' – that small dark race exterminated by the Celtic invaders – once crowded for hiding. Whether inspired by race memory or nature spirits, the leprechaun tradition lingered on in Ireland to culminate eventually in brooches and souvenirs at tourist stalls.

I had one personal encounter only. Walking alone on a winter evening, I heard small feet pattering behind me. When I stopped, they stopped – but not immediately. When I ran, they ran. I went faster and faster through the woods. Easier to recount precisely were the experiences of an old artist, Mr MacIlwaine, and our dairymaid, Miss MacAdoo, a red-headed lady weighing over eighteen stone. MacIlwaine, whose small oils of the Irish countryside occasionally travelled to exhibitions, often painted in our demesne. One evening he strolled away, leaving a sketch of Kelvey lake on his easel. When he returned the picture had been finished – 'by fairy hands', he said. Hurrying to the dairyhouse he related this to Miss MacAdoo, who laughed derisively. Next morning all her milk had turned sour. MacIlwaine, who lived to nearly a hundred, has gone, Miss MacAdoo has gone, and the breed of dairymaids has gone, but the fairy painting of Kelvey lake hangs at Castle Leslie, and it is curiously different to MacIlwaine's other work.

The head forester lived in the prettiest of the lodges and the farm steward in a big house beside the cut-stone yard with its old clock and pigeon loft. Nine men worked on the farm and four foresters planted and hewed in the woods. The walled garden with its yew hedges planted after the Crimea War by Tom Leslie sloped down to the lake.

The head gardener, Mr Bryce, inhabited his own lodge, and six old men fiddled away in the glasshouses while a couple of boys dug outside. I think that actual gardening bored Mr Bryce – what he enjoyed was tasting the grapes and peaches to see if they were sufficiently succulent for the big house, or making up sheaves of sweet-smelling lilies and heliotrope to fill the drawing room with scent. Never out of a smart suit, with a gold watch chain across his waistcoat, he seldom left the hothouses except when, to my grandmother's annoyance, he was arranging flowers in Castle Leslie. I heard her expostulating, 'Bryce ought to leave the flowers for me to do. I find him tiptoeing around my boudoir. I suppose he wants to read all my letters.' But Mr Bryce had taken control years before and he would still be stepping back to admire his own floral creations ten years hence. On occasion he attended shows and won prizes, and quite regularly he 'invented' a new dahlia which he named 'Lady Leslie' and presented to my grandmother. This did not appease her at all. She wanted the head gardener to take a spade in his hand, remove his panama hat and get out of that suit. But she could not break tradition. Head gardeners were a law unto themselves.

Meanwhile Papa, clad in green tweeds and cap, enjoyed himself with the foresters. He loved trees and the primeval forest which stretched down to the shores of our lake inspired him to write a ballad – 'The Great Wood of Truagh'. Staring from our nursery window, we learned that the lake had hardly changed since the great elk came down to drink. A fine specimen head of this extinct species dug from a nearby bog hung in the billiard room.

Holiday governesses might be employed to see that hands were washed for meals, but they had not sufficient energy to curtail our freedom. We were now big enough to be allowed to run wild and did not need watches; the farm clock or the distant rumble of the four daily trains told us the hours. Jack and I went our own ways in this wilderness. We both came close to the beauty of nature and made real friends of the country people with their laughing eyes and wonderful exactness of speech. We felt that we belonged here. The Leslies had been Members of Parliament in Dublin and argued with passion against the Union of 1800 forced through by George III. Pa had found and would proudly read out the list of landowners ready to accept bribes and peerages if they voted for that Union. Against the name of Mr Leslie of Glaslough King George's minion had been forced to record: 'Wants Nothing.'

Since that unhappy New Year's Day 1800 when the Dublin Parliament was closed and Irish Members were forced to go to Westminster, the Leslies had remained indignantly on their Monaghan estates. Eventually they sold their Dublin house and, like the rest of the country gentry, took their social life in London, but when the Famine struck they remained in Ireland and strove to feed refugees who arrived from the west. The big iron soup cauldrons still lay rusting in the farmyard. When our great-grandfather inherited the property he became a Member of Parliament, but he could not wield the influence of his forebears in Dublin. The woes of Monaghan seemed inexplicable in Westminster. So the Union of England and Ireland had thrust the Leslies into that curious vacuum called the Anglo-Irish aristocracy. But after three hundred years sitting by their lake they had become Irish – or thought they had. Jack and I simply did not feel alien. We belonged to this earth, to these trees, to this rushy lake. We were part of the landscape.

The only friends we had of our own age were John and Charlie Madden, who lived in a large fortified house, Hilton Park, twenty miles away. Very occasionally Colonel and Mrs Madden would bring their sons to lunch, and while the grown-ups strolled and gossiped we would lead our guests to the walled garden. A key from a secret drawer allowed us to sneak in by an ivy-covered door and, hidden from possible gardeners' view by ten-feet-high yew hedges, we reached the long elegant glasshouses where grew the peaches and grapes. These were only served to grown-ups and had to be saved for important visitors. The glasshouses were always locked and Mr Bryce kept the key, but ventilators remained open through which Jack and I could wriggle. We handed out the fruit to John and Charlie, and then away we would creep stuffing it into our mouths.

Mr Bryce counted everything he grew. The disappearances puzzled him. Finally he complained to Granny Leonie that *someone* from the house must have been stealing. She looked into the key drawer, and looked at me – I fled because of the dilemma into which a direct question would push me. Mama always said that she would forgive anything as long as one did not tell a lie. But when one told the truth she became so angry!

Lady Leconfield, who owned famous Petworth House in Sussex, came to stay every summer, bringing a lady's maid, but not her husband. Lord Leconfield could not move without his valet – and his valet disliked Ireland. Violet Leconfield was very tall and angular and, said Gran, because she had no children, rather sad. Once or twice Lady

Leconfield asked me to sit with her, saying wistfully, 'Tell me about yourself.' I dared not move for my pockets were full of white mice and when these escaped they set up house with ordinary mice and had piebald babies in odd corners. Carrying them around was absolutely forbidden. Jack's pet kid was also forbidden the house, where it tended to disappear. One afternoon Lady Leconfield led me into the drawing room for one of these heart-to-heart talks that never got very far because of the need to keep my pockets sealed. On this occasion she called out in shocked tones, 'It looks as if some sheep have been on the sofa.' Well, yes, those black cherries did look like sheep droppings. Then we saw the kid curled up asleep on the cushions. Bells had to be rung and Lady Leconfield learned nothing about my soul.

Two summer holidays were partly wasted by taking cures in Europe. Dr Kocher's injections, in Berne, had made me uglier than ever and I was not sent again to him, but one July Mama took me along as her companion to Mont Dore in central France where for three weeks we breathed steam and sipped water from the hot springs. Patients lived in a hotel and had to buy hooded, blanket-thick, teddy-bear outfits in which to walk breakfastless to the *établissement thermal* each morning. There, we stripped off and wandered about in steam rooms where old peasant women swished the floor with brooms and hoses. Then we sipped a glass of water from the springs, were dried with hot towels and, resuming our teddy-bear disguise, returned to breakfast in bed. Whether the cure benefited my chest I cannot recall. No one had yet noticed that the one thing that stopped my wheezing was starvation. Mama suffered from chronic bronchitis caused, she said, by four winters of icy Madrid winds following her girlhood in Samoa and the Philippines.

Aunt Anne did not try Mont Dore, but in the following July she took me to Vichy. Here, amidst the bilious millionaires of the world, no possible cure for a child could be devised, so I was once more reduced to high jumps on the hotel bed. The boredom of strolls with all those dressed-up, dieting grown-ups tried me sorely. But I loved my aunt and she allowed me to play around with her newly purchased Paris clothes. I would try on glinting evening gowns and shawls, strutting to amuse her.

We stayed in an enormous and, I suppose, very expensive hotel. Barney Baruch, the famous financier who would come into my life later on, arrived there to treat his liver, and for company he brought Clare Sheridan and her daughter Margaret, both of whom had the innards of mountain goats. Clare, who had never recovered from a kind of *folie de grandeur* induced by her days in the Kremlin, criticized the hotel decor and scoffed at the rich invalids. Margaret, with her intellectual gifts, never suffered from boredom. She taught me to copy the grown-ups, to bow to the *maître d'hôtel* on entering the dining room, and to drop compliments concerning the food while he led the way to our table. We did not realize that he and the waiters thought our juvenile graciousness excruciatingly funny. Margaret read French and English fluently. I could read by now, but very slowly and Aunt Anne made the mistake of giving me *Black Beauty* to keep me quiet during the afternoon rest. Such fare was far too vivid. I choked with tears over the death of Ginger, the cab horse, and could not stop weeping. Doctors went padding along the hotel corridors visiting their millionaire patients, and my aunt's French maid, who found me unable to raise my head from the sopping pillow or indeed to catch my breath, became so alarmed that she begged my poor aunt to send for one. He diagnosed 'une crise de larmes', which was very obvious.

It was a relief to leave Vichy and get back to Ireland. We loved to visit the Herd's cottage, where sixteen children grew up stout and merry on oatmeal porridge. The Herd and his wife had red-gold hair and looked like Vikings. In a strong Antrim accent she would say, 'I dunna care to see wee children hungry,' and fed the neglected waifs of a neighbour along with her own. Every child in this cottage had an allotted job. The youngest importantly took his own little can to the well as soon as he could walk. None of these children felt unwanted. Not so my contemporaries. The daughters of Lord Enniskillen, who lived in beautiful eighteenth-century Florence Court twenty miles to the north, became aware from the very beginning of the crime of being born girls. 'Three girls, poor John,' I heard our grandmother say, until at last there came a boy, a Viscount Cole, to inherit the name and estates. Females were wanted in very small quantities by the upper classes. They had to be married off and that cost money. Girls without dowries became, as Lady Mary Wortley Montagu had put it, 'fit only for retirement'.

But there was no plethora of girls in the Leslie family. My grandmother Leonie had produced four boys; in fact I was the first girl since Great-Aunt Olive had been born in the sixties. Having no sister, I felt myself quite a rare bird and Mama doted on her only daughter – yet all around I could soon see how the pattern of life depended on the male. And the Great War of my childhood had wrecked many homes simply because social usage decreed that houses and estates must go with a name and the name went with men only. The added anguish caused when heirs were wiped out and their sisters could not inherit seemed all the more illogical since certain peerages did descend in the female line, so homes could be held together and complete devastation of family life did not result when the boys were killed.

All around us echoed this chant concerning slaughtered heirs. Old Sir James Stronge, who lived in Tynan Abbey four miles away, had lost his only son in the war. Four stout-hearted daughters remained, but they were 'just girls'. When Sir James died their home would have to go to a distant cousin.* Caledon, the splendid house visible from our hills, was safe. Lord Caledon, born in the same year as my father, had with three brothers survived the war – no dearth of males there – and the third son had already made his name as a soldier.†

My father's great friend, Lord Dufferin, was the youngest of four sons. Freddie Dufferin had been unusually close to his brother, Lord Basil Blackwood, who was killed in 1918. Many years later I would read in Lady Cynthia Asquith's diaries of this bond, and she, who had been Basil's beloved, would use a unique phrase to describe her own pain at his death in action – 'A whole language gone. . . .' Freddie and Brenda Dufferin often came to stay at Castle Leslie, and they brought their son, Ava,‡ a brilliant boy who was considered the best brain at Eton. As he was five years older than me I could but admire from afar and my admiration was tinged with envy – because it was impossible for me to be clever and I needed cleverness far more than he did. We could, however, trawl for pike together and I was better than him at getting a big one into the net. It was something to be able to beat a boy at anything.

Mama and Brenda played bridge; sometimes Lord Dufferin would be drawn in, but my father kept out of these sessions. On one occasion only did Mama force him to take part. The rules of bridge were explained, and smirking, for he realized he had the right kind of memory, Pa played an extremely good hand and won. 'But never again,' he said, and when asked he would retire to his writing desk.

* The cousin was Sir Norman Stronge, former Speaker in the Northern Ireland Government, who, together with his son, was murdered at Tynan Abbey in January 1981.
† Later he became Field-Marshal Lord Alexander of Tunis.
‡ It was then usual for elder sons using a courtesy title to be called by it, not by their Christian name, so, until he inherited, the Earl of Ava was addressed as Ava not Basil.

Once or twice I overheard Brenda and Mama talking of the great love which had existed between Freddie's brother, Lord Basil Blackwood, and Lady Cynthia Asquith. She had been married to the Prime Minister's younger son (Asquith's elder son was killed in the war) and while her spouse was off in the trenches she did not hesitate to entertain Basil on leave. Mama disapproved. Although Lord Basil had been killed eventually – and a heroic death casts an aura of virtue over immorality – she thought the acceptance of a lover while 'that poor husband' was in the trenches 'not very nice'.

'You're so American,' Brenda would say with her impish laugh.

One summer our grandparents went off to stay with friends on the Continent. Such visits bored Papa Jack, who would have been content to idle away his days dabbing at his own oil paintings, but of course Granny Leonie revelled in a month or so at Cap Ferrat with her adoring swain, HRH the Duke of Connaught. She collected writers and interesting people who lived in the South of France, and the deaf old duke – Queen Victoria's favourite son – was entranced to find Somerset Maugham and Noël Coward at his dinner table, even if he could not always grasp the witticisms my grandmother relayed into his ear trumpet. The duke had loved her for forty years and now that he had grown old while she, his junior by ten years, retained her sparkle, she considered it her duty to bring him into the fun. Margaret Sheridan, who visited them, described to me the elegant manners of these ageing people – characters left over from a world which had disappeared in 1914.

During this particular summer, while our grandparents remained away, Mama ran Castle Leslie with her own staff imposed on the existing servants. Pa invited friends to stay who proved of a different calibre to those of the older generation. Lord Pembroke arrived with his ladylove, Lois Sturt,* brightest of the Bright Young Things. Cocktails, which my grandmother did not permit, were shaken beneath the Bassano in the drawing room and we heard the clink of special ice made in a hand machine (there were no refrigerators and the eighteenth-century ice-houses in the wood had long been abandoned except by bats). We adored Lord Pembroke and Lois. On the whole I've noticed that people who are having illicit love affairs are merrier with children than people who are not. Lord Pembroke had, however,

* Daughter of Lord Alington.

left Lady Pembroke in the cold and we heard that Queen Mary was sore displeased.

Lois was the first woman I ever saw wearing evening trousers. She asked my mother's permission to come down to dinner in a gold lamé pyjama suit. We hung over the bannisters listening while they danced to the gramophone, and there were shrieks of mirth when Lois did high kicks.

Lord Pembroke was so charming that I offered my greatest treat – climbing the church tower. The stone church, built in 1666 by the Scottish Bishop Leslie, lay just beyond an old bowling green. The church key was at my disposal, being held by an elderly churchwarden who lived in a gate lodge. Lord Pembroke accepted my invitation and strapped a camera on his shoulder. We had to climb four tall rickety ladders to reach the top of the tower and in the danger lay delight. The house party was astounded to see us waving from the tower, and having taken snapshots Lord Pembroke pulled out a penknife and cut his name in the lead guttering. Weeks later, when my grandmother returned and learned that Lord Pembroke and Lois had stayed at Castle Leslie together, she flew into a tantrum – 'Queen Mary will think *I* invited them' – and she tore an entire page out of the visitors' book.

This was a pity for on it was the name of another summer visitor, W. B. Yeats, who had amused Mama by his habit of declaiming poetry aloud as he strolled by the lakeside, ignoring her presence if she happened to be around. Still more amusing were mealtimes, when Yeats completely silenced my father. Pa liked to hold forth to a rapt audience and so did Yeats. They couldn't do it together and the better man won.

Towards the end of that summer, when my parents' house party was still a sore subject, some grown-up remarked that Lois Sturt was *fast*. Granny, noting my presence, rounded on me. 'You don't know what fast means do you?' I had no idea of the secondary meaning of this word, but answered cheekily, 'Yes, I do.' Then I made a shot in the dark. 'It means a gentleman sleeps in the dressing room.' A horrified silence fell over the company until my innocence became obvious. I had watched this scandalous couple and noticed that, while Lois was given the mauve bedroom, Lord Pembroke slept in the adjoining dressing room. My guess at a definition of the word was astute.

Among the useless qualities I had inherited – perhaps from some Red Indian ancestor – was a good head for heights. I could climb any tree and look down fifty or sixty feet without a qualm. This propensity terrified my mother and I liked to torture her by climbing a certain tall

Douglas fir and waving from the topmost branch. One upward glance gave Mama vertigo and she would hide her face on Papa Jack's shoulder while crying out, 'Get her down. Why have I such a daughter?' This phrase I would hear often in the coming years and it always gave me pleasure. Why indeed? Why had I been born?

8
Animals and a Couple of Human Friends

In our forest kingdom I came to realize the temper of the human race. We were as fierce and cruel as the race of rats. No other mammal except rats knows blood lust. Nature's hard laws held sway over lake and forest; hawk swooped on small bird, pike gobbled chicks of duck and moorhen, fox feasted on rabbit, otters caught fish, badgers added beetles to their diet of roots. But swift killing for food in no way measured up to man's killing for pleasure. My grandfather was proud of his pheasant shoot. The head keeper reared poults as tame as farmyard hens and prettier, which would in time fly high when they heard beaters drumming and then fall to the guns. On the day of a shoot, sticks holding bits of paper marked each stand and an enormous luncheon of meat pies which could be kept hot for hours was devised in the flustered kitchen. My mother and grandmother disliked that artificial creation of 'game' which resulted in heaps of beautiful gleaming feathered bodies. In fact I recall Mama sitting weeping in a car. Maybe the distant Redskin blood of Granny Leonie revolted, for the ancient teaching of those tribes declared that man, who had to live by killing, must revere animal life, only take what he needed, and give his own body back to the forest after death. No such philosophy entered the heads of the beefy gentlemen who stood about in mittens waiting for pheasants to be driven overhead.

We were seldom allowed out on the day of a shoot lest we disturb birds or get in the way. To stand for hours beside a gun watching dead and wounded birds tumble out of the sky was, I thought, a doubtful pleasure, but the work of the ardent delicate-mouthed dogs fascinated us. Keeper and under-keeper had reason to be proud of their labrador retrievers.

Already my father, a great shot in his day and still delighting in his skill at bringing down snipe, was turning into a naturalist – rather as he had evolved from Protestant landlord into Catholic Irish Nationalist. We overheard the county whispers that he did all this just to annoy his father, but I don't think so. His naturalist instincts had been gradually aroused, as ours were now, by the vermin board. The destruction of natural fauna to preserve game remains the most reprehensible side of organized shooting. Pheasants reared like poultry in a yard owe their existence to careful attention, and this means that the wilds have to be denuded of natural inhabitants. The beautiful bodies of foxes, hawks and magpies hung rotting on the vermin board, a shameful proclamation that man is 'Lord of Creation'. Foxes were trapped in gins and magpies were poisoned with strychnine. 'I'll mix them the queer posset,' our otherwise benign keeper would mutter. During migration wild duck of all kind rested on the lake and my grandfather, proud of his duck shoot, devised long wooden bridges and hides in the marshes at the lake's far end.

Meanwhile Pa noted the numbers of species which landed alongside the usual mallard – teal, shoveller, widgeon, golden-eye and pochard sent us squealing to our nature notebooks. Great crested grebe and little grebe were of course sacrosanct, so were coot and herons, otters and badgers and the morose cormorants whose stinking droppings killed all trees on which they perched. Our grandfather said that cormorants usefully kept down the pike who were gluttons for baby duck. These sharklike fish could even pull small cygnets under water, so that out of the five or six hatched in the rushes by our two pinioned swans, only two or three ever survived, presumably by perpetually riding on their parents' backs – an enchanting sight. Occasionally wild swans landed, but these would be given no rest by our own angry pair, who drove intruders from one end of the lake to the other until they accepted defeat and flew away.

In springtime our grandfather also turned naturalist and saved the corncrakes' nesting sites. With mechanical haycutters on the increase, these birds were finding it hard to find long grass in which to weave their nests. Papa Jack had heard their harsh cry by the lakeside since his boyhood and as the terraced slopes had to be scythed by hand, he decreed that the long grass should remain undisturbed until complete silence on some July night made clear that parent birds and their families had flown. The biggest heronry in Ireland – or so we called it – lay in the sparse trees that grew on our marshy islands and in spring

94

we would stare up at twig nests, listening to the clapping of beaks as baby herons called for food. Sometimes a cold yellow eye peered down, meeting one's own disdainfully. And in the sandy soil of the pinetum – a tree-garden planted with unusual specimens around 1800 – lay the vast badgery. These gorgeous animals were very difficult to glimpse but on one happy occasion my father and his foresters came on an outlying brood. Pa and his men were felling a dead tree in the Great Wood; after it crashed three baby badgers marched out from the stump in procession. Their parents must have been waiting in the under-growth. Unafraid and unhurried, the cubs regarded the happening with equanimity, as if a storm had uprooted their nursery.

Otters proved rarer and even more difficult to see. As trout were already devastated by the pike (alien fish launched in Irish waters), my father had no difficulty in persuading local fishermen that these glorious lighthearted river creatures did no harm, they were so few and so shy. However, one morning, out with the under-keeper, we suddenly came on two otter cubs who had caught an eel and were playing tug-o'-war with it. They were so intent on their game that we stood unnoticed until a breeze carried our scent and they vanished.

Over the whole place, incessantly eaten by foxes, shot and trapped by man, but impossible to curb in numbers, loped millions of white-tailed rabbits. They were a plague to the farmer, eating the good grass and leaving weeds, burrowing holes that could break a horse's leg and generally doing damage and no good (except when a hungry poacher boy carried one home to the pot). Mama had once visited Australia and said it made her feel sick to think of eating rabbit, but Granny Leonie, bemoaning the difficulty of diversifying food, kept ordering 'rabbit pie again'. I did not care what I ate, but Jack with his natural vegetarian tastes had to be forced to swallow meat; it was as if he had carried over this revulsion for animal flesh from a former life. When he saw rabbits cut open in the kitchen and tiny unborn bunnies lying inside, he became yet more queasy.

Pheasant shoots only took place during a short season, but the wild animals called 'vermin' were continuously exterminated, their exquisite bodies nailed up to taint the wind. And all the year round, two men, 'the trappers', set their snares and gin traps. Trapping on the estate was let for a nominal sum in order to keep down the pestilential rabbit population, but they trapped foxes as well, and of course badgers and otters were sometimes caught by these cruel devices. I knew the trappers well; in fact they and the country people were our only grown-up friends in the world. Pity was not unknown to them, and one man told me of the day when he found a gin trap had been dragged out of the soil by the fox whose leg it held. He searched for but could not find the trap for a week. Then he came on the dead vixen, her leg mangled by the iron jaws and around her lay the carcases of rabbits which her mate had caught and carried to her. Dying slowly in pain, she could not eat. 'Ah would not have liked to see it. . . ,' said the trapper. I only wished that all the world could have viewed this death to understand the reality of trapping. The nights, clear and frosty or warm and fragrant, were often rent by the scream of a snared rabbit, but it was the pain inflicted by the gin trap which truly indicted us.

Fox-hunting did not exist in County Monaghan, it being impossible to gallop over bogs and through forest. Later on, when I discovered the stone walls of County Galway and the pleasure of galloping after hounds, I wondered how cruel the sport truly was. I could realistically recall the hideous alternatives. Trapping entails the most prolonged agony, shooting means that a number of wounded foxes creep away to die slowly, but a kill by hounds ensures instant death. The worst that can happen to a hunted fox is to escape and get pneumonia. To die gasping in an earth hole, little lungs choked with phlegm, may approximate the gin trap. My own incessant bouts of asthma enabled me to imagine what wild animals often undergo. Old age comes to all – to fox and to human – then, and then only, physical weakness must make death a friend. I would be much older when I came to dislike wearing fur coats. At this time I did not associate pelts with trapping.

Jack was a diligent naturalist; he knew the correct Latin names of animals and plants. To the displeasure of our elders, bats became his speciality. Not only did he recognize every species of bat, but he collected them. A tall, glass-fronted bookcase which stood in his nursery floor bedroom became a bat zoo, or perhaps bat condominium would be the appropriate word. Live bats hung sleeping from the shelves and were fed with slivers of raw meat. At night Jack let them fly loose, which necessitated keeping the windows closed. The fragrance of bats' droppings and raw meat permeated the corridor and housemaids refused to enter my brother's room for fear of catching bats in their hair. In vain Jack explained the charm of these pets, who recognized him and squeaked when he brought their food.

Every animal carries its own form of flea, but the bat variety happens to like humans. We dusted flea powder on ourselves, but not on the bats for fear it might harm them. The sweetest was a long-eared bat

Jack with his grandmother Leonie at Glaslough in the
winter of 1921–22

Views of Castle Leslie, Glaslough. The landscape photograph is reproduced by kind permission of Desmond Leslie

Top: Aunt Anne, Mrs Bourke Cockran

Above: Before the row over breakfast in bed (see page 83)
left to right: the author in sunhat, the Dowager Lady Caledon, Mama,
the Dowager Lady Rossmore, Lady Charlotte Graham-Toler, Madame Wolkoff
(former lady-in-waiting to the Czarina), Granny Leonie

named Micky who travelled to England and back in my brother's pocket. On one occasion, when Jack crossed the Irish Sea with Aunt Anne, she allowed Micky to enjoy his nightly flight in her *cabin de luxe* – surely the only bat to whom such a privilege has ever been accorded? The stewardesses in their frilled caps had no idea what was going on. Aunt Anne was such a sport she even allowed Micky to land on her neck.

Micky lived a year or more and eventually died in London. Jack wanted to give him a funeral in Kensington Gardens. While embalming Micky he placed the remains in a small tin box which he then mislaid. Months later plumbers were called in to pull up my bedroom floor and investigate the cause of a lingering unpleasant smell. They found no clues, until turning out a cupboard we came across a little box which contained Micky's remains, inexpertly mummified and extraordinarily unfragrant.

According to ill-written, lock-encrusted diaries kept at this period, I was besotted by dogs and ponies. Willie Dawson, who had come to us in 1898, and been stableboy, second coachman and finally a slow, rather dangerous chauffeur, taught me to ride. At first, proximity to horses aroused asthmatic sneezing fits, but the allergy faded and eventually I discovered my own medicine. It was very simple – to eat lightly. When confined to bed I had noticed that food increased wheezing. So I fasted and eventually deduced what no doctor had ever realized. My particular asthma was caused by stuffing! Mama had always been keen on feeding us up – the gasping which started when I was a year old resulted. Overeating in damp weather automatically made my bronchial tubes swell. No psychological reasons came into it. Had Jack and I been psychosomatically delicate we could hardly have survived.

During these years when we were turning from bewildered children into sullen teenagers, the women of the family dominated us. Mama with her American predilections and Granny Leonie with her pioneer energy, musical talent and European wit grew close, whereas my father and grandfather remained distant figures. Both these men were bored by children. Papa Jack must in the past have desired heirs. He should have rejoiced when his four sons arrived, but he took no interest in their upbringing and when they were born apparently all he ever said was, 'Another damned boy!' Delicate Uncle Seymour amusingly recounted his own first memory of his father. Seymour was four years old when his mother took him to spend a winter with her sister Jennie Churchill in Paris. When his father arrived to stay, little Seymour noticed with surprise a moustached stranger in his mother's bed. He did not remember ever seeing him before and asked anxiously, '*Qui est ce monsieur, Maman?*'

I think we realized fairly early that our own father did not exactly dislike us – he would merely have preferred us not to have been born. Maybe affection lay buried in his nature but although he now occasionally spoke to me and even allowed me to accompany him with the foresters, he rarely uttered a word to his sons. In fact he behaved as if they did not exist, and sometimes they wondered if this might be his unspoken wish. When the time came for the boys to go to boarding school, Mama arranged for the preparatory years. Pa merely insisted that they should not go to Eton. He and his brother Norman had been there together. Pa said they had landed in a bad house, yet he never ceased returning to Eton. He wrote a great deal about his college and never missed the Fourth of June where he cut an impressive figure. But both boys were sent to Benedictine schools – Jack to Downside in Somerset and Desmond to Ampleforth in distant Yorkshire. This kept them well out of the way and Pa could continue to be a famous Eton character untrammelled by offspring.

I think I was Pa's favourite. Something in my unaffectionate nature appealed to him whereas he scorned the boys' yearning for a father. I remember the occasion when a temporary governess told Jack at Glaslough station, 'Go and kiss your father goodbye.' The little boy approached shyly and stood on tiptoe. Pa looked down and said coldly, 'Do sons usually kiss their fathers?' Scarlet-faced, Jack retreated and I saw the governess's expression of amazement.

Why, I wonder, couldn't he bear to touch us – to lift us up or swing us around like other fathers? Mama revealed intense affection streaked with rage. I, in particular, maddened her, for with each year I became less as she wished me to be, and some inner nastiness caused me to revel in that fact. Having shown early promise of beauty, I grew steadily less attractive.

Now that we were older, Jack and I were occasionally taken from forested Monaghan to the Donegal coast for bracing air. Mama had a theory that leaves distilled green chloroform which rendered 'potty' all except the Celtic Irish. However that may be, it was wonderful to find ourselves suddenly launched on a bicycling trip from our Donegal shooting box. Jack and I covered miles together, eating sandwiches and picking blackberries. One evening we entered a lonely cottage below Ben Bulben. An old woman lived there alone and she invited us to sit by her fireside for a 'sup of milk' scooped out of a tin by the door. She radiated content and strangely stirred the marrow of our bones for we saw many unhappy grown-ups. When we left Jack asked, 'Aren't you ever lonely?' She laughed and this was her reply: 'How could I be lonely when I have my mountain?' And we looked up at the fantastic outline of Ben Bulben dark against a violet sky.

We knew little Gaelic though Robin Flower, greatest of Gaelic scholars and superb translator of *The Islandman*, often came to stay and when my father took him on expeditions – to see haunted places or the great ring fort which had once been Emain Macha where Deirdre of the Sorrows found her love – we would squeeze into the car and listen.

I was fourteen when Margaret Sheridan arrived for the summer, and fired me with the ambition to become intelligent. Her mother had been in and out of our house ever since I could remember and all the young responded to Clare Sheridan's glamour. For a time she had sent her son Dick to Jack's school in Switzerland and, wearing a huge leopard-skin hat, she took them out to tea, impressing the other boys. Her daughter Margaret was embarrassed by what she called 'Mama's self-dramatization'. Perhaps it was inevitable that a girl unusually mature for her age should dislike her mother's propensity to shock. Margaret's cynical, entertaining, heart-rending descriptions of family life in Turkey and Algeria filled me with wonder. According to her, we ought to laugh at grown-ups, flout their beliefs, jeer behind their backs, think for ourselves. I tried to emulate Margaret's independent outlook but her brilliance could not be copied. My cousin was self-educated except for a couple of years at a New York girls' school and occasional French tutoring. During the period when she had been 'adopted' by her aunt, Lady Wavertree (Wilfred Sheridan's sister and wife of Lord Wavertree, famous breeder of race horses), Margaret had never attended school. She simply read and assimilated. At fifteen she spoke perfect French and fluent Arabic while her knowledge of history and literature paralysed me. Margaret's copious diaries and witty letters reveal that she could write as well in English as in French.

Margaret jeered when I picked up *Tarzan of the Apes*. I did not argue (until then I had believed Tarzan to be a true story), but switched to her own favourite author – Anatole France. Although I could haltingly read French the transition proved tough. I battled on and two months later found that I enjoyed *La Revolte des Anges*. Anxious to establish communication with this enchanting older girl, I tried to change gear. Our rooms adjoined and during the long-drawn-out sum mer evenings, when the grown-ups strolled out to play tennis and golden light streamed sideways through the beech trees and the lake shimmered in haze, we would curl up on a sofa and converse.

On special occasions when there was no house party Margaret and I might be allowed down to dinner, but our evening meal usually arrived upstairs. The sight of us giggling in dressing-gowns pleased the older generation, who had no idea of the sarcastic plays we were writing about them. Margaret's pen could make vicious swipes, yet she retained a certain innocence. Difficult to be Clare Sheridan's daughter and not know the facts of life – but did she? Boys never entered our discussions and the stinging amoral laughter emanating from the pages of Anatole France gave no clue to actuality. I could not foresee that within two years Margaret would metamorphose into a beautiful young woman surrounded by gentlemen admirers and that I would be left out of the circle.

When the summer holidays ended and we all returned to London I resumed the daily trek to Miss Faunce's school with a light heart, for I was now able to understand what the teachers were talking about. Margaret stayed with us for a few months, reading over my school work and commenting with a certain acidity, but her criticism stimulated, and I turned into a new person under her spell.

Occasionally Clare took us to Brede Place for the weekend. The wonderful six-hundred-year-old house was still without electricity or bathrooms. Although we had all heard the ghost on summer evenings, it was during a winter snowfall that Margaret and I experienced our real encounter.

There were certain nights at Brede Place when everyone felt uncomfortable. Stephen Crane, who lived there in 1900, wrote, 'The wind plays the old house like a harp.' The most haunted end of the house was that which adjoined the ancient chapel. Especially frightening was the Tudor oak staircase beside it. Snow lay deep on the ground and the servants had decided to sleep in the kitchen end of the house where the ghost feeling penetrated less strongly. Margaret and I went to bed together. Our room adjoined a large timbered room leading to that Tudor staircase where no one willingly walked by candlelight. We slept together in an oak four-poster. Clare came to kiss us goodnight and tuck us in. She laid her candle on a table and without mentioning that it was 'one of those nights' she bolted the small oak door leading to the haunted end of the house. After she had departed Margaret and I lay side by side too frightened to move. Then suddenly we heard sounds in the empty room next door – as of furniture being pushed around. We did not dare speak when the bolt shot back on our side and noisily the door opened. Streaks of moonlight came through the window and we could see across the room. Nothing entered. Finally, rigid with fear, we fell asleep. When I awoke, early morning sunshine streamed in; looking at the door I saw that its opening had not been my imagination – it stood ajar. I fell back into sleep until 'Cookie' arrived to wake us. When we saw her timorously closing the door we asked, 'Who opened that last night?'

'Oh Miss, I did hope you wouldn't notice – Mrs Sheridan told me she had bolted you in safe.'

This is my only ghost story, but it is true and without explanation. The bolt drew back on our side and the door opened on its own.

When the time came for Clare, Margaret and Dick to leave for Algiers, I suffered dismally. I wished I was Clare's daughter, to be whistled from one country to another; Margaret, on the contrary, who delighted in the British Museum Reading Room, wished she was me. We discussed running away. Together we visited a pawnbroker behind Paddington Station to see what my small pearl necklace would fetch – £10, and, as I recall it, the fare from Southampton to Algiers was £30.

They departed on a dank day of fog, and Mama produced a fresh shock. Just as I had established myself at Miss Faunce's, I was to be uprooted and dumped in a boarding school. My parents wanted to go to Italy and next term, instead of leaving me on the nursery floor with Nanny and young Desmond, while the Dufferins 'ran the house', I was to be placed in the Convent of the Sacred Heart at Roehampton. Writing letters to Margaret would be my only solace.

That Christmas we spent at Clandeboye in Northern Ireland with the Dufferins, a visit which was hardly suitable preparation for a nunnery. Pa devised comic carols which we sang to much drinking of punch. Before we left Clandeboye, Veronica Blackwood, the Dufferins' only daughter, a curiously attractive girl of seventeen, *jolie laide* and desperately unhappy, left for a finishing school in Paris. I will always remember her weeping departure from that big hall, filled with stuffed grizzly bears. Veronica kept saying, 'Everyone has a mother except me,' while Lady Dufferin, elfin and flirtatious, shook cocktails. Lord Dufferin, the kindest of men, somehow failed to communicate with his daughter, and Ava, her brother, who was now at Oxford, would have

been embarrassed to throw his arms around her. Certainly I could not
have brought myself to do so – it was my natural reaction, but I just
stood there foolishly watching. Anyway she didn't want *me* – a girl of
fourteen – she needed the men of her family.

Ava at nineteen was very different from the boy who had first fished
pike with me. He had dazzled Eton with his scholastic talents and the
lucidity of his mind was impressing contemporaries. He was going to
Balliol College, Oxford, as a Brackenbury Scholar. I asked him once
how he got the title Ava and he paused a long while before replying,
'My grandfather was Irish and Queen Victoria told him he must add
an Indian place name to celebrate annexing Burma so he chose Ava
(the ancient capital of Burma) although an old serving woman had
cursed him from the palace roof.'

I liked Ava less now that everyone expected him to become Prime
Minister, but when he came on to stay at Castle Leslie, his flickering
self-doubts were revealed whenever we rowed out on the lake. Breaking
ice as we went, he tried to talk about the person he meant to become.
I was too young to understand the gropings of that sensitive mind. I
rather resented his success. The grandson of a great statesman,* the
son of delightful Freddie Dufferin and of amusing puckish Brenda, the
owner of a first-class brain – how could he fear for his future? But
Ava was not of ordinary calibre. Restless and hungry for truth, he
wondered why we were on earth and found no comfort in my maudlin
assurances. To cheer him up I invited him to a forbidden adventure.
We crawled over the glass conservatory roof and a pane broke beneath
his weight. Somehow avoiding broken legs, he pulled himself onto a
ledge and helped me invent excuses for the smashed glass. Our parents
could not have guessed the subjects we debated while rowing on the
lake, one to each oar. But if his place in the universe bothered Ava, at
least he had the British Empire to fall back on! He came of a great
pro-consular family and carried a proud name. It would surely be his
role in life to serve. Two of his uncles had been killed fighting for that
Empire, and now that war could never happen again, it looked as if
he had but to step onto the ladder's top rung. He would not have to
die for his country – the dying was over. Ava must become a great
parliamentary fighter righting the world's wrongs. Subduing my envy
for the machinery of his mind, I sulkily reminded him that as he was

* The First Marquess of Dufferin and Ava was Viceroy of India and Ambassador to
France.

a boy – an elder son – all the gates lay open. It was people like me who were going to find it difficult. But Ava kept on fussing about his place in eternity. He suggested that if the rainbow existed for us humans only because our eyes were adjusted to the spectrum, might not the material reality of the whole world vanish if we were not there to touch it? I puzzled at this concept. Then he said that our bodies alone prevented us walking through walls. So here we were dangling amidst the stars, held in the shell of our senses – and hard put to know what was rainbow and what was mist! Looking back over the years, I can see the sombre black eyes suddenly lighten with laughter, and against his questioning I hear the tinkle made by melting ice in the rushes. It was the end of Ava's boyhood.

9
More Schools

Towards the end of January we all returned to London, which lay wrapped in peasoup fog, and the Dufferins settled into our Westbourne Terrace house. On the evening before they left for Italy my parents drove me out by taxi to the suddenly selected Roehampton convent, and left me utterly bewildered in a bare, much-polished room called the parlour. Mama burst into tears as I followed a nun from her view. Up long corridors and many stairs I found myself ensconced in a private room instead of a dormitory, for which Mama had chosen to pay extra. These nuns in no way resembled the jolly Irish nuns in Monaghan, and the following weeks reduced me to the near idiocy of pre-Miss Faunce days. I stumbled through a new curriculum, unable to grasp an entirely different form of education. No library existed and during each three-month term girls were only supposed to read their textbooks.

Church history had hitherto passed me by, but now heresies became our daily fare and I began to wonder what sort of lunatic asylum I had fallen into. Every morning a nun woke us holding out a dish of holy water with which to splash a blessing. Then, after a brief face-wash in a tin basin and the hasty donning of navy serge uniform, we pulled on veils (black on weekdays, white on Sundays) and gathered in the corridor to file silently to chapel. As the girls got no fresh air or exercise before this daily service, which was slowly droned by an ancient priest, they tended to keel over. Occasionally a nun fainted, but nuns seemed able to slide out of their pews as they collapsed. Still in silence we then trailed to the refectory, veils were removed and grace intoned. If holiness did not descend it could hardly be from lack of trying.

As Mama had signed on for every 'extra' from piano lessons to private bedroom to bacon and eggs for breakfast, I found myself, with embarrassment, one of the privileged rich who were handed a plate of hot food instead of white bread, margarine and tinned jam. What Mama could not sign for was the privilege of becoming a Child of Mary. These girls were selected for 'goodness'. They wore ribbons with medals around their necks and top-class Children of Mary sported pale blue ribbons with silver medals worthy of a court function.

Study hours were long and serious. All morning we sat in classrooms and, after a brief hour when we stood around a hockey field, we returned to the study room which was large enough to house desks for over a hundred girls. At six we had tea followed by another march in veils to the chapel and at nine we went to bed.

Whatever talents I had developed at Miss Faunce's school cut no ice here at all. Theological discussions had never taken place in my home. I had never opened a history of the Church or even *heard* of the Great Schism. In this convent I had to go back to square one. A respite came on Sundays when, after two morning masses, we could write letters. Luckily I had brought plenty of notepaper. Letters of other girls were censored but Mama had requested that mine to her and Margaret should not be read. So my long weekly scrolls were handed in to the Mother General sealed. I enjoyed this privilege. I also managed to wheeze my way out of one morning mass.

On Sunday afternoons we could by arrangement see relatives in the parlour or walk them down a special garden path. My cousin Kitty Fitzmaurice took the long bus ride out of London with her French governess and there we were – face to face in the shiny parlour where a nun sat bowed over a book pretending not to eavesdrop. Kitty had, on the whole, been more strictly brought up than I had – in fact those roof excursions had given Jack and me the status of daredevil cousins. Now I saw her eyes gleaming at what had befallen me. When we walked on the allotted path and could talk freely, Kitty's grim governess, whom I had previously feared, followed at a discreet distance. Mademoiselle glowed at my predicament. It would be good for Kitty to see what parents could do to their children. Lord Lansdowne must seem indulgent by comparison.

Up and down the path, softly talking, walked other girls with their visitors and before long Kitty noticed that no ribbon hung around *my* neck. I tried to describe the steps necessary to become a Child of Mary but the final blue accolade denoted virtuous behaviour difficult to analyse in this convent where all were so studious, so good and so devoid of chance to err. 'You'll never have one,' said Kitty and how right she was.

I made two friends. One of these girls, a pretty little bouncing rosebud, had been in the convent seven years and wickedly kept a powder compact in her knickers. She would become the film star Vivien Leigh, and when I met her later I often wondered if that long sojourn at Roehampton had sapped the only thing she lacked – health. My other friend was the sole day girl, Winifred Paget. She walked from her father's house, Ibstock Place, every morning and had been made to swear she would never post a letter or take a message from any girl in the school. The incarceration was complete, as if we were in prison.

Very few visitors turned up on Sunday afternoons for what could hardly be considered a cheerful outing. But I was lucky, and my beloved great-aunt Mary Crawshay taxied out at vast expense. The close friend of Dr Axel Munthe, and many other amusing European characters, she was famed for a special brand of wit – so Victorian and so light – impossible to catch for repetition. It had always been entertaining to go to tea in her house in Upper Berkeley Street. On the last occasion I had dropped in, Queen Ena of Spain and the exiled King George of Greece were eating scones while Aunt Mary made them scream with laughter about Her Majesty's marital troubles and *His* Majesty's amours. From caustic remarks concerning my father I had long known that my great-aunt was not enamoured of Roman Catholicism, and this visit to the convent, the parlour and the path was hardly likely to change her views. She brought me two books as gifts – *Dr Dolittle* and one of the *William* books – innocent enough. But during the three months of term, we were not allowed to read *anything*! The books were immediately confiscated and placed in my trunk.

What Aunt Mary wrote to Mama I do not know but, on returning from Italy, my mother paid one indignant Sunday visit and upset the whole establishment by refusing to keep to the allotted garden path. She decided the time had come to end the experiment, but although I loathed the place I volunteered for a second term. My form was going in for an examination and I wanted to have a go.

So after Easter holidays in Ireland I returned to the convent. Mama threw a fit on discovering that the girls were permitted just two baths a week and changed bathtowels at mid-term only. Then she learned that each girl possessed one serge dress and wore it every single day winter and summer. Out of kindness I did not tell her that we were shampooed once only – at the beginning of term when our heads were fine-combed for nits! The nuns received their habit on entering and this lasted a lifetime. All that incense must have been rather necessary.

Up until examination week I strove to master each subject. When the science paper was placed before me I leaped at it. No single question resembled anything I had met before but I tried to work out logical answers, and when the result finally came through I had passed what was called the Junior Oxford and Cambridge, although the examiners remarked that I used very curious methods of deduction.

The strictness of our regime was nothing compared to the austerity which nuns of the Sacred Heart inflicted on themselves. The first shaft of pity I ever knew for a grown-up person struck while I was talking to a young rather beautiful Mother. (The teaching staff were called 'Mother'. The 'Sisters' were a lesser breed employed as servants.) We were celebrating the fiftieth anniversary of an old nun entering the order and when this young woman came to my room with the printed commemoration card we chatted for a few moments. I saw her expression as she handed me the card. 'Fifty years . . .' she murmured, and a bleak shadow crossed her face. I knew she was wondering how to bear it. She never guessed what her expression revealed or that my heart tightened for her. Why did women enter the harsh Order of the Sacred Heart? Years later when reading *Frost in May* by Antonia White – a classic written about the same convent in 1900 – I came to understand the psychological pressures.

Soon after examinations I developed a high temperature and was told to carry my sheets down to the sanatorium. A week later orders arrived that I be sent home by taxi. The serge dress and black stockings were left behind as convicts leave their garb, and after a brief convalescence my parents began to trot me around. No sooner had I teetered to my feet, fresh from the clang of convent bells, than I found myself taken to the Cavendish Hotel where famous old Rosa Lewis always opened her arms joyfully to our family. In Rosa's sitting room Mama and Pa were meeting the Arthur Vincents, owners of beautiful Muckross House in Killarney. Mrs Vincent, the only child of a Californian millionaire, had been one of Mama's earliest friends. Her daughter, Rose, who was my age and the loveliest thing I had ever set eyes on, accompanied them. At fourteen Rose was already well groomed and wore silk stockings. She looked at me coldly and our parents' tentative efforts to evoke friendship did not work at the time. Later, when

Mama was not so keen on cementing bonds, Rose would turn into an adorable, impossible, contradictory, exciting friend and I would attend *all* her weddings.

Rosa Lewis was as usual opening champagne and, having handed us strawberries out of the bubbling glasses, she suggested that we 'run around'. Jack and I set forth while Miss Vincent remained aloof with the grown-ups in that wondrous little room whose walls were plastered with signed photographs of royalty and 'dear, dear so-and-so'. We children were flattered to be included in the gallery.

During that pre-luncheon hour, when it was the grown-up habit to quaff champagne, Jack and I explored Rosa Lewis's rambling hotel. The corridors were lined with sporting prints and the bathrooms had deep tubs encased in mahogany. The chintz-hung bedrooms had not been tidied up, and they looked exactly like rooms at home with boots and clothes flung all over the place. People lived here for years without paying a bill. No one ate at the Cavendish although a dining room existed, but the popping of corks went on all night and much of the day – paid for, Pa said, by 'rich Americans thrilled to be allowed a glimpse of London high life'.

'I've heard there are secret passages,' whispered Jack. We searched carefully and sure enough most rooms seemed to have an alcove with an unobtrusive door leading down steps. Of course we did not know that Rosa Lewis had been a pet of old King Edward, or that she ran this hotel as a rendezvous for secret amorous liaisons; but the air of dereliction and mystery was most pleasing.

That summer we did not return to Castle Leslie because Aunt Anne had rented a seventeenth-century manor house on the Isle of Wight. We travelled across the Solent with a cavalcade of servants which included our London cook and her kitchenmaid daughter Amelia, who carried a dripping cod fish all the way. An island car with chauffeur was hired and Amelia caused immediate trouble by falling in love with the chauffeur, who did not respond to her advances, but could not avoid taking his meals in the kitchen. Nanny, in charge of seven-year-old Desmond, disapproved of romance below stairs and took the chauffeur's side. Every morning he drove us to the beach for swims which were not allowed to exceed twenty minutes at a time. We were impervious to cold and would have remained for hours in the sea. While we circled around doing the breast-stroke Nanny would sit on the beach watching Desmond build sandcastles.

Mercifully, we were, except for the first week, free of any form of governess. This liberation sprang from one of Mama's less successful 'brainwaves'. She had invited her London masseuse for a holiday which entailed 'keeping an eye on the children' and giving the elders occasional massage. This good lady arrived and immediately flew into a tantrum because when Princess Beatrice (the youngest child of Queen Victoria and now governor of the island) came to lunch Mama did not include her at the table.

During Cowes Week the harbour became full of yachts owned by friends of our parents. Lord Birkenhead invited us out to his steam yacht to amuse his daughter Pamela, and off Jack and I drove in Aunt Anne's car with our 'keeper' sitting between us. Jack and I still indulged in fist fights. As stitches had been necessary after former battles, I ought to have learned my lesson, but on this drive to Cowes we descended again to physical combat. The fight started over the possession of a water pistol which I tried to take by force. A mistake. Jack was now stronger than I and could deliver lethal blows. The masseuse-governess sitting between us had a large bosom which caught several of our punches. Her screams brought the car to a halt, the chauffeur descended and pulled her out to safety. Jack and I fought on. Placing one foot in my middle he managed to hold me pinned to the seat while leaning forward to bang me on the head with the lead pistol. The chauffeur intervened, bravely snatched the weapon, placed the hysterical lady on the front seat and drove us all back home. I'll never forget Mama's outrage when she saw us. 'Cowes Week and you were supposed to make nice friends!' she moaned. I had been rather badly hurt and the gash in my scalp had to be disinfected. We did not reach Lord Birkenhead's yacht that day, and in the evening the indignant masseuse phoned for a taxi and departed. She sent Mama an enormous bill and a threat to sue if she developed breast cancer from our blows. The pistol was confiscated and we never took to fisticuffs again.

On the next visit to Cowes Pa was in charge. We realized what a lot of fun we had missed by brutish antics, and were now on our best behaviour, but Pa wasn't accustomed to looking after children. He fancied lunching with Rosa Lewis, who kept open house in the villa she always rented beside the Royal Yacht Squadron which was the stuffiest yacht club in Europe (even refusing membership to Queen Victoria because she was a woman). Rosa's idea of lunch consisted as usual of champagne and strawberries. Jack and I were thirsty and swallowed several glasses, then we munched hungrily through plates of luscious fruit. People came and went. Jack and I sat tipsily on the

lawn with a blonde lady surprisingly dressed for midday in a tailored
suit of black sequins. The strawberry bowl became empty. Rosa went
off for a nap. Pa had disappeared. We wandered out in the garden to
play, and play we did. Jack had a fertile brain and immense courage.
'Watch,' he said, 'I am going to stop cars driving away.'

Lord Birkenhead came out of the front door, stepped into his limousine and the chauffeur started down the narrow drive. Jack rushed
out from the rhododendrons and lay down across the avenue. It was
impossible to advance without crushing him. After much hooting, the
chauffeur got out with the obvious intention of lifting this unknown
body out of the way. Quick as lightning Jack leaped up and ran into
the bushes. Then he emerged further down the drive to repeat the trick.
Again the car had to halt or squash him. Out got the chauffeur and
away ran Jack. Owing to the time it took for the chauffeur to get in
and out of the car, the procedure could be repeated indefinitely. Birkenhead did not try to help his driver, but peered out with an expression of consternation which kept me doubled up with laughter in the
rhododendrons. Finally Jack tired of this ploy and allowed the car to
move on.

We hung around for an hour or so, very bored and occasionally
climbing up the verandah to look in upstairs windows.

'Hi you – not allowed,' called a gardener. As we slid down, Pa
reappeared.

'Come on,' he said, 'the Birkenheads will give us tea.'

Thoughtfully we trotted at his heels, clutching our unused bathing
suits and longing for a swim. The promenade seemed to be thronged
with people Pa knew and he kept stopping to talk. On the Birkenheads'
yacht their pretty dark-eyed daughter Pam Smith showed us her cabin.
We did not dare relate our escapade at Rosa Lewis's house and when
her father arrived in a dinghy we assumed what we hoped were angelic
expressions. Lord Birkenhead never recognized his tormentors.

Yacht races, ice-cream, scrambling aboard, returning by dinghy,
fireworks – all this imprinted on our minds the excitements of a
yachting regatta. So did the swift walk with Pa to see a small house on
the sea front, beyond the Royal Yacht Squadron, called Rosetta Cottage. This was the house which his grandfather, old Mr Jerome, used
to rent in those distant days when gentlemen could enjoy regattas in
their own small boats as the fishermen did. Here Aunt Jennie had
accepted Lord Randolph Churchill's marriage proposal.

'If my grandfather had not brought his girls to Cowes and rented this house – no Winston!' commented Pa.

The rest of that blazing hot summer we spent happily enough. The old manor house was haunted, which frightened the life out of Mama and the servants. Even prosaic Nanny complained of the unaccountable smell of madonna lilies which we learned later was the trademark of this particular ghost. During the reign of Charles I, the heir to North-court, a fine house a few miles away, had been engaged to the young lady of this manor. She then fell in love with a visiting Frenchman, and the suitors fought a duel on the lawn beneath what was now Mama's window. The betrothed was killed, the Frenchman made off and the girl remained alone husbandless. Midnight thumps on the oak stairs and the recurring inexplicable perfume caused the three younger maids to insist on sleeping in one room. But I was never frightened. I had been inured to ghosts by Brede Place.

Towards the end of that summer Pa invited a friend of his to stay, Major Ronnie Bodley, who had quite a history. Possessed of extremely good looks, he had originally married a beautiful English girl who divorced him after the honeymoon for physical cruelties of a lurid nature. Pa was very comic about it all and we listened agog to his account of the evidence given in the British court-of-law – hot pennies dropped on her arms to arouse passion, horse-whipping on hotel balconies, etc. The press of Europe had gone to town because in those days English judges did not grant cruelty divorces without scars, bruises and eye-witness accounts. In this case the staff of a Paris hotel had given dramatic interviews to reporters. So had a shoeblack in the street below. 'Old Etonian enjoys his honeymoon,' ran Continental headlines. After the divorce Bodley had retired to the Sahara where he ranched sheep and wore dramatic Arab robes becoming to any man. He had met our cousin Clare and chased with her around the desert demanding marriage. Her brother Oswald joined the party and put a stop to all such notions. At least Oswald said he did. Dickie, aged ten at the time, claimed separate responsibility. Margaret, fresh from Lady Wavertree's schooling in the South of France, had joined them in some oasis when Clare came down with high fever in the caravanserai, and her account differed. Margaret said that her delirious mother made her own deci-sion. 'If that man is too lazy to drive a car and thinks I am going to do the work when we're stuck in the sand, take him away and hang him.' Her children did not have to resort to this solution – the en-gagement was broken.

Mama and Aunt Anne were longing to see Ronnie Bodley, especially as he wrote asking to bring his new wife – an Australian girl of twenty. So he arrived with Betty, who was a little slip of a thing and very lovely. She had been polishing off her education on a world tour when she caught sight of Ronnie standing in white Arab robes and headdress outside the Laghouat Hotel. He knew that his handsome face in this get-up could hardly fail to arouse attention. Ladies in search of romance halted in their tracks. Betty had ended her cultural tour right there in Laghouat by marrying him.

Before the Bodleys arrived Pa had great fun reading aloud the novels which Ronnie and Clare had in tantrums written about each other. Bodley's book, called *Opal Fire*, based the heroine on Clare and described her amorous adventures. 'A cad's book,' we learned. In retaliation Clare produced a novel about Ronnie, entitled *Green Amber*, depicting him as a dishonest desert sheep farmer.

I was, of course, longing to see this gentleman and when he arrived my letters to Margaret grew long and detailed. Echoing the grown-ups I used the phrase, 'He looks like a Greek god.' She wrote back crushingly, 'Since when have Greek gods had tip-tilted noses?' But by then the Bodleys had come and gone. Temporarily tamed by his young wife, Ronnie had proved rather charming and Betty had not yet discovered what nasty medicine he could administer. She would learn. And Mama would learn. But in good time.

10
More Schools and the Sahara

Westonbirt College, a new girls' school which had opened in Glouces-
tershire, received much publicity in the press. The converted home of
Victorian magnate Sir George Holford, creator of the world-famous
arboretum, Westonbirt was vaunted as on a par with any boys' public
school. This, in the England of the day, was high praise. The teachers
had all received university degrees. An illustrated article about Westonbirt caught Mama's eye and she conferred with Mrs Paget, the
vivacious French mother of Winifred, who had been my friend at the
convent. We heard with delight that we would be sent there together
– to a boarding school which actually possessed a library!

In London I felt some regret at not returning to Miss Faunce's
establishment, but this new college, with a swimming pool and gym,
certainly had allure. Winifred Paget and I were expensively outfitted at
the school tailors in Sloane Street. The uniform list was long. Every
imaginable garment had been designed according to the Board of
Governors' decree in grey and red. Unlike the convent, where one navy
serge dress sufficed winter and summer, for hockey as for study, Westonbirt clad its two hundred and fifty girls in different outfits for every
activity. We started off with a grey tweed overcoat and numerous
skirts, blouses and sweaters. We wore grey tunics with red sashes for
gym and silvery Greek tunics for dancing class. For smart occasions
there were red-grey silk dresses and of course there had to be *hats* for
church and other outings.

Arriving via school train and bus at a vast house of extraordinary
architecture, I found myself gazing at its skyline of carved ornaments
and obelisks. 'But what period *is* it?' One could hardly guess for this
1850 mansion had been built like a Tudor dream.

Westonbirt proved a worthwhile if brief experience. True to press reports we were indeed allowed to spend Saturdays tearing over the country in the wake of fox-hounds, and õccasionally we managed to open a gate for Mrs Crawford, our headmistress, as she galloped by in top hat and sidesaddle rig. When parents came down to see their chicks at half-term, Pa arrived with Mama. Pa had heard that Old Brown, Sir George Holford's stud-groom, taught us riding and he spent a happy afternoon reminiscing with him about 'the good old days' when my grandmother had attended the big house parties. Meanwhile Mama also enjoyed herself, for she had met a beau of her youth – Lord Glasgow – whose graceful daughter Grizel Boyle* led the dancing class. In her grey silk Greek tunic, which made even the most awkward girl attractive, Grizel would whirl around demonstrating the arm poses of Athenian nymphs.

As the diplomaed professors knew how to teach, the weeks passed swiftly, until chickenpox swept through the school. Girl after girl developed spots. The sanatorium overflowed and parents arrived in cars to take their darlings home. Winifred and I and the Briscoe George sisters (who would later come back into my life) hung around each other's necks, determined to get infected together, but I remained immune, and my friends did not feel ill until the last day, when they avoided reporting spots for fear of missing the school train home.

It was December when I returned to London, never dreaming that I would not see Westonbirt again – or indeed that it would become famous and extremely difficult to enter. *Our* mothers merely wrote announcing their daughters would arrive, as if conferring a favour on the school. Winifred, drooping and voiceless on the train, was met by her loving parents and whisked home where the full horror of chickenpox could be revealed. I found the Dufferins again in our London house. Mama was in America and Jackie arrived for the last time from Switzerland. He was to be sent to the preparatory school attached to Downside College in Somerset.

For Christmas with our great-aunt Olive Guthrie we travelled up to her Scottish home – Torosay Castle on the Isle of Mull. From the ferry, the *Lochinvar*, which brought us to Mull from Oban, we entered an open boat which stalwart islanders rowed to the jetty. When we clam-

---

* Lady Grizel Wolfe-Murray, as she became, died in a lifeboat when the ship on which she was travelling back from the Middle East was torpedoed during the Second World War.

bered over the snow-covered mountains of that wild lovely island, Jack
– Alp-accustomed – proved his mountaineering superiority. His legs
never tired on a steep climb nor did he run out of puff. Aunt Olive
took us to tea in old Duart Castle, stronghold of the Macleans, and
there we listened to the stories of ninety-year-old Sir Fitzroy Maclean,
who had ridden in the Charge of the Light Brigade at Balaclava.

On New Year's Eve Aunt Olive gave a ghillies' dance. People drove
to it from all over the island and several stayed the night. Jack danced
well for his twelve years and having gone through his paces in Highland
flings he was not too shy to ask Lady Massereene to waltz. She was
a tall, dark creature, an old friend of Pa's and famous for her amours.
She wore, not very suitably, a gleaming white evening dress, backless
and with the thin shoulder straps fashionable at that time. Jack's head
reached her shoulder but he waltzed manfully and only when they
stopped did we notice that she had powdered her bare white back and
that my brother had been helping with the coal fires. The ghillies gazed
in astonishment at the imprint of a black hand in the centre of her
ladyship's spine.

When Mama returned from America she decided that one term at
Westonbirt was enough. I was now just fifteen and eager to learn
something somewhere, but the joy of being allowed to keep my cocker
spaniel Kelly in London compensated for lack of teachers. For the next
year or so I would be dressed in grey and red because trunks of
Westonbirt uniforms had travelled home with me, but apart from being
togged up in school colours I was now free, like Margaret Sheridan,
to read and read and read. And also like her, but less successfully, to
write and write and write. In a surviving diary, marked 'Volume III
Part II' (happily the rest has been lost), I describe Kelly's life in detail.
Every walk in the park is recorded – 'She is too adorable, the way she
tears around in circles with her white teeth gleaming and her little pink
tongue hanging out.' And there are illustrations of horses – not from
life, but careful ink drawings of horse anatomy; every bone and tendon
and ligament is given its Latin name. For now I wanted to be a vet. If
not a Great Poet or a Great Artist why not a Great Vet? I tried to
discover how to set about fulfilling this new ambition, but there were
nasty hurdles to cross in the form of examinations. A whole page of
the diary describes the dog show where I meet Fowler, the under-
keeper from Glaslough, showing his Irish setters. Then Kelly is taken
out walking by Nanny and lost in the park. Much telephoning of

police and at nightfall she is picked up and returned by a constable who dries my tears.

Suddenly, towards the end of February, Mama decided she could not stand London another minute. We must depart for Algeria to stay with Clare in the Sahara. This meant I would be reunited with Margaret, on whose long weekly letters I had depended during the past eighteen months – through the convent trials, through Westonbirt and through our variegated holidays. I was wild with excitement. Mama took bookings on a Dutch ship sailing from Southampton to Algiers, bought thick felt sunhats on the line of topees and what she imagined to be suitable camel-riding breeches. Off we went – she and I and her lady's maid Sarah. People of Mama's vintage thought personal maids were a necessity like toothbrushes. Clare never travelled with a lady's maid, but then she was unique – also she knew how to use those belonging to other people. Not only would she donate tips but exotic mementoes and a fund of splendid stories with which the lesser servants could be regaled. Lady's maids regarded themselves as a notch above housemaids – in the hierarchy they came just after housekeepers and, right up to my day, at big country houses each sat in precedence according to the rank of her mistress. When ambassadresses went visiting, someone in the lower quarters must have known the date on which each envoy had been accredited to the Court of St James so that servants' hall protocol could be correctly kept.

Despite her years in Samoa and the Philippines, Mama had never really abandoned the social niceties of the white man's world, whereas Clare had shed luxuries like personal maids when she ran off to the Kremlin. Clare however never made a cup of tea or boiled an egg for herself. She always found someone who would be delighted to cook for her, sew and wash for her, build for her, carry tons of clay and set up pedestals for her. On a desert island there would not have been much to choose between them – in fact my mother might have proved the more ingenious at opening coconuts.

So there we were. Within ten days of 'the idea', Mama and I and Sarah awoke to the blue Bay of Biscay. On 5 March 1929 we entered Algiers harbour, and my diary assiduously records: 'As we drew into the docks I espied a large grey figure on the quay and recognized Dick Sheridan who goes to school here.' The next week was spent exploring the Kasbah with Dick, by now a huge fourteen-year-old. Lord Wavertree, his uncle, was staying at the Hotel St George and during dinner I heard him raging to Mama because Clare would not send Dick to

Harrow. She had spent the £5000 he gave her for Dick's education on alabaster pillars rolled by camels across the desert.

Dick was supposedly being educated by the Rev. Fry, the English chaplain in Algiers, but of course the boy grew bored. He still took violin lessons (abysmal squeakings!) and in the evenings attended art class. He asked if I would like to join this and Mama, remembering that I had once been pronounced artistic, brightened until she heard that the models posed nude. Lord Wavertree, purple in the face, ranted on, 'Can you beat it – that boy aged fourteen drawing naked women. . . .' Intimately as I knew Dick, I felt rather relieved we had not got to sit side by side sketching naked bottoms.

After a week in Algiers we left by train running south all night towards the oasis of Biskra where Clare had built what she swore would be her final habitation. At dawn we had to tumble out of our sleepers and catch a smaller train. I was riveted by the wild barren gorges and scatterings of little tents. It was past noon when we reached Biskra and there stood Clare and Margaret on the platform. My adored girlfriend was looking rather pale and cross for she had undertaken the fast of Ramadan in order to 'get closer to Arab friends'. It was torture not being able to eat or drink during the twelve hours between dawn and sunset. 'But not as bad as when Ramadan falls in midsummer and thirst grows excruciating,' she said. I felt a little dispirited. Margaret seemed to have grown away from me. We had been able to write each other easily, but now it seemed difficult to talk.

My diary describes Bab el M'Cid. Clare had purchased three date gardens on the outskirts of Biskra, designed a house and directed Arab masons to build it of mud. 'The house is white and has three big rooms and several smaller ones. Margaret has a lovely room, pink with a blue and pink brocade bed, which she has turned out of for Mummy and me. Clare sleeps in the drawing room which has orange walls with birds and glass fruits hammered in by her and there is a very useful sunk garden. We look over the dry river bed to a few palms and then desert to the Atlas Mountains miles away.'

The sunk garden was indeed useful for into it the goat and her kid could not climb. It was teatime. Haafa, the Arab boy factotum, was away buying a ram to kill for feasting at the end of Ramadan and no one knew how to milk the goat. Having learned to milk a cow on the farm at home, I became a hero, for I could entice and tie up the goat and while Margaret held the kid I induced a jugful of milk. Tea was important, for Mama had collapsed exhausted by the journey and poor

Sarah was in tears. We all sat on cushions in the useful sunk garden except Margaret, who slunk away.

'Don't speak to her,' said Clare, 'she has another three hours till sunset and it is terrible for her to watch us sipping tea.'

Two days later the firing of guns and cutting of sheep's throats marked the end of Ramadan, and I hoped that Margaret would break the barrier which seemed to have grown between us. She certainly cheered up when able to join us at meals, and she developed enough energy to take me off for long rides in the desert. On the feast of Id Margaret donned the garb of an Arab woman and we went to watch the crowds praying on a hill. Then we visited the Bash-Aga, who threw a long scrutinizing glance at Margaret in her jewellery and brocade and said in French to her mother, 'What a pity I cannot have her as one of my wives.' At Bab el M'Cid the ram had been slaughtered and roasted pieces were being distributed to Clare's friends. At that period she knew and liked only Arabs.

Next day Clare and Mama, Margaret and I, all four, developed septic throats and high temperatures. The lovely white house was not designed for furious sick women. Sarah burst into fresh tears and only brightened when Haafa, the Arab boy, who had fallen in love with her, placed a turquoise ring on her finger – engagement ring or gift she would never know, being unable to converse in Arabic or French. However Haafa's protestations were obvious. As Clare's illness made it impossible to enter what my diary refers to as 'the drawing room', the low Turkish brass table on which meals were served had to be carried outside. Haafa knew only one dish, which was the usual Arab couscous – a form of semolina into which oddments can be dropped.

Mama began to dislike the desert. She could not ride with Margaret and me and she hated sitting cross-legged on the ground during meals – she said it pulled her suspenders and made ladders in her silk stockings. The camel-riding outfit remained unpacked. And she soon tired of couscous.

'Don't speak to Clare, she is like a wounded bear,' she warned me, but by the time we were convalescent and eating out of doors Mama dared to venture a suggestion. 'Wouldn't it be nice to put some chicken in the couscous?' she asked.

Clare bellowed for Haafa to whom she always spoke in French.

'Kill the cock.'

'Oui, Madame,' replied Haafa and set off on a horrid chase after the cock.

'Not now,' screamed Clare, but it was too late. Triumphant and bloodstained, Haafa reappeared and next day we tried not to gag at fragments scattered in the semolina. We were guests after all, and self-invited to boot. However, Mama so insistently complained of the villainous countenance of the night watchman that Clare hired a second night watchman to watch the first. Then Sarah reported that Haafa's little brother slept on the kitchen floor instead of going home to the village. 'Insanitary,' decreed Clare, 'and he eats all the food.'

I was torn between the wonder of our surroundings, the glorious rides, Margaret's preoccupation with her Arab phase and a vague uneasiness aroused by our warring mothers. Mama and Clare were boiling up into one of those feuds which were easy to dispel in places like London, where each could rush to friends and say how impossible the other one was. Here it was different. Happily, the rains were ending and we did not have to face the annual drama when the river bed turned into a gushing torrent and the mud house sank ever a little lower, but a last storm did turn the dust roads into deep mud and for several days we could not leave Bab el M'Cid at all.

Then the Arbuthnot family arrived to stay in a hotel. Clare fell on their necks, forgetting that she liked only Arabs. The moment Margaret recovered she went off on a tour of distant Roman ruins with David Arbuthnot and his sister, who were older than I and better company. I felt myself deserted until Dick arrived from Algiers. He could never equal what his sister meant to me, but we had been chums since babyhood, and we went out riding in the desert together, talking about life and what we would do with ourselves. Clare worshipped her only son but she let him grow lonely. There were no boys of his own kind in Algiers and the intellectual pursuits of Margaret were beyond him.

One evening riding back over the sand dunes he looked at me with a shy grin.

'I'm not allowed into the harems now,' he said. 'If they found me with the women they would kill me.' It was something for a fourteen-year-old to be able to say that. 'Will you be my first sweetheart?' he asked innocently. I did not want to be anyone's sweetheart. I wanted Margaret. But I acquiesced. I did not realize that Margaret had reached the age when young men interested her more than I did.

Some of my diary entries are happy. One day when Dick and I go riding we run into an Arab procession with drums and exploding rifles which frighten our horses, so we make off to the race course to see French officers playing polo. Then we set our mounts towards the hills.

'We rode along a desert track for several kilometres; once we passed a couple of Arabs with a donkey and a camel. Finally we reached a great sand dune between the mountains; we tied up our horses and after a half-hour of hard climbing on our feet, reached the top – it was, Dick said, "one great miracle". Around us lay the small mountains and in the distance the great Atlas range – to the south stretched the Sahara.'

But on our return that evening Mama had had another brainwave. She had remembered Ronnie Bodley's sheep ranch at Laghouat some hundred miles away across the Sahara. Telegrams were dispatched and arrangements made for a hired car to drive us to this distant oasis. Three days it would take. When Clare was told she closed her eyes. 'All I need! . . . To hear that you prefer that rotter to me.' Dick and I munched uncomfortably through the next meals while our mothers, sitting cross-legged, argued with each other.

Margaret had not returned from her tour with the Arbuthnots. I was going to have to leave without bidding her farewell. I said goodbye to her beautiful grey Arab horse, but that was not the same. And Dick kept whispering how much he wished we would not go. 'I can't stand Ronnie Bodley,' he said. '*I* prevented Ma marrying him.' Away we drove in the hired car. Haafa bowed sorrowfully to Sarah, Dick waved wistfully, Clare could hardly bring herself to say goodbye. On the way to Laghouat we stayed at Bou Saada. Mama did not see why Sarah should not be taken to watch the Walid Naïls dancing, although she avoided explaining their careers. For centuries the Walid Naïl girls left their tribe to earn dowries as prostitutes in Bou Saada. They put their earnings into jewellery and were hung with heavy gold and silver bracelets and head ornaments. They danced in public, accepting what each man could pay. When a Walid Naïl grew sufficiently rich she returned to her tribe and purchased a husband.

It was evening when we reached Laghouat and drove ten kilometres beyond the oasis to see Ronnie riding out on his Arab stallion to meet us. Betty entertained us delightfully, and for weeks I was again riding in the Sahara and visiting Arab chiefs. Occasionally we drove to Ronnie's desert sheep ranch where his Arab partner, blue-eyed with a red moustache, always feasted us on roasted sheep and oranges in a large tent.

Ronnie's friends proved interesting. The son of the local Bash-Aga drove us off to his country place in the mountains, a charming white house in the entrance of a ravine with flowering gardens and eighty servants. After lunch six of the wives came in to see us, but none spoke French. My diary recorded: 'They could neither read nor write, nor count, and spend their time dressing up, talking and staring at the ceiling.' It was a relief to visit the stables where superb Arab horses were kept and loved.

Ill-health seemed to hit Europeans rather often in the pure desert air. Stricken by tummyache I was taken by Ronnie, who had a septic finger, to the fort of the Foreign Legion. I hated the military doctor who merely remarked, 'Mademoiselle est gourmande,' and poured castor oil down my throat until I vomited. Worse befell Ronnie, who was asked to lay his hand on the table and suddenly had the little finger amputated at the joint without any form of anaesthetic.

Despite the pleasures of races, processions and feasts with Ronnie's Arabs, perhaps I was not all that sorry when we returned to Algiers. Mama again hired an Arab driver who appeared at 8 a.m. and drove like Jehu until 6 p.m., never blowing his horn and putting on full speed whenever he saw a flock of sheep.

A Dutch boat took us from Algiers to Genoa. Reaching Florence we found Pa and Jack waiting in the hotel. We ignorant youngsters were handed guidebooks and ordered to go forth and learn about the Renaissance. One day our parents took us to tea with Mrs Keppel, the most interesting and famous of Edward VII's mistresses. She proved to be one of those ageless charmers, wearing a white silk gown with a huge white picture hat. We strolled around her Villa l'Ombrellino high above the city and I noticed her pearls, those famous pearls given her by the King. As we drove down the hill in a horse cab our parents' conversation concerning Mrs Keppel's past seemed very difficult to comprehend. I still did not know what the word 'mistress' meant.

We were back to London for the 1929 General Election. Pa cared little for politics except those of Ireland but he was a natural orator and ready to display his power of repartee on behalf of any friend standing for Parliament. Unhesitatingly he went to Limehouse, a slum district near the docks, to scrape up a few Conservative votes. When Pa mounted the platform he was introduced as a 'famous authority on Irish literature', and at the end of an hour's debate the bewildered workers wanted to know whether he was Conservative, Socialist or a 'bloomin' Communist'! Of course Pa was really a mixture of the lot but his Eton friends were Conservative and it was they who had asked him to speak.

Meanwhile Jack was struggling to understand Downside, the Benedictine monastery school which had been chosen for him. The head-master, Father de Trafford, came of a well-known English Catholic family. The boys were terrified of him and with good reason, for he alone beat them, and did so with a curious religious ferocity unlike other headmasters of that college before or since.

Jack had only just vanished to Downside when Mama received a phonecall saying he had pneumonia and the authorities requested her immediate presence. I was taken along for company in the school guest house. When we reached Jack he was gasping for breath while a doctor was ramming a thick needle into his lung to draw off liquid. The sounds he made trying to breathe and cry out at the same time chilled our blood. Pneumonia was an agonizing experience in the days before penicillin. A week later we left him to convalesce. There were aspects of Downside that Jack liked – the beautifully sung Vespers and bicycle rides over unspoilt country to medieval churches. But the school atmosphere was very peculiar, especially concerning sex. One day in the sanatorium a trained nurse casually sat down on a boy's bed to chat with him. A monk entered and was so horrified that he had her sacked forthwith.

While our parents light-heartedly continued their social round in London I encountered a new kind of education – Miss Wolfe's classes. This famous old lady had once been governess to Pa's cousin Elsie, now Lady Lansdowne, and for some years Miss Wolfe had run classes for girls in her fine house in South Audley Street. It was a marvellously snobbish arrangement. Miss Wolfe only accepted pupils whose parents were friends of 'dear Elsie'. We sat in her drawing room working at different tables and often at different subjects. It was very peaceful reading the tomes which Miss Wolfe would pull from her library shelves and, marking her own favourite passages, thrust on our desks.

When a question was asked, whatever the subject, Miss Wolfe would stop everyone working and dart to her bookshelves, pull down a volume and read out what she considered pertinent. 'And what do *you* think?' she would ask, closing the volume. She was a tiny old woman with enormously thick spectacles, insectlike in appearance rather than human. A few helpers were employed. A lesser teacher sat with the younger girls and an erudite professor came to discuss politics. The chaos of these classes was conducted with a certain artistry and we learned a lot because all our studies interested her personally. No one could fail to pick up something of Miss Wolfe's discriminating taste.

And being dreamy I noticed that the plaster work of her ceilings was very good indeed.

During the next year and a half I walked daily across Hyde Park to attend Miss Wolfe's classes and a certain amount of bookish information lodged in my mind. But I hankered for Margaret. Never would I get over the loss of her friendship. The era of communication which had meant so much to me was now closed, for she did not write after our mothers' disagreement.

I don't think that Mama ever saw what an insult our visit to Ronnie Bodley had seemed to Clare. They made it up later, but by then Margaret had stepped off into a world of male admirers where I could not follow. None of the girls I met in London possessed anything like her fascination and intelligence.

There was a sequel to the Bodley visit. One hot August, when most people were out of London and the Dufferins did not want our house, Mama allowed the Ronnie Bodleys to stay there. Three servants remained. Ronnie was going through a bad patch, his sheep were not selling well and he caused poor little Betty much terror by waving a revolver and threatening suicide. Then she found him lying (on Mama's bed!) weeping about another woman. That ended it. Our servants were of course enthralled, and the stories they related could only have been gleaned by listening at doors. They had never known quite such enjoyable guests.

11
Finishing Off

We still peered with awe into Norman's unused room at the end of its corridor on the top floor of Castle Leslie. My grandmother had kept it untouched for twenty years. On the walls there still hung trophies of his army days in India – the hooves and antlers of animals he had shot – and on tables stood those yellowing photographs of his sweethearts and his polo ponies. Norman had been exceptionally attractive to the opposite sex, and even Granny Leonie, who revered her son's memory, could not refrain from laughing about his memorial service in London. In those days everyone wore deep black at such functions, but on this occasion three separate women arrived dramatically in flowing crepe bonnets, each believing herself the sole love of Norman's life. My grandmother found herself distracted by so many 'widows' glaring at each other.

On Norman's birthday our grandmother would spend a long time alone in his room and a bunch of dried flowers with rosemary for remembrance always lay on his bed. A curious sad atmosphere lingered in this room. Norman had loved the place he was to inherit and his thoughts from wherever he had gone seemed to drift back. Although buried in a distant military cemetery, he remained alive to us. We knew exactly what he looked like from his portrait in Rifle Brigade uniform on the stairs. Having broken the entail when Pa had become a Roman Catholic, my grandfather must have been perplexed about inheritance until Jack, the logical heir, was born.

I had two surviving uncles, Seymour Leslie, born in 1889, and Lionel, who arrived in 1900, only fourteen years before me. Lionel had gone into the Army and was training to be an officer when war ended. Then, wearing the Cameron Highlander kilt, and gallantly if not very musically practising the bagpipes, he sailed with his regiment for India. Illustrated letters about jungle adventures reached his parents until, after four years in India, Lionel resigned his commission and decided to *walk* home. He crossed the Himalayas, explored Tibet and part of China, and considered bringing back a beautiful Tibetan girl but wrote his mother that her betel-nut-stained teeth put him off.

Then Lionel became a rather famous explorer in Labrador and the title of his book (with an introduction by kind cousin Winston), *Wilderness Trails in Three Continents*, exactly depicts his personality.

We adored this tough schoolboyish uncle, nearer to us in age and ambition than any other member of the family. Outings with Lionel were always intriguing. One day I accompanied him to the Monaghan shoe shop. The owner greeted him joyfully. 'Captain Lionel – do you remember those boots I sold you ten years ago?'

'Yes,' said Lionel in his slow solemn way. 'Yes, I do remember. They were very good boots. I walked across China in them.' And he was not exaggerating.

Seymour, our other uncle, could not have been more different. An exuberant intellectual, he had suffered agonizingly throughout childhood from a tubercular hip which kept him flat on his back for ten years. He could not follow his brothers to Eton but educated himself from books held by an overhead gadget. By the age of sixteen when he was able to walk, though limping, Seymour had taught himself perfect French and German and became the best-read member of a hard-reading family. He pluckily insisted on 'cramming', as it was called, for an engineering course at London University.

In his memoirs* Seymour evoked the picture of that world into which he grew up. 'To exhibit the idleness of the Edwardian menfolk it is sufficient to glance at my father's day. He had long since retired from the Army to study painting and did excellent caricatures in the manner of Leech and very indifferent portraits in oils. His London day was like his father's before him.' This consisted of strolling through Tattersall's looking at horses, or skating at 'Niagara', the smart ice-rink, or riding in Rotten Row, maybe giving a paid mistress lunch in the appropriate basement grill of a hotel reserved for such purposes, or, if the mistress was a 'lady', attending her drawing-room tea where riots on the sofa were almost *de rigueur*.

Seymour describes how he fought his way out of the vacuum of

---

* *The Jerome Connexion*, John Murray, 1964.

social life. 'By now I was in economic rebellion, determined to be an electrical engineer, but this proved difficult to explain to Edwardian ladies of fashion. "An electrical engineer?" exclaimed Lady de Trafford. "But how *very* curious! Do you mean you could come and mend my electric bells? My butler has been complaining. . . ." '

Seymour was determined to be independent and pay his own way. 'There was no "vocational guidance" in those days, no estimates of IQ and I could hardly have chosen a more unsuitable career, though later it merged successfully into something quite different. . . . It was certainly good shock treatment to escape from the Edwardian hot-house into the purposeful middle-class atmosphere of London University.'

Seymour, unlike Lionel, was musical and took modern Russian scores to puzzled country house parties where he sat at the piano playing excitedly. 'Isn't it marvellous?' he would demand of tone-deaf English sportsmen. Aunt Jennie lent him her leather-bound Debussy and he lent her Stravinsky, Scriabin and Rachmaninoff.

By the time the 1914 war broke out Seymour had gone to America to join General Electric. In 1915 he returned to England for a post in the mammoth armaments firm of Vickers Ltd. At war's end Vickers decided 'to beat swords into ploughshares'. Seymour learned instant Spanish and spent a year in Madrid, trying to sell Vickers' buses, which were perched on tank chassis. In 1923 he went to Russia selling grain elevators to the Bolsheviks. In Moscow he found Clare Sheridan having tea with the Litvinoffs in that guest-house/palace which is now the British embassy. Returning to London Seymour opened the Chelsea Book Club, a bookshop of unique character, and wrote an avant-garde novel called *The Silent Queen* about an American millionaire who invented a silent toilet. This book, with its curious theme, became a best-seller, but Seymour did not follow it up. 'Too many writers in the family,' he said. Instead, he became publicity man for Queen Charlotte's Hospital's Save the Mothers Fund. Everyone was bored by hospital charities but Seymour was so amusing he raised thousands of pounds. While organizing charity balls to wipe out the dangers of puerperal fever, Seymour also wrote articles for *Vogue* entitled 'Our Lives from Day to Day'. Reading the first of these tongue-in-cheek effusions (dated 19 October 1927), I can see why *Vogue* would not let Seymour go for years! No journalist had ever written in such vein about London society. 'For all its calm and friendly atmosphere, October is one of the most important months of the year in the stern struggle for survival of the socially fittest. We revise our address-books, but those whose names are quietly eliminated never know why or how they have dropped out of things. Had they been to the right parties, worn the right clothes, seen and read the right plays, said the right things – in a word, acted à la *Vogue*, all might have been different.'

The circulation of *Vogue* soared, mothers died less in childbirth and Seymour darted meteorlike around London. Seymour knew everybody and was witty about scandal. Lionel knew nobody except fellow-explorers and Alaskan trappers and he cared nothing about London society. The two uncles came often to Castle Leslie and each in a different way helped me to grow up.

As I approached seventeen I was sent with Winifred Paget and another girl, Elizabeth Darrell, to Paris 'to be finished'. This outmoded phrase was not as bacchanalian as it may sound. We knew French from mademoiselles but English girls were always expected to acquire polish and poise in Paris. I needed these more than most. An odd streak in me remained resentful of any attempt to cultivate the art of alluring the opposite sex. This was what all mothers hoped of their daughters – maximum sex-appeal with the minimum of sex-experience.

A new dieting fad had become the fashion, and in this I not only participated but forced my friends to extremes. We all wanted to be thin and longed to look depraved. More intent on banting – slimming – than on irregular verbs, the three of us arrived in Paris. It had been decided not to send us to one of the smart finishing schools but to a family who specialized in improving English bumpkins. The Mesdemoiselles Amourys welcomed us in their apartment and strove to impart 'polish'. The discipline we imposed on ourselves included skipping one hundred times while wearing thick woollies. One night Liz stood out on the balcony to cool off and pneumonia resulted. A nurse had to be installed and Liz's mother arrived from London. Liz confessed and I accepted the blame. But it was really not my fault when, soon after the convalescent girl had returned with her mother to London, Winifred came down with serious influenza. *Her* mother, briefed by Liz's mother, arrived raging, and when Winifred was well enough she took her home. I found myself left alone with the Mesdemoiselles Amourys, who by this time regarded me with extreme disfavour.

At Christmas Mama had another of her brainwaves. I did not seem to be shaping well, and she decided I must be encouraged 'to get over the hyena stage'. Instead of returning alone to the Mesdemoiselles Amourys, I was to attend the Sorbonne and stay with Madame Lermantov, a delightful old Russian lady, once married to a diplomat under the Czarist regime. Mama had known Madame Lermantov in Madrid and heard that she was now exiled and living in financial straits in Paris.

The prospect delighted me. Moreover, Uncle Lionel, no longer an Arctic explorer, was studying animal sculpture in Paris, and I envisaged long days of serious work at the Sorbonne followed by interesting outings with him. Winifred, who was remaining in London to become a debutante, gave me a knife so that I could defend myself against apaches on the Metro. Life was looking up.

Madame Lermantov proved a perfect darling. I grew to love her and to suffer Russian-fashion when small troubles made her weep. Starting with Stendhal, I began to get my teeth into French literature.

The evenings with Lionel surpassed expectation. He was not only working under a French sculptor but sharing digs with a French girl. She was a dancer at some night club where her costume consisted only of gold paint. After the performance she had to wash the gilding off with glycerine and drink two pints of milk to reduce the danger of blood poisoning. I had never met anyone like this. Nor for that matter have I done so since. She came from Arras. Her life had been hard and she was not shy of talking about it, or the trials of dancing naked.

When summer came Madame Lermantov tried to expand my acquaintance, by introducing me to some young Russians who were earning their living as artists and taxi drivers. They lived in a penniless community run by a very old French sculptor, Alfred Boucher (his group, *The Runners*, stands in the Luxembourg Gardens). This new life proved a revelation. Old Boucher, bearded and friendly in his dotage, had known Rodin intimately. Ten years younger than Rodin, he had won the Prix de Rome and attained early fame. Boucher then helped Rodin to gain recognition, and also helped Rodin's son, who was treated with the disregard which many great artists show towards their offspring. I had the wit to recommence a diary and note down the anecdotes which old Boucher recounted.

My last evening was memorable. Pierre Panchenko, a Russian exile, who drove a taxi after dark (night club clientele paid best), had married and was holding a wedding feast. The bride was a quaint little French artist in Boucher's community. All the inhabitants of the huts built around the courtyard took part. The Russian music made one's blood burn, and Pierre, fortified by much vodka, jumped up to perform his native Caucasian dance. Crossed swords were laid on the floor and Pierre, a huge man, whirled lightly over them, his legs spinning out the

Gladys, Duchess of Marlborough, a painting by Boldini (1916).
Reproduced by kind permission of Jane, Lady Abdy

The debutantes: Rose Vincent
and Winifred Paget

Marjorie Ide, the author's mother, dressed for Court

Right: Jack as a Guards officer
Below: Desmond at the age of fifteen

Sir Shane Leslie with Lord Dufferin and his son Ava at
Glaslough in 1924. They are holding a big pike

The author's first husband, Paul, on horseback

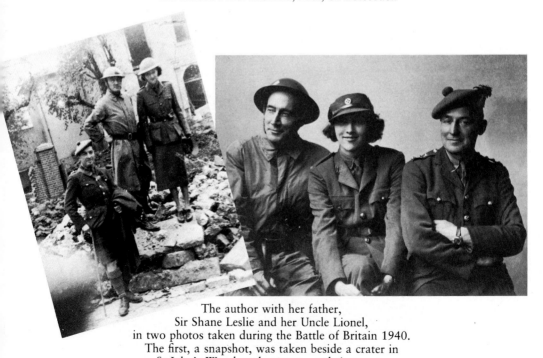

The author with her father,
Sir Shane Leslie and her Uncle Lionel,
in two photos taken during the Battle of Britain 1940.
The first, a snapshot, was taken beside a crater in
St John's Wood as they were on their way to
the formal studio session which
produced the second photograph

intricate steps. Faster and wilder thrummed the balalaikas until it all became too much for the exuberant bridegroom. Snatching up a sword Pierre tried to kill himself, shouting, 'I am so happy I want to die!' Chums rushed at him and tore the weapon away – with difficulty for he was exceedingly strong. The bride flung herself weeping onto her bleeding husband, and bandages were fetched, coffee was boiled, dawn pinked the sky. I pranced home ill with excitement and dreaded the anticlimax of having to travel home the next day. No one ever behaved like this at weddings in London. English men were so dull.

12

Debutante

The thirties had crept in and those twinkling tunes of the twenties were changing to a more sombre beat. Over the next nine years how dark the shadows would grow.

One morning in my Irish home, I entered my grandmother's bedroom to find her seated at her dressing table which stood in a bow window overlooking the lake. She was shaking with emotion. 'Look,' she said, pointing to a newspaper clipping stuck in her mirror. 'I have been sent that and I am going to keep it there in case I ever forget what human beings can do to each other.' The clipping showed the photo of an unhappy-looking man walking along a street in his underpants with a large star pinned to his vest.

'That star shows he is a Jew,' said my grandmother, and her trembling hands kept dropping her silver brushes.

'But why do they want to do that? And who are *they*?' I asked. The outrage seemed so peculiar.

She pulled down the clipping and read the German caption. I had never heard the term National Socialist and the haunted, humiliated expression of the man's face puzzled me. That newspaper clipping was my first inkling of the 'regime created by tiger cubs reared on an ashheap' which was to smash our world.

We had a few years to go yet. Among my grandmother's close friends was Count Herman Keyserling, the philosopher. He did not come to Ireland, reserving his brilliance for lecture tours in other parts of the world. (This was a relief, for Grandma said he was inclined to disdain ordinary mealtimes, muttering, 'You go home to eat – here I will sit and tink.') Now Keyserling had had his passport taken away so he could not leave Germany, but his son Manfred, a tall handsome

boy, came to Castle Leslie. He talked with passion of his own generation which felt that class should disappear and that dawn light lay
ahead. This passionate desire for comradeship was interesting in one
born into the old Russian-German aristocracy. Manfred was the only
boy we ever met from Central Europe and no tinge of Nazi ruthlessness
showed in his vibrant, hopeful views.*

During our slide towards Armageddon, Irish country life continued
in unawareness. I would visit County Meath for the fox-hunting and
photos abound of lawn meets with maids wearing floppy caps carrying
trays to riders – stirrup cup to be quaffed in the saddle. Other photos
show sporting ladies in tweed skirts, flat-heeled shoes and cloche hats,
marching around at smart shoots. Hampers of food stand everywhere.
As in Edwardian times, the moment people got out of doors they
thought it necessary to stuff.

When the time came for my debut in London society I determined
to attend a course in modern French fiction at the polytechnic. Mama
fussed in case these lectures collided with important dances. How had
her tiresome daughter ever heard of the polytechnic? Occasionally my
parents took me to country house parties. I started off at Bowood, the
Lansdownes' magnificent house in Wiltshire, where Kitty, now a lovely
young creature, was already 'out' and enjoying her hunting. 'An egg
for tea for Lady Kitty,' the footman would call, and for the huntress,
mud-bespattered in her sidesaddle habit, a boiled egg would be added
to the heaped plates of scones and cake. Less pleasure was shown by
the elders when Kitty scratched her face in briars while out hunting
the day before her own great ball.

At Bowood the young people would be carefully placed at dinner to
sit next to suitable prospective spouses, and mothers scolded daughters
who did not make alluring conversation to young men – the right
young men of course. But no one entered the portals of glorious
Bowood who was not very right indeed.

Yet I heard on the family grapevine that Kitty herself was rebelling.
Her grandmother – my great-aunt Consie – had regarded Kitty's fingernails with displeasure.

'I don't like that bright pink.'

'Oh, don't you! I think it is so pretty,' Kitty had riposted. This bold
reply was repeated in hushed tones. It showed what even the best-
brought-up girls were coming to.

* Manfred Keyserling fought in the Germany Army and lost his legs at Stalingrad.

My parents often stayed at Eaton Hall with Bendor, the Duke of Westminster. Mama used to take her fortune-telling cards, hand-painted for her long ago in Samoa by Robert Louis Stevenson's step-daughter Teuila. She enjoyed telling fortunes in the secrecy of her bedroom until one evening the cards showed every symbol representing death and disaster for one of her friends. When in the following week the most unexpected tragedy hit, Mama decided never to pack her cards again.

On several occasions I also was taken to Eaton Hall. Bendor had, as a young man, married Sheila, the sister of George Cornwallis-West, who had married my great-aunt Jennie. They produced two daughters and one boy, who died at the age of seven. The tragicomedy of being a girl in English society was nowhere more apparent than in this vast Victorian mansion which no girl could inherit. Bendor's name was seldom mentioned without the accompanying sigh: 'But he has no son.' One might have thought that the only function of an English duke was to beget yet another duke. Sheila had divorced him but her two daughters, Ursula and Mary, often appeared at Eaton Hall.

Ursula, a tall, blonde wraith and the mother of two boys, must have been ironically aware of her remissness at being born a girl unable to carry her father's name. Bendor had tried a brief second marriage to a famous horsewoman. His third duchess was Loelia Ponsonby, dark, vivacious and many years his junior.

When I was first taken to Eaton Hall that delicious Parisian dress-maker Chanel, who had long been Bendor's mistress, was also staying there. I watched agog what was to me an elderly house party and tried to make subtle conversation at dinner. Chanel's evening gowns were memorable for she always wore the same model – consisting of layers of deep silk fringe. She said these dresses were her favourite design and easy to pack. She appeared in a different colour each night – black, white, red, deep blue – no bother. That was what Chanel liked. No bother with clothes or men.

Mama seldom enjoyed staying in the enormous house. On one occasion she had found her sheets were damp. When she rang, asking that they should be aired, the housemaid did not know where to find a hot cupboard. And then Mama had discovered an unfed parrot. She made Bendor ring bells and shout at minions to fill the empty seed dishes – but the 'parrot boy' had disappeared and no one knew where the seed was kept. The park was huge and very beautiful. When lonely I could row out to an island on which lived an equally lonely monkey.

The house parties consisted of twenty people or more, eyeing each other rather unhappily, while Bendor showed himself good-natured and petulant by turn. I liked him, but he obviously did not know where to turn next for diversion. He needed to work in some leper colony to get his priorities right and discover himself. As it was, he fretted amidst toadies who were ready to dash off to Norway with him for the fishing, or to the South of France for the sun, but within hours he would change his mind and then appear cross with himself and everyone else. Yet how could this man have struggled out of the net he was born into? My father was fond of him. Bendor took him off for long confidences to complain of the lack of true romance, saying he was 'tired of handing out pearl necklaces'. Pa, scornful of women who ran after *him* for poems and Bendor for pearls, would turn such grievances to laughter. But the richest of England's dukes remained mighty sorry for himself.*

The shooting parties at Eaton Hall were those I disliked most. My father no longer cared about this kind of pheasant shooting, when the best guns in England stood out with their loaders bringing down thousands of hand-reared birds, and I always hated the sight of mass killing and, although it had nothing to do with the huge heaps of slaughtered and wounded pheasants, I found it repellent that the shooters' faces always looked so red!

Another duke who turned my father into a sort of best friend—confidant was Sunny Marlborough. He also had a fund of hard-luck stories, starting with boyhood. His parents had parted in distressing circumstances right back in the seventies when the aristocracy did not go in for divorce. His father, known as the 'Wicked Duke' (with reason), had been a brother of Lord Randolph Churchill, and his mother, known as 'Goosie' (also with reason), was one of the Duke of Abercorn's seven daughters. After bearing four children, she had divorced her spouse whose infidelities exceeded what even the meekest Victorian wife could be expected to put up with. Sunny, the eldest son, who then carried the courtesy title Marquis of Blandford, spent much time at Blenheim with his father who, he said, 'never spoke a kind word to me'. Sunny had fallen in love with a girl who did not possess enough money to keep up the acres of Blenheim roof, and his arranged marriage to Consuelo Vanderbilt has been revealed in detail, giving

* The second Duke of Westminster would be an old man before he found happiness with his fourth wife Anne – the Irish owner of Arkle, greatest steeplechaser of all time.

however only her side of the story. Sunny became a Roman Catholic but this gave him little spiritual tranquillity. At the time of my first visit to Blenheim he was married to Gladys Deacon, an American of immense erudition and sadistic wit (whose father had caused quite a sensation in France by shooting her mother's lover dead in a Riviera hotel). Unfortunately Gladys had sought to improve her beauty by early facial surgery. As Grecian profiles were then the thing, she allowed wax to be inserted on the bridge of her slightly tip-tilted nose, with dire results. The wax ran down slowly under the skin, dragging her lovely face into a frog shape. Later the wax had to be cut out of folds beneath her chin, but nothing could pull her face back into place.

Mama did not come on my first visit to Blenheim. She had grown wary of damp sheets in ducal houses. Pa took me alone. The only other guests were cousin Randolph Churchill, now a good-looking bombastic twenty-year-old, and a very beautiful Australian girl who was about to come out in London. Randolph had lured her to Blenheim where she was obviously expecting a large interesting house party. When Patricia Richards, as she then was, realized that Pa and I were the only other guests, her face fell. And Randolph's strategy grew only too obvious.

We all arrived in pouring rain. The duke met us and tea was carried into one of the drawing rooms (there were many in Blenheim). The duchess did not appear for a long time. We waited hopefully, as no ·one could pour tea except the hostess. Finally we heard, not footsteps, but the claw-clatter of many little dogs. 'Watch Sunny – he hates her guts – great sport!' whispered Randolph. In came the duchess, surrounded by a moving carpet of King Charles spaniels. Gladys Marlborough was extraordinary to look at. Absolutely hideous and yet exotic, with golden hair swept back in a bun and strange blue eyes staring out of the ruin of that stretched face. She advanced in her dirty old clothes, shook hands and waved us graciously to chairs. From then on she devoted herself to my father, who was able to produce the sort of cosmopolitan witticisms she enjoyed.

After tea Randolph took us for 'a snoop' through the immense organ room and past several uncleaned Rubens to the room where his father had been born. We may have seen one-sixteenth of the house on this tour.

Eventually a maid was summoned to lead the young ladies upstairs to their rooms. The duchess lived on the ground floor – 'in a wing of my own', she remarked with an acid glance at her spouse. Patricia and

I rang the bell and a housemaid appeared to take our dresses away to iron.

'Where is the bathroom?' asked Patricia.

'Oh, miss, I wouldn't know that.'

We waited a long time and then explored. Eventually at the end of a corridor we found a bathroom, the tub set deep into a mahogany box. A little tepid water ran from one tap.

Coming down to dinner in the fluffy dresses suitable for *jeunes filles*, we found the three men waiting and then our hostess swept in with her spaniels. I don't think she had washed much or combed her hair, but she wore a blue evening gown with a train, and this train she had pinned up on her behind with a large safety pin. Purposely she showed people that she did not care what she looked like.

We went in to dinner. The pictures were splendid, the food uneatable and the conversation stunning. I had never heard anything like it. Marlborough sat looking like a rat caught in a trap, while the duchess delivered her poisoned shafts. Poor little man, I thought. He was forced to listen while his wife told us girls why we should not get married. 'I didn't marry,' she said, 'until I'd been to bed with every prime minister in Europe – and most of the kings.' The duke did not smile. Pa lifted one eyebrow. Randolph's eyes never left Patricia's face. Then the duchess got on to Anatole France and what a lark it was going to bed with *him*. My Anatole France – Margaret's pet author! I began to feel very sophisticated. Meanwhile two footmen in dirty cotton gloves served tepid food which had been carried from some distant kitchen.

Patricia and I had adjoining rooms and I was in her room saying goodnight when a step sounded in the corridor. Randolph had made his way from the bachelor wing. Patricia clutched me nervously. 'Don't leave me,' she whispered. Boldly I stepped over to the door and opened it to his knock. Randolph did not look too pleased and pulled me out into the corridor. 'Look here, coz,' (he always called me that), 'take this and go to your own room.' He'd bribed me before – a few bob here and there at Chartwell to answer phonecalls and say he was out – when it suited him. But if I took a bribe now it would have to be a mighty big one! I scorned his pound note, turned back and jumped into Patricia's bed beside her. There we sat stolidly, in our nighties and dressing-gowns with cold cream on our faces and the be-ribboned slumber helmets of the day holding our short curls in place.

Randolph was stymied. All he could do was ask for a corner of the eiderdown and hold forth about his future as Prime Minister. An hour passed, and then he had to go. His eyes were cold when he bade me goodnight.

Next day it continued raining. We walked the terraces in mackintoshes while Pa and the duke vanished into some remote corner of Blenheim to look at papers. When teatime came Randolph and Patricia were missing.

'Where's that pretty Miss Richards?' asked the duke suddenly.

'Couldn't you see?' replied Gladys, 'Randolph is hoping to seduce her among the cabbages' – her exact words remain in my memory.

At this moment they entered, Randolph looking furious and Patricia flushed with temper. That night we were left in peace. Randolph had to leave early in the morning.

'How does one get away from this dreadful place?' Patricia asked me. 'I shall never come again.' One began to see why chaperons were considered necessary. Blenheim was the only country house at which I ever stayed where girls were left unguarded.

Within weeks Patricia, who had real beauty – beauty of bone – became the 'Deb of the Season'. A few months later she married the ninth Earl of Jersey. Maybe she never did return to Blenheim, but I spent many subsequent weekends there because the duchess had taken to me and I was fascinated by her unusual mind, and Pa liked rummaging in the library. I was always sorry for the duke, he looked such an unhappy man, but the entrancing, unutterable Gladys would take me off alone and talk for hours about her lovers. Half of what she said I could not believe. She showed me the revolver she kept 'to shoot Sunny if he ever dares to enter my rooms'. I found her patter good value. So did H. G. Wells, who turned up unannounced one weekend when some college was acting a Greek play on the terraces. Crouched under an umbrella, I could not bear to miss a word of this excellent performance, but H. G. Wells got bored and made off towards an indoor tea. By the time I joined him, the duchess was well launched. 'What I can't make out, Mr Wells, is why you are gorging in Blenheim Palace when you spend all your time decrying people who live in big houses!'

H. G. Wells beamed and stretched for another cream puff. 'Well, I'll tell you. I don't mind the big houses exactly – nor people like yourself – and I never refuse a good tea . . .'

'But you haven't been invited. . . .'

'No matter,' continued H. G. Wells. 'You interest me.'

For once the duchess was reduced to silence.

Later on in London a film producer begged me to ring up the duke and arrange for the shooting of some scenes at Blenheim . . . I did so but Sunny angrily refused. 'Make a film in *my house*! Certainly not.' Wondering if it was quite fair to trigger off an argument, I then phoned the duchess. She roared with laughter. 'If Sunny goes away you can bring your common friends and of course they can make movies all over the place.'

But Sunny did not leave Blenheim that summer, and I never managed to get the film crew there.

For some reason the duchess kept the letters I wrote her in 1933 when she was leaving Blenheim and demanding a divorce. Her biographer, Hugo Vickers, handed me these letters forty-five years later. I see that I addressed Gladys Marlborough as 'My dear friend', and pleaded to meet her alone in London – 'Mum wants you to come to dinner but that would not be the same. I just long to be with a real person.'

Maybe she kept my letters because in them I relayed Clare Sheridan's compliments on her 'man's mind'. To a callow girl, these two extraordinary women, with their bizarre talk about famous lovers, had a fascination which was lacking in debutantes. I tried hard to appear sophisticated and one of my letters ends, 'Wishing you the best of luck in the divorce – With love – Anita.'

During the London season debutantes went to dances every night, wearing their prescribed white evening dresses. Presentation at court proved an interesting experience. Mama and I borrowed trains from friends and these satin lengths were attached to our shoulder straps. The required ostrich feathers had to be affixed in our hair by a little man in a hurry. Every hairdresser in London was putting the final touches to the crimped heads of his customers. Nanny looked me over and the cook and maids came up to gurgle appreciatively at the curious image that was me dressed up for a royal court. Before we even stepped into the limousine hired for the evening Mama was getting a headache from her tiara, but there was no method of easing its weight. For an hour or so we had to remain on display in broad daylight as cars queued in the Mall. The public could put their noses to within two feet of the window and allow their comments to be heard. A few spoilsports pulled down window blinds – an attitude out of keeping in a democracy.

Inside Buckingham Palace we passed slowly from one large gilded room to another. King George V and Queen Mary sat stiffly on their thrones, bowing graciously and looking just like the king and queen in a pack of cards. Mama, having been presented on marriage by Granny Leonie, was able to present me. I was then 'done' until marriage, when the process would have to be repeated.

Deb dances were seldom enjoyed by young girls. Unable to dance except with a man who had been formally introduced, nervous chicks clung to their families. Lord Enniskillen's motherless daughters, with whom I often stayed in Ireland, used to be sent off with a harassed chaperon. They had never danced with a boy in their lives before being thrust into a London ballroom, and Ann, the eldest, told me that she always looked for long window curtains to hide behind. Then she would miserably wonder if her shoes were showing.

As dancing was so important at functions it seems curious that English males were never taught to keep time. Waltzes resulted in bruised toes and an Englishman's idea of fox-trotting consisted of marching a lady backwards. In the USA boys did not scorn dancing class and whenever an American moved off in an English ballroom an expression of rapturous amazement would spread over his partner's face.

I longed for adventure of any sort and one day complained to my cousin, Desmond Vincent-Jones, about the lack of it in a deb's life. He was a naval lieutenant, doing a course at the Royal Naval College at Greenwich, which enabled him to attend many balls. Sitting out amidst the potted ferns, I muttered, 'What I'd really like is to visit an opium den.'

My cousin assured me he could manage that – the officers of his acquaintance knew all the best dens. I was impressed and Desmond arranged for me to go out to dinner with him. He picked me up in an open sports car and we drove miles down river. My heart leaped to my mouth when eventually we stopped in a dark lane. I had no idea where we were. 'Shhh,' Desmond kept saying as we tiptoed towards a warehouse in a rubbish-filled garden. It was quite dark and not knowing exactly what one did in an opium den I felt a little nervous. My cousin rapped three times on a door and scuffling could be heard. Then a Chinese face peeped out.

'It's all right – just a young lady who wants to try your pipes,' said Desmond. I thought this a bit much, but stepped inside and there by the light of an oil lamp I saw the floor covered with bodies lying sprawled in disarray. Occasionally they snorted unpleasantly. Then suddenly the figures leaped up with yells and shrieks. I turned to flee.

What a trap Desmond and his naval pals had spent the day rehearsing. The Chinese man was the Crown Prince of Siam, who was also attending the course at the Royal Naval College. Several girls climbed out of sacking, all weak with laughing – except me. We drove off to supper and I tried to think it as funny as the others did.

Because of our grandmother, Jack and I were always invited to the most interesting receptions in London. These took place on the eve of the opening of Parliament at Londonderry House. Full dress uniform was worn and Lady Londonderry, draped in diamonds, stood at the head of the stairs giving the same warm welcome to us youngsters as to eminent statesmen. She liked to be called Circe – 'able to tame the swine in every politician'.

When my grandmother took me to balls it was different. Gazing across the room through lorgnettes, she would spy the most amusing people – never young however. I would find myself suddenly at ease, laughing and joking with some elderly ambassador who treated one naturally. It took only a few weeks in London society to perceive that it was almost impossible for a duke to retain any character – such was the sycophancy and so hot the chase after ducal heirs. Earls also appeared to find it difficult to conceal their conceit at inheriting a title devised for sea-raiders but grown singularly inappropriate for men about town.

Very different to these formal dances were the parties Clare Sheridan gave in her St John's Wood studio. She would collect artists and writers to dine by candlelight on red wine and spaghetti. Talk blazed like a poked fire. Fascinating James Stephens, author of *The Crock of Gold* and *The Charwoman's Daughter*, would sit there looking like a leprechaun, teasing the company in his marvellous Irish voice.

Pa did not care for bohemian evenings. He liked big dinner parties and he would only go to balls which took place in grand private houses. Mama seldom accompanied me to dances because, in her own words, it bored her to see my sulks. Her beau of the time was Vyvyan Holland, the erudite son of Oscar Wilde, who had survived the trauma of his boyhood and of knowing the father who had always been so kind to him hideously punished. For several summers Vyvyan came to stay at Castle Leslie and in London he accompanied Mama to first nights and what he called 'interesting parties'. These were not deb balls.

Sent to dances alone, I soon learned how to slip away from the unfortunate chaperon into whose care I had been placed, and within weeks of being launched into society I had a young man – the one young man no mother would allow to any country house party or invite to any dance, because on several occasions he had shown that 'he did not know how to behave'. The climax had occurred when he vainly tried to bribe to silence an elderly housemaid who found him in some lady's bed, and in the same week he had his licence taken away for drunken driving. His parents were old friends of my grandmother, who had introduced him to me before she heard these stories.

In a flash this scion of a noble house realized how useful I could be to him because at seventeen I could drive! No tests were needed in those days; one just bought a licence. By day I drove John's sports car wherever he wished and at night he hired a chauffeur to bring him to any house where I would be attending a dance. How thrilling it was to slip out onto the balcony and spy that shadowy figure waiting at the corner beside his car! Then came the nonchalant climb upstairs to find my wrap and I would run down to the front door and creep out unseen. Safely in the car, we would drive to an odious place called the Ace of Spades on the Great West Road, and here, if we'd brought bathing suits, we swam in a canvas tank. One could also – if possible after a large dinner and before a lobster supper – eat scrambled eggs. The timing of all this kept me in a fever, because I had to get back to the dance before anyone grew suspicious. Sneaking in under the lighted awning, I would find my way upstairs and explain to the unfortunate chaperon, who could not go home until she had deposited every girl safely, that I had been 'sitting out'.

It was not difficult to scandalize in those days. When Winifred Paget took up tap-dancing I joined the class. We wore red shoes with steel tips. I found these extraordinarily comfortable and caused consternation by wearing them on walks in the park. Mama gave me up as a bad job. I had not even inherited her American spun-glass legs. Besides, she had other fish to fry.

We were lucky on one score. Our entire family were pets of Lady Cunard, who often rang up to say she was not using her box at the opera that night. This news would be a signal for frantic disentangling phonecalls to people we might be dining with and dressing up in spangles to rush to the underground, for it was considered perfectly *comme il faut* to travel to Covent Garden in full evening dress.

Lady Cunard, unique, twittering and ruthless, was married to Sir

Bache Cunard, a fox-hunting baronet of large fortune who liked living among his broad acres and was bored stiff by London musical life. Lady Cunard, once called Maud, had bejewelled herself and become Emerald. She collected people who could talk well at her dinner table and insisted on general conversation. Jack and I were *never* invited but she got my father whenever she could and we knew ourselves lucky to sit in her box. Because of her we got to know all the operas.

Royal Ascot was considered a highlight of the London season. Applications for the royal enclosure had to be made months ahead. Every debutante went and officers of the Brigade of Guards were advised to make an appearance in grey top hat and morning coat. Still being mad about horses, although I'd lost the urge to become a vet when I realized the difficult exams entailed, I looked forward to Ascot week. But I was unlucky. Granny Leonie was away in the South of France with the Duke of Connaught, and Ma and Pa had had a tiff there the year before when a sudden cloudburst had turned the course into a quagmire and flooded the tents. A bookie was killed by lightning and Mama, in her trailing chiffon gown and huge hat, had to clamber onto a chair in the luncheon tent. There she stood marooned while waiters waded around, paddling crates of food to safety. Gallant gentlemen in top hats rushed to rescue damsels in distress, ruining their own trousers in the process. Standing on her chair, Mama saw Pa carrying one of his 'alley cats' to safety before her. A row ensued and she swore never to go to Ascot again.

When my turn came, she had left London and Pa disappeared. Taking a seventeen-year-old daughter to Ascot was not his idea of amusement. But my badge had arrived and I was longing to swank around the royal enclosure and see the King and Queen drive down the course in their open landau. Aunt Anne had given me two of her expensive cast-off Paris dresses – one strawberry pink and one deep orange – and I had bought a wide-brimmed straw hat – picture hats they were called – with ribbons that could be changed. What a guy I must have looked setting off alone by train from Paddington wearing the draped pink dress with the hat wound with pink velvet ribbons! I had been well schooled in etiquette – no lady in the royal enclosure might approach the bookies but a gentleman was permitted to go to the rails and place bets for her. Unfortunately I had no man to back a horse for me but there was plenty to see.

Queen Mary was there wearing one of her famous toques and giving the impression that she kept an eye on you personally. In fact she was about to send a message to a certain artistic peeress ordering her to leave the royal enclosure because of her hat. The lady had asked for it. She was wearing a round sailor cap with 'HMS Good Ship Venus' in gold lettering.

As the afternoon wore on I grew hungry. Everyone else kept going off for lunch in one of the club tents where members led in their own parties. None of that merry throng could have dreamed that any parents would send a girl alone to the royal enclosure.

Next day, in the burnt-orange dress this time and sporting orange favours on my hat, I placed a couple of sandwiches in my handbag, and eventually I sat down on a bench to eat them. It is not all that easy to munch secretly and I probably imagined that the laughter of a group of pink-faced young gentlemen standing nearby was directed at me. Dislike enveloped me. *They* were able to bet, *they* belonged to clubs and could eat when they chose, just because they were male.

It was an olive-skinned gentleman with roving – very roving – eyes who came to my rescue. Aly Khan, son of the Aga Khan, happened to be standing nearby. Looking up, I caught his amused glance under the grey topper. We had met at a dinner and he stepped forward jauntily.

'How about some strawberries?' he asked. I leaped to my feet and Aly led me into one of those club tents where everyone else was having such a delicious time. Strawberries and cream? A second helping? Yes, please! Aly was the only person to be kind to me that day, and I never forgot it.

It was a relief when the season ended and it was time to go back to Ireland. One could not be a deb twice. That phase was over, and if my ambition throughout had been to annoy Mama, I had succeeded wonderfully.

13
The Ominous Thirties

During all this time I continued to view my father through long-distance lorgnettes. Sometimes I felt sorry for him. Obviously he had fallen between two stools. The son of an Ulster landlord, he had evoked fury by espousing with passion the cause of the Irish Nationalists, led in Westminster by John Redmond; then he had seen Redmond throw away Asquith's promised Home Rule when war broke out in 1914. Redmond died of a broken heart when his brother had been killed fighting for England, and Ireland tossed Redmond's memory into the dustbin after the execution of Irish leaders in 1916.

Bewildered and hurt, torn by conflicting loyalties, a poet not a soldier, my father had done what he could to bring America into the war. During 1916 he worked with Sir Cecil Spring-Rice, the British ambassador in Washington. Pa tried to serve England by cajoling the Irish-Americans to enter the conflict on the Allies' side and he tried at the same time to serve Ireland by editing a literary magazine embellished with Gaelic verse. Neither country gave him thanks. Sir Cecil Spring-Rice found that his counsels to British politicians were disregarded and finally he was thrown out of his ambassadorship. He died, like John Redmond, of a broken heart. Both were Anglo-Irishmen who loved two countries and strove to make them understand each other.

Pa had then found himself unwanted in the new Irish Free State and all he could do was seek to reconcile the two cultures – the English culture, evoked by Eton and Cambridge, in which he had been brought up, and the old Celtic culture which he had found for himself and loved so dearly. *He* did not die of a broken heart – Jerome blood abolished such tendencies – but to the end of his life, while he worked to weave peace between opposing forces, he would not cease to blame

John Redmond for encouraging Irishmen to fight in English regiments 'without placing Home Rule on the tip of the proffered sword'.

Pa felt near enough to me to burst into my bedroom one night and wake me from sleep. 'I've failed to persuade the Home Secretary. They'll be hanged tomorrow.' He had been appealing for clemency for two Irish extremists whose bomb had blown up by mistake and killed people in an English city. In those days capital punishment seemed a natural penalty and I could only blink sleepily and say, 'I'm sorry, Pa. Dev [De Valera] will hate the English even more.'

Pa never spoke to me as an individual. Once when I tried to approach him and explain the heavy, leaden feeling I got when forced into society, he just said, 'Why don't you get married and go away? You'd feel less futile,' and went on with his writing. I stood by his desk and the stuffed snowy owl he was so fond of gazed coldly at me through its glass dome. There was no more to be said.

Pa was welcomed by London hostesses for his witty conversation, but he presented a very different picture on the occasions when he happened to attend a meal at home. The family bored him. Not only did he never speak, but if we ventured an opinion his eyes would close like those of a parrot – the bottom lid moving upwards. I think Mama enjoyed going out with him but she was inclined to interrupt – a lethal fault in any wife – and they led separate lives. Being extremely talkative herself, she seldom noticed if he spoke or not at home. When occasionally she did notice his silence and closed eyes, she would rise, to the consternation of the butler, and sweep out of the dining room. Jack and I had grown accustomed to such scenes, but our inability to digest food in such an atmosphere remained and every now and again, when Mama was trying out a new dish with her famous cook, she would notice this and it added to her anguish. 'What! You aren't eating! Poor Mrs Young will be hurt.' So we chewed and swallowed manfully, whatever emotions wrecked our digestive juices.

Pa never gave us any presents nor did he remember our birthdays. We simply did not interest him. Yet he was capable of sudden generosity if an idea caught his imagination. Money bored him and he wrote entirely for pleasure, but when one of his books caught on and the publishers sent an unexpectedly large cheque, Pa hurried off to Cartier and spent the entire sum on a bracelet for Mama. It consisted of three sapphires and diamonds alternately, to commemorate her three children. She burst into tears of surprise when he handed it to her. And we were equally surprised. So he *had* noticed us – or at least our number!

I continued to miss Margaret. Clare had brought her daughter to London a year before I came out. At parties she dazzled in white Grecian dresses with a flower in her dark hair. Scorning eligible young men, she remained in love with the Sahara. People should have left her alone to develop her potential but they couldn't let her be. She had to be fitted into a niche and there were no suitable niches in England for such a girl. I knew one man who wanted to marry her – he was a mutual friend – a writer as clever as herself and mad about the East. But they were held apart by lack of money. It seemed so illogical that this mentally well-matched pair should have allowed such an issue to separate them, especially as her own mother never ceased moaning at the mistake she and Wilfred Sheridan had made. 'We married so late and within five years he was killed.'

Barney Baruch, the American financier, took pity on Margaret. When she told him how she longed to explore the Northern Sahara and to study the Tuareg tribes, he bought her two splendid desert-worthy vehicles. Eventually, I learned with a heavy heart that she was to marry a French Army officer much older than herself and vanish with him into French Equatorial Africa. Her mother gave her the white house at Biskra as a dowry – alabaster pillars and all. Clare was already tired of it.

The following winter Mama tried to tear me away from fox-hunting around Dublin for another plunge into London society. On my eighteenth birthday she altered my life in an unexpected way. She gave me a fringed shawl of white silk covered with hand-embroidered flowers, which had been her court dress in Spain, where she wore it with a high comb and mantilla. Grateful for this marvellous present, I twisted and turned around the house in it until Mama casually remarked, 'Why don't you learn Spanish dancing?' Inquiries revealed that a well-known Spanish dancer, Elsa Brunelleschi, gave instruction in Westbourne Grove, ten minutes' walk from our house, and from that moment on I was taking lessons, clicking fingers and stamping my heels till the plaster fell off our ceilings. The embroidered shawl was eventually put away in tissue paper – it was a museum piece, much too heavy for dancing – but I had a long cotton gown made with a frilled skirt, and for an hour or so every morning I practised the turns and stamps taught by Miss Brunelleschi. Mama found her old castanets and on these I trilled away. The only other tall, blue-eyed girl attending these dancing classes was Vivien John, youngest daughter of Augustus John; the other pupils were small, dark and Latin-looking. I had discovered a new kind of fun. If not a great poet or vet, why not become a great dancer?

'Aren't you ever going to tire of it?' Mama soon asked, wishing she had never given me the shawl. But I did not tire of such discoveries. One day I went straight from dancing class to tea with Granny Leonie in her house in Great Cumberland Place. She looked at me with horror. 'Dear child, please go upstairs. You need a bath.' Peering in the mirror I saw a grubby face framed by locks still damp with sweat. Tearing off my clothes, I jumped into a bath and later reappeared apologetically in the drawing room.

'She's learning to dance, sir,' my grandmother said into the ear-trumpet of HRH the Duke of Connaught.

'Well done,' beamed the courteous old gentleman misunderstanding what I was up to. 'So important for a girl to dance nicely.'

The height of my dancing career occurred on the night that Mama gave a fancy-dress party. Everyone had to come dressed as film stars. Mama looked amusing as Mary Pickford, the world's sweetheart, and I chose a Spanish actress so that I could wear my frilled skirt. Towards the end of the evening guests sat around on the drawing-room floor and I performed a Spanish dance, castanets and all. Although shy to speak I was never shy to dance. I believed I did it rather well. Anyway Miss Brunelleschi was not there to criticize and Ma's guests applauded enthusiastically. Ava (now Basil Dufferin) sat beside me afterwards. He'd become Under-Secretary of State for India and his career looked as if it must develop according to plan. His surprise and his compliments seemed genuine. 'You dance wonderfully,' he said. 'I couldn't believe my eyes.' This was high praise for, despite his brilliance, Basil lacked ability to communicate. Added to a couple of glasses of champagne, his words went to my head. If only I could go and live with those Spanish gipsies in caves and practise all day long, what might I not become? Of course Mama's guests had never seen real Spanish dancing – or, if they had, did not recognize the intricate technique. What amazed them was that Marjorie's daughter could stamp around at all.

Soon after, at Winifred Paget's house, I met C. B. Cochran, the most famous impresario of the time. How could I have had the nerve to tell him about my Spanish dancing? I did however, and he arranged an audition. I was about to go off to Ireland to help Lady Lavery's daughter train horses but this new temptation prevailed. Nervously I climbed on a dark stage, handed my music to the pianist and twirled around shaking my frilled train.

Cocky was kind. 'I haven't any place for Spanish dancers at the moment but you can be a dancing showgirl in my new production *Nymph Errant*. We start rehearsals next week.' So I became a Cochran Young Lady. Granny Leonie was disgusted, Mama could not believe that I, who loved horses and country, should be ready to miss a summer in Ireland.

At first the rehearsals seemed intriguing, but then, as the dancing showgirls had less and less to do, I began to wonder if there were not other ways of becoming a great something or other. Gertrude Lawrence was the star of this Cole Porter show, but when one had heard a song fifty times even her most avid fan could be ready to call it a day. It might be exciting for me to meet girls who were not debs, but after a month in Manchester Mr Cochran's Young Ladies seemed quite as dull as the products of Mayfair – in fact, although I would not have admitted it, even duller.

Nymph Errant ran for six months at the Adelphi and when the curtain came down for the last time I saw Gertrude Lawrence turn to her leading man and burst into tears. I was surprised that she felt no relief at no longer having to sing the same songs over and over again.

My great-aunt Mary Crawshay, who had diligently visited me at the Roehampton convent, came equally diligently to watch the musical cavorting of *Nymph Errant*. Afterwards she had me to tea and talked about Sarah Bernhardt – but it was the great Duse she remembered most clearly. Auntie Mary evoked Duse's artistry in an unforgettable phrase: 'When Duse came on the stage I felt a cold wind touch the back of my hands.'

Every now and again Pa took me to spend the day at Chartwell, where I grew to know Winston's daughter Sarah, who was my age. We were both bored by the political talk at meals. Instead of listening to Winston and jotting down everything he said in my diary, I spent idiotic hours giggling with Sarah. I told her about Mr Cochran's Young Ladies and she joined them. Next time I went to Chartwell Clemmie looked at me coldly. Her daughter was 'kicking over the traces' and wanted to marry the comedian Vic Oliver.

Randolph appeared occasionally and when he did turn up Winston would listen lovingly while his son held forth and one could see how much this irritated the older men present. Randolph was at the time entranced by Tilly Losch, the Hungarian dancer, '. . . the most delectable woman,' he called her, adding, 'not like you – no one will ever call you delectable, coz!'

When Sarah disappeared onto the boards I came to know Mary, the youngest. She was only about twelve – beautiful of feature and touchingly fond of her home. I remember walking in the gardens at Chartwell with her. 'I'm *never* going away,' she said. 'I'm going to live here for ever and ever – with Papa.'

Clemmie swept around calmly. She was the perfect hostess, the perfect wife, and to Mary the perfect mother. Randolph and Sarah did not seem able to communicate with her. Diana, the eldest, had been desperately unhappy when after her first London season she came with her mother to Castle Leslie. 'Will nothing ever happen?' she had wept, embarrassing me greatly. 'Mama says I am not a success and only Papa is ever nice to me. He takes me out to the Savoy Grill and tells me not to worry even if my eyelashes are sandy.' Diana married the son of Sir Abe Bailey – the South African magnate. Later, when that proved unsatisfactory, she married the politician Duncan Sandys and produced three interesting children. Sarah made a name for herself before the footlights, Randolph took his own line and only the delicious, tremulous Mary was left.

One girl who came out in the same year rebelled as strongly as I did, but in a different way. I was very fond of her actually and, although many people found Unity Mitford peculiar and indeed enraging, her way of doing kind things unobserved made me like her even more than her obstinate refusal to flirt with eligible gentlemen. The least handsome of an outstandingly beautiful tribe, she quarrelled furiously with her sisters, who held opposite political views, and eventually, through the eldest, Diana, who left Bryan Guinness for Sir Oswald Mosley, she found her idol – Hitler. *He* wasn't any mother's idea of an eligible gentleman – but Unity wanted a bandit. When we were glum debs Unity would often talk about getting 'kidnapped for the White Slave traffic'. She thought it would be such a lark escaping on the way to South America.

Unity became besotted by Hitler and Granny Leonie expressed disgust when she gave the Nazi salute at the German embassy. But the Unity I knew was sad and serious and pathetically in love with the Führer. I remember one evening when she dined with us and repeated Hitler's disparaging comments about Anthony Eden. The other guests looked shocked, but it was Unity who drove one of them, a girl who had no car and little money for a taxi, to her distant home in the suburbs. And that is how I prefer to remember her.

Clare Sheridan was now living in Paris. She had a studio flat in the Rue Bonaparte and as she and Mama had made up their tiff I went to stay with her. Clare had always loved my father and on occasion she maddened Mama by saying, 'Anita is really my daughter. . . .'

Dick, resolutely guarded by Clare against martial aspirations – 'No son of mine is going to die for his country' – was consistently risking his life at sea. He graduated from small sailing boats to joining the crew of a Finnish windjammer – the *Lawhill* – and sailed before the mast to Australia and back. Clare had never recovered from the shock of learning that her husband had been killed in the trenches within hours of Dick's birth. 'At least that sort of thing can never happen again,' she would say.

Dick reappeared in Paris wearing a black sailor sweater and driving a fast car. We thought of doing a course at the Sorbonne together but my diligent student days were over, and Dick's never really began. I enjoyed his company just as much as when we rode Margaret's Arab horses in the desert. But we were grown up now, and wondering what on earth we were to do with ourselves.

Maybe we could become authors. Dick had accumulated good material and he wrote a book about his sailing adventures called *Heavenly Hell*. Having inherited and sold Frampton Court, the Sheridan family home where he was born, he spent the proceeds on buying magical Brede Place from his Frewen uncle. After laying on water, electricity and central heating, he decided he did not want to live there and let it for twenty years.

Dick then settled down in London to write a play. He was eager to emulate his famous ancestor and become Richard Brinsley Sheridan II. Clare fussed about his approaching twenty-first birthday. Two hundred years previously a curse had been laid on the eldest sons of Frampton – none had ever inherited. (Dick's father was a second son; the elder brother was killed in the Boer War.) The sale of the big house and its several thousand acres relieved Clare's mind, but she remained uneasy.

While Dick laboured at his play I remembered the notes I had made concerning Rodin. Old Alfred Boucher had died but his anecdotes lay in my diary. Taking myself off to Castle Leslie I spent a happy winter alone with my grandparents writing a life of the great sculptor. It was good for me to do the research and it made me write letters to numerous people who had known Rodin. I would come in from riding to a hot bath and jump into bed – for my room was icy and the eight servants must not be overworked making fires. There, unheated but happy, I gradually compiled a biography. The seal was set on my writing career when, on hearing my intention, both my parents laughed scornfully. 'Write a life of Rodin? You're not up to it!' I'd show them.

In the evenings at Castle Leslie Granny Leonie would play the piano – a soft-toned Bechstein chosen for her by Paderewski – and talk about her past. For taxation reasons she had to spend six months each year out of England and this exile from her London house was a sore trial. She had never been a country person. *How* bored she became and how wasted she felt in the isolation of Monaghan forests! She puzzled at my contentment there, while enjoying young company and giving out much of herself. Once she said, 'You know, if we forced you to do this – to spend a whole winter with grandparents in the depth of Ireland – I would think it the cruellest thing!'

I could not understand her commiseration. To me the peace and beauty of that Irish home was balm. We all had to go away on 1 April. Then the house would be closed, save for the housekeeper and her minions. This routine had been in force for over a hundred years – since the old Georgian house stood where the Victorian pile now blinked its sixty plate-glass windows at the lake.

On occasion my grandparents took me to stay in the viceregal lodge where their friend James MacNeill had become the first (and only) governor of the Irish Free State. The parties were very grand and no one else of my age ever got invited. Heaven knows why kind Mrs MacNeill made me an exception. Once I sat next to W. B. Yeats at lunch and he regaled me with anecdotes about his Sligo boyhood and about Mark Twain, whom he had met in England.

During the hunt ball season I would be sent to Dublin to enjoy myself. The Irish hunting fraternity were not stuck up like the English and it became the custom to ask me to finish off the evening by doing what they called my 'snake dance' – this being, of course, a version of the tarantella taught me by Miss Brunelleschi. Black velvet dresses were not considered suitable for unmarried girls but I had bought one with a wide skirt and I could hardly wait for the moment to show off. Spanish dancing was the only thing I did well.

Before we returned to London my grandmother talked to me seriously. She said, 'You must not regard yourself as a companion to me.' But I loved her company. She was more amusing than girls of my own age, far wittier and certainly wiser. She had a premonition of war and wanted me to snatch a husband while the going was good.

'You can't linger on for ever in the family home,' she said, 'though it's lovely for us to have you, Anita dear. Youth does not last for ever. I did not marry until I was twenty-six but suitors were crossing the Atlantic all the time to ask for my hand. What is wrong with you? Don't you like society?' Then she added thoughtfully, 'Not that it really exists now. The world I married into disappeared in 1914. All the sons of my friends were killed in the first six months and one cannot build up a country when a whole generation has been wiped out. I pray you will not have to face what we went through.' I saw her hands with the old-fashioned gold rings twitching nervously. Her favourite son had been taken – surely not the grandsons as well? Surely not young Lord Erne, our neighbour, whose father had been 'missing presumed killed'. Surely not Basil Dufferin, whose uncles had been wiped out?

One day the Ernes brought Anthony Eden over from their home, Crom Castle. He and Mama sat on the terrace arguing about which was the more terrifying – Germany or Russia.

'There's nothing to fear from Russia,' he insisted. 'The last thing she wants is to expand. Look at little Estonia and Lithuania.'

'But Russia is so sly and strong,' countered Mama. 'She hasn't changed since the Revolution. How can you not be afraid?'

Anthony Eden laughed. 'Only Germany can endanger us.'

After his departure Mama tried to puzzle it out. 'Why should I, an ordinary American woman, have more commonsense than all those politicians put together? Russia's game is so obvious – '

Another visitor who would walk over when staying with his elder brother Lord Caledon was Harold Alexander, the youngest general in the British Army. Lady Caledon had, like Granny Leonie, produced four boys and no girls. The eldest of each batch, my father and the Earl of Caledon, were both born in 1885. Lady Caledon's younger sons, Herbrand, Harold and Sigismund Alexander, had all married delightful women and produced children, but British primogeniture remained supreme. Three great houses – Caledon with its Nash façade and domed library, Tyttenhanger, a superb Elizabethan manor near London, and 18 Carlton House Terrace – remained the property of Erik, the dreamy bachelor who happened to be the eldest and carried the title. When his brothers came to stay they were treated as if still in the schoolroom and their wives suffered severely from the lack of fires in bedrooms.

Lord Caledon obviously never intended to marry but he had a ladylove – a marchioness who had tired of her husband and teenage children. Midge, as she was called, was forbidden by the dominating dowager to stay in Caledon House so she took up quarters indefinitely in our best guest bedroom – the mauve suite. Cars were not allowed to cross the Border on the direct road linking our estates, so Midge would drive to pick up her beloved where County Monaghan ended and County Tyrone began. One day, overexcited at the impending meeting, Midge drove her car bang into a stone bridge and severely injured her leg. This meant *weeks* in bed in the mauve room with Erik Caledon walking over for every meal.

To amuse the Alexander brothers Desmond wrote a play in verse for his model theatre in the former footmen's wing. On Desmond's ingenious little stage, three feet across, we could manipulate puppets while speaking their lines. The Alexanders would steal away to watch these topical playlets, which caused them to weep with laughter, especially the one concerning Lord Caledon's reluctant marriage proposals to Midge. This masterpiece ended: 'Hush. Hush. Whisper who dares? Little Earl Erik is saying his prayers!'

We all felt that, with luck, Germany might get tired of National Socialism. And Mussolini was by all accounts so well read! Or so said author Hugh Walpole, who came to dinner soon after a visit to the Duce and spoke highly of his erudition. Walpole's lavish praise caused cousin Clare to leave the table in a tantrum. 'She could never resist taunting men,' explained my grandmother, who adored her niece while regretting some of her tendencies. 'So unwise to taunt men,' she continued. 'In the end they forget their manners.'

Hugh Walpole held his head in his hands. 'But Mussolini *is* delightful when you get him onto literature. . . .'

'She never did,' exclaimed my grandmother tartly. 'And now you must go after her and apologize.'

'But what for. . . ?' asked Mr Walpole.

'It does not matter what for. Just do it nicely and bring her back.' Granny Leonie knew how to make men mannerly against their will and Clare was led back, somewhat pink still, before the butler had time to notice that the conversation had got out of hand.

In 1936 Lady Gwendeline Churchill brought her daughter Clarissa to stay in Castle Leslie and sixteen-year-old Desmond fell in love with this Garbo-like beauty. The only method he could devise to catch her attention was to take her out riding. Unfortunately, on Clarissa's last day he sought to ingratiate himself by lending her his own frisky mare. They were miles from home when the horse ran away and a tree branch concussed his cousin, who lay dreamily on the grass while local cottagers bathed her face. By the time Desmond got Clarissa back, her mother was standing with the luggage waiting to leave. Cries of 'Where have you two been through lunchtime?' changed to '*What* have you done to my daughter?' Clarissa was carried upstairs glazed of eye and muddy of coat and the departure had to be postponed. Poor Desmond slunk away to devise other methods of courtship.

I did not agree with Granny Leonie's insistence that a woman on her own could not live interestingly. Yet such admonitions made sense when so few jobs existed. Cousin Clare was an exception, possessing great artistic talent. Although aware of my own lack of genius I remained set on adventure in the single state.

Because I loved her, I tried to please my grandmother, and I listened to her talk about the old Edwardian code. She expounded the logic which permitted amorous liaisons to married women. 'The terrible thing about divorce is that it upsets *the family*. It's the family that matters – you just have to lump it if someone you marry falls in love with someone else – and remember there are always other fish in the sea. . . . ' My generation laughed at the restrictions of her byegone age. None of us would have been censured, as Clare had been, for walking alone across Hyde Park. Nevertheless all the girls I knew remained virtuous. The fear of what might befall those who were not, in those days before the pill, kept even the scattiest on the straight and narrow path. A few girls were said to be 'fast', but no one knew exactly what that meant.

So there we were – on display, with our looks and what fortune we might happen to possess – to be picked over as if in a slave market. At least, there all the others were. Scowling and unbid for, I stood wondering how to break out of the ring! What no one ever mentioned – and the subject was surely pertinent to girls being trailed on the marriage market – was the sexual deviation natural to many Englishmen. Men were assessed by mothers for their financial assets or their titles or perhaps for the kind of life they had to offer, but the word homosexuality I never actually heard.

We were schooled in what young men might not be permitted to do to *us*, but there was never a class to explain what they might be wishing to do to each other. The British educational system for boys was very curious indeed. It has become the fashion lately for writers of memoirs to dilate on the perversities prevalent at preparatory schools; everyone – from outraged heterosexual Randolph Churchill to outraged homosexual Robin Maugham – has revealed the nasty approaches to which they were subjected, aged eight to twelve. But at the time a pall of secrecy lay over the possible eventualities facing sensitive little boys sent to boarding schools where masters – presumably without sufficient mistresses to keep them happy – held the double power of beating and caressing. Children are not wont to tell parents of their searing experiences. The aristocratic ladies of England might have been well advised to attend more assiduously to the sex life of small sons, helpless in half-understood embroilments, and less to that of eighteen-year-old daughters. But our only instructions were to keep men at bay without losing their interest!

I never encountered lesbianism but oddly enough this subject was not completely taboo. Mama of all people suffered an attack which she recounted so often that all my generation knew of it and giggled hysterically. A certain French *comtesse* – 'Bobbie' she was called, which might have given fair warning – was a frequent guest in country houses. Mama found her amusing and, when discussing the delights of hand-embroidered underwear in Paris, invited Bobbie to come to her room to see her crepe-de-chine cami-knickers (in those days we all wore this one-piece garment). When Bobbie arrived expectantly Mama greeted her in flowing dressing-gown which she flung open with exuberant American cries. 'See the lovely quality of this silk, all hand-made. . . .' Apparently Bobbie pounced like a panther and astonished Mama had to run for it down the corridor. I was rather shocked when I heard a girl say, 'Poor *Bobbie* – what a sell!'

Despite the great passions among upper-class English women, such as that of Vita Sackville West and Violet Trefusis, which must have been known to many, the mothers were never afraid of lesbians seducing their daughters whereas they were afraid of males.

When my grandmother took me to tea with Vita Sackville West and her fascinating husband Harold Nicolson, Granny Leonie gave me to understand that Vita had written a very shocking novel – *The Edwardians* – which 'let down her caste'. People whose upbringing placed them in the know were not entitled to reveal. Harold Nicolson made me laugh about his diplomatic memories of Madrid where he had been in the British embassy in the years when Mama was acting as her father's hostess. 'She was the spoiltest thing,' he said, 'and she's never liked me since the day some admirer sent her a box of cherries. They were delivered in error to our embassy and, not knowing who they could be for, I ate them before the mistake was discovered. She has never liked me since – has she?'

'No,' I had to answer truthfully.

The only girl I knew well who married a homosexual paid for it heavily. She was four years older than I, the daughter of one of Pa's peeress alley-cats, and I think she vied for his favours with her mother. Certainly she wrote a pathetic dedication to him in her own privately printed book of poems. 'To Shane who understands. . . .'

Her mother pushed her into the marriage. It was a very smart affair at St Margaret's, Westminster, and as I watched her walk out of the church in a clinging white satin gown, her smile was so forced that I felt a cold chill. The groom made no pretence about his predilections and yet we did not really know what drove him. I heard the vague talk – 'He'll change now' – but of course he couldn't change; he didn't even try, and when this girl felt she could no longer compete with the footmen, she fled and then secured a huge endowment. Eventually, her nerves affected by the strain, she committed suicide.

My grandmother continued to entertain in her drawing room crammed with inlaid French furniture, but being an instinctive person she was getting a little frightened, and not just because of the disappearance of the world she had known. Edwardian society had finally vanished, she told me, after Lady Ellesmere's ball in 1928 when the hostess, outraged at the new habit of gatecrashing, had ordered several uninvited persons to depart. This firm stand had been admired on the night, but next morning reporters got hold of the story and rang up Lady Ellesmere, who unwisely blurted the names of people she had asked to leave her house. For the first time ever the vulgar press got right in on a society scandal. Caught in the street, the girls named gave hasty interviews blaming each other, and for two months newspapers reported their tale-telling in headlines. When Lady Ellesmere complained about the journalists, a cruel caption ran: 'If Lady Ellesmere does not like the heat she should not come into the kitchen.'

And while the social columns wallowed in this bathos, Hitler's black wings were spreading over Germany.

14

Matrimony and All That

My own vintage tended to marry young. Patricia Richards married Lord Jersey. Veronica Briscoe-George became engaged to handsome, swash-buckling Lord Selby, broke it off and then, while Winifred Paget congratulated her on a marvellous escape, announced that it was on again.

Rose Vincent, whom I had first met with our parents in the Cavendish Hotel, had become an intimate friend. Her American mother had died leaving her a huge fortune but there were legal strings, so at eighteen she chose a tall unsmiling Scotsman, Lord Burgh. As I watched the pale little bride floating in a dream down the aisle, I recalled with a stab of emotion her explanation to me: 'You see I get my own money if I marry – otherwise I'll have to wait till I'm twenty-one.' Kitty Fitzmaurice had married Edward Bigham, eldest son of Lord Mersey, and Winifred Paget decided to marry Guy Carleton, a horsy young man with a quick wit.

Very few girls departed from the well-beaten track. Betsan Horlick, whose grandfather had invented malted milk and who had sat next to me at Miss Wolfe's classes, created consternation after she married John Coats, an apparently conventional stockbroker. Betsan had also got her fortune at eighteen by marrying, and this couple opted out of social England to become vegetarian lecturers at the Theosophical Centre in India – causing bewilderment and sour comment among the dowagers.

Mothers of the time used an odious phrase about the wilder spirits among their daughters, saying, 'A couple of babies will settle her down.' This irritating prognostication made our hackles rise, yet it proved true among my school friends. Of the girls who had sat beside me at Miss Faunce's, Betty Shaughnessy and Rosemary Peto had both married at eighteen, Betty to produce two children for Lord Grenfell, and Rosemary six for Lord Hinchinbroke, a strong-viewed politician, later Earl of Sandwich. Betty and Rosemary abandoned their spouses after nursery shackles loosened, but throughout their youth they were caught in the domestic net. Beautiful Patricia Richards's marriage to Lord Jersey hardly survived the nursery stage, nor did that of Rose to Lord Burgh. However, most of the others were as their mothers wished – 'settled down' by the physical effort of maternity despite a plethora of nannies and servants in attendance.

I felt a strong revulsion towards the settling process and certain mothers muttered that I was a bad influence on their girls. After the deb stage we did talk of free love and reincarnation, both being topics which turned the older generation mauve with disapproval. When I first heard of the danger of world overpopulation I remarked to my mother, 'But there are too many people in the world.' She answered pontifically, 'But not of *our* class.'

Among the eighteen-year-old brides I knew there was one whose marriage would last – and through what trauma. This was Angela, the daughter of that Mrs Dudley Ward who for many years made the Prince of Wales behave like a gentleman. Angela chose her man and he chose her. There was no outside pressure. She married Bob Laycock, a handsome, very masculine, outstandingly intelligent officer in the Blues, never dreaming of the stress she would have to endure when he vanished for weeks in the western desert after leading a commando raid in an unsuccessful attempt to capture Rommel.

It was impossible to ignore the reason why most girls got married. Matrimony represented their only mode of escape. Those who did not marry had to linger on in their parents' homes and these were cages, gilded or occasionally ungilded. Despite my grandmother's directives I was left free. I happened to be the only girl born into the Leslie family for fifty years – since Great-Aunt Olive Guthrie had arrived in the old house. Before her, many little Miss Leslies had been brought up by the lovely lake. Some had 'married well' becoming marchionesses, and some had not married at all, being too grand to step down a rung. My four great-aunts had all found suitable husbands – at least the matches appeared 'suitable' on the outside. Their descendants also behaved 'suitably'; the boys won titles and the girls married titles. We seemed to have a flock of connections in the House of Commons as well as in the House of Lords.

My father's friends covered a wide range. One of the most curious was Tallulah Bankhead, the actress. Her reputation was such that any party at which she turned up became 'spicy'. Mama would never have dreamed of inviting Tallulah to the house, but once when she was away in Paris Pa threw a party of his own. I tiptoed down to get myself introduced to Miss Bankhead, hoping thereby to gain kudos with my friends. She threw her arms around me, exclaiming joyously, 'Oh, Shane's lovely clever daughter. You must come and see me.'

Swooning at the compliment I asked, 'When?'

'Any evening. . . .'

As always, when Tallulah was present, the party waxed wild. Oswald Frewen, Clare's brother, arrived from the country to scrounge a bed for the night and he joined in immediately, dancing around in his motor-cycling goggles. Tallulah was, according to her custom, turning cartwheels in the centre of the drawing room when Mama appeared in the door. For some reason she had unexpectedly returned from Paris and her expression of outraged bewilderment at what was taking place under her famous Spanish madonnas sent guests scuttling. There was talk thereafter about such entertainments being 'bad for the servants'.

I had got Tallulah's address in Farm Street and I called there occasionally. She was always kind and I sat in her little house feeling tiresomely undecadent amidst ladies whose eyelids glistened with incandescent violet grease. Although I found myself tongue-tied in such company, I was able to impress friends later. 'I've just looked in on Tallulah – a friend of mine you know.'

A lady who would gain far greater renown than the already legendary Tallulah was at this time among Mama's bridge-playing companions. Ernest Simpson's sister, Mrs Kerr Smiley, had in fact asked Mama to prevent her brother marrying what she called 'a tiresome divorcée who has chased him over here'. Laughingly Mama said she had something better to do. Later when Wallis Simpson came to bridge parties Mama liked her. I remember her verdict. 'Wallis is very quiet and so well groomed, and when playing bridge I keep looking at her beautifully shaped eyebrows. The nearer you get to her the more attractive she becomes.' It was not long before Wallis met the Prince of Wales, and he got very near indeed.

When the Prince became King it was difficult to maintain that all seemed satisfactory. Winifred returned from that year's Buckingham Palace party held for afternoon presentations in lieu of an evening court, and she, who had looked forward to royal glamour, pronounced sore displeasure. Edward VIII in a morning suit sat not on a throne but, in Winifred's words, 'in a sort of armchair and the furtive bored little man made no effort to show interest in the proceedings'. He kept glancing towards the window hoping it would begin to rain, so that his guests in their trailing dresses and big hats would have to go home early.

The country as a whole disliked their king being dominated by a woman. Eventually my grandmother, so loyal to royalty, and so discreet, admitted that she had been appalled at certain 'distasteful behaviour'. She had known the Prince of Wales quite well as a young man. His grandfather, Edward VII, had regarded her as an intimate friend, and in George V she had always aroused a certain quizzical interest, so it became natural for her to talk to the young Prince of Wales sympathetically. She could see how onerous he felt the chores of his royal station to be, and she tried to cheer him up and to build some liaison between him and his stern father. Pathetically the Prince told her, 'When my father sends for me in his study my tongue clings to the roof of my mouth and it all goes dry.'

The rumours concerning the King's infatuation were – to put it mildly – causing concern. Queen Mary thought it might be helpful if some hints were dropped by a tactful older woman, and so Her Majesty went to tea with the old Duke of Connaught, at his residence, Bagshot Park. There she suggested to Leonie and the duke that it might be wise to pay a visit to Fort Belvedere and comment gently on what is better not done in public. My grandmother could not help noticing that, despite the nervous tension of the moment, Queen Mary ate two large slices of chocolate cake. 'What a digestion!' she commented.

Next day Granny and the duke drove over to Fort Belvedere to see the King and after tea they went for a stroll. When they returned to the house, my grandmother, reared in the Edwardian tradition, could hardly believe her eyes and ears. Mrs Simpson sat down and, holding out her feet, gave the order, 'Take off my little muddy shoes.' And the King of England knelt down to do his job.

'It's no good trying to stop that sort of thing. He likes it,' said my grandmother. She immediately grasped the impossibility of altering this entanglement. But Mama, retaining her American outlook, continued to stand up for Wallis Simpson, defending her with adjectives like 'respectable' and 'soignée'. Mama held on to the principle that it did not really matter bringing down a throne as long as no one became 'piggy'.

Switching back to ordinary life in contrast, we always had a nice young window cleaner who came once a month with mops and pails to wash every window of our five-storey London house. Around this time he set up his own little business and called it the Coronation Cleaners. Mama agreed it was a good name.

Two months elapsed and the cleaner did not turn up. Mama pulled his card out of her desk, saying, 'I'm going to walk around to see if he is ill.' She came back in tears. 'I felt something had happened. When I reached the address and looked down into the area there was a canary in a cage singing and a young woman feeding it. I asked where the window cleaner lived and she looked up at me in a queer way. 'He's dead,' she said. 'He fell from a third floor. I'm his wife. He thought the name would bring him luck.'

In 1936 Mama took me to New York where she and Aunt Anne wished me to marry a rather nice young American of their choosing. Ben, the nephew of one of their closest friends, was tall, fair, athletic. Indeed, he had been captain of the team which America sent to the Olympic Games and he could not have been more charming. The trouble was that *I* had not picked him, nor he me. We used to talk about the way we were shoved together – 'with the tact of a sledge-hammer hitting you on the head,' Ben said. For three months we went around New York. He showed me the high spots and explained in detail the American art of 'spooning'. I could almost have fallen in love, if it had not been for the fact that all this had been arranged and everyone wanted us to get married.

Ben worked long hours in a bank, which surprised me. Rich Englishmen did not work; they lived on their country estates and interviewed agents. Sometimes they became masters of fox-hounds, or went into politics, but only younger sons worked in banks! Ben was the eldest of three boys. A big fortune loomed. It was odd.

Aunt Anne's penthouse at 1136 Fifth Avenue, filled with tapestries and French furniture collected long ago by Bourke Cockran, was very pleasant to live in. My Empire bed, standing on a raised dais, had belonged to Madame Tallien – and ought to have evoked romantic dreams. At the weekend Ben often fetched me to go to his aunt's mansion on Long Island while Aunt Anne followed in her car driven by the German chauffeur (she had a Swedish butler and a French lady's maid, so the servants' hall of that penthouse was quite cosmopolitan). Ben's aunt had been a great beauty, but tragedy marred her life and now she was turning into an eccentric of variable and violent moods.

The terraces around her house had a curious glint – they were built of old paving stones she had seen being pulled up in a street in Italy and had purchased to ship across the Atlantic. She still looked wonderful, having the indefinable presence of a woman who dominates men. Wearing long strings of pearls, she would hold court in a room lined by Chinese panels which she had brought from the ends of the earth. Having never before seen my mother against her American background, I realized for the first time that she belonged to this continent – not to sooty old London or the dripping woods of Monaghan. I belonged back there, but she did not. Among these exuberant friendly extroverts – the American men and the women who were her own sort – she blossomed. It was only her pride and her Puritan sense of duty that had kept her from running back to the land that had bred her.

Clare Sheridan had asked Barney Baruch to invite me to dine in his house – hung, I quickly noticed, with very fine pictures. 'Is that a Gainsborough?' I asked, eager to make intelligent conversation. The handsome old man put on his pince-nez and walked up to peer at a small golden label. 'Why, yes it is,' he said, 'what a bright girl you are. I never know what Mrs Baruch hangs on the walls.'

I liked him. There was no humbug about that man. 'Winston and I became very close at the end of the war,' he said, 'and we've never ceased to feel that England and America have got to run in tandem if Western civilization is to survive.' He was not enamoured of Clare, having had too much trouble looking after her for Winston's sake, but he loved Margaret. 'I'd do anything for that poor kid,' he said. 'What do you think of this Frenchman she has married?' I tried not to look angry; instinctively I hated that Frenchman and wished that Margaret had not vanished with him into Equatorial Africa. 'I gave her two desert trucks,' said Barney Baruch. 'What else do you think I could have given to stop her doing this foolish thing?'

Towards the spring, when New York snow was turning to slush, Barney Baruch invited me to stay at his plantation in South Carolina. There, sitting out on the terrace while cicadas filled the night with tiny violin-playing, I found the old statesman ready to become my friend – as he had been Margaret's. He taught me his own philosophy. Several things he said then remained as guidelines to me in the future. Once, when Mrs Baruch, a large, gentle, undominating woman walked past, he turned and said, 'Do you know, she has never said a cross word to me in her life.' I always remembered those words – the greatest tribute any husband could pay a wife. On another occasion he confided,

'Although I was President Wilson's adviser and have made my name as America's greatest financier, no good school would accept my daughter because I was a Jew. Mrs Baruch is a Gentile but I am a Jew. What do you make of that?'

I was puzzled. At my English schools – and they were supposed to be the top – there had always been some Jewish girls. I explained this and added, 'I did not much like them because they were so clever. Lessons seemed too easy to them.'

He guffawed. 'We are a clever race, but I had to learn things from scratch and I'll tell you now how I made my fortune – simply by studying human nature. All these youngsters come to me bleating about their degrees in economics, and I tell them there's only one thing worth studying – human nature.'

In the daytime we went riding under the trees hung with veils of grey moss or swimming in the sea. 'You ride better than you swim,' said Barney Baruch. 'I suppose you've had more chance to learn.' This was only too true. 'When we get back to New York,' he went on, 'I'll have you given lessons. You must learn to keep your head down. I don't like to see a young girl no good at a thing. You hold your head too far out of the water.' I wondered if I should tell him that I could do Spanish dancing, but resolved not to. I was out of practice and getting a bit stiff. Better to concentrate on the crawl. 'Poluka' he used to call me and seeing I did not know what the word meant he explained. 'A poluka is a no-good black boxer who just keeps trying.' Slightly indignant, I would get out of my wet bathing suit and when we did return to New York I took swimming lessons very seriously indeed.

When the *Queen Mary* made her first Atlantic crossing, Aunt Anne and I were on board for the return journey to England. Quizzically and a little sadly Ben and I said goodbye. Aunt Anne was furious and hurt that her plans had not materialized. She kept saying to me in her cabin, 'You had a row didn't you? What was it about?' We never had a row. We were just averse to snares.

The Baruchs were also on board the *Queen Mary*, and at Southampton, when we were all hanging around staring at the gangplank, Barney Baruch said, 'Don't forget what I've told you. It is only human nature that counts. If you want to make a fortune study human nature.' An enigmatic man. He used to say, 'I don't look like a Jew – I look like a pope, don't I?' Yes, he looked like a pope and held forth like a pope.

In September 1936, Dick Sheridan came of age. Clare had settled in

London. Her studio in Woronzow Road, St John's Wood, was decked with flowers for the celebration party, and she had a tall iron candelabra made to carry twenty-one candles – 'a light for each year of his life'. It was a wonderful party and lasted till dawn. When I went home, Clare embraced me almost fearfully. 'Thank God he's made it – if Frampton had not been sold he might not be here. I was so afraid.' She was referring to that curse laid on the lands of Frampton Court by an old woman who had been turned starving from the door centuries before. Not wanting to upset his mother, Dick had not told her that one acre, the acre beside the river where his grandfather insisted on being buried, still remained in his possession. He was intending to sign the plot away to the local council.

Soon after his birthday Dick went off to Biskra. He thought that in the Sahara he would be able to write a play. A girlfriend went with him. A few months later, in the spring, when Clare was working on a bust of the dancer Serge Lifar, I went to see her and she told me, almost casually, without ceasing to pat in pieces of clay, 'Dick has had his appendix out. They had to fly him over the desert to the French hospital in Constantine. Quite an emergency.' It meant no more to her than that.

Two days later I heard that Clare had left at an hour's notice, having received a telegram that peritonitis had set in. She reached Paris on a Sunday. No plane service to Algeria then existed and there was no train till late that night. Calling on the concierge of her old apartment in the Rue Bonaparte she learned that a telegram had arrived for her which the postman refused to leave for a person no longer resident. The concierge assured her that a door of the post office would be opened if she rang. So there, alone in that French post office, Clare tore open the cable which said that Dick had died. When she came to her senses, she was lying on the floor while a kindly postmaster tried to pour coffee down her throat.

She found refuge in a friend's apartment where a doctor gave her sedatives. She decided he should be buried at Port Vendres on the Mediterranean coast. Having seen him laid among the peasants and fishermen of that little French village, she travelled on to Spain where the Civil War was raging. Then she moved on to Biskra where she tried to rest. Margaret joined her from Brazzaville and they sat together in the date grove of Bab el M'Cid where Haafa, the Arab boy, sought to comfort them. He kept meeting Dick's smiling ghost in the garden.

Like the Irish country people Arabs accept the reappearance of the dead as a natural happening.

Not very long after Dick died I married a Russian. Paul Rodzianko was reputed to be the greatest living horseman. I met him in a country house where he was training steeplechasers and he seemed so different to other men, like a blast of north wind from the steppes. I found him fascinating. But not for long. It was like having a talented bear at your heels, or like inviting the north wind to tea – things blew round and round, one danced with the wind but then grew exhausted and the gale roared on. He seemed to take it for granted that I would marry him, but for many months I pushed the possibility to the back of my mind. He was fun to go around with, quite different to anyone I had ever met. One day Pa stopped me on the stairs and said, 'Your mother is giving me hell because of Paul Rodzianko.' Then he passed on. It bored him to discuss anything with his children.

I thought of Paul waiting outside in his little car, that car bought with what he had earned by teaching horses to jump and riders to sit correctly. There was never a grumble out of him. He had been a rich man in Russia – his mother was descended from Strogonoff who discovered Siberia for Czar Ivan the Terrible, and since the Revolution he had lived by his own talent. He had extraordinary brilliance with horses and it was imposed on knowledge. Just before the war he had won the King's Cup three years running at Olympia. I admired his resilience and his courage even more than his artistry.

Paul was thirty years older than I and despite the very real attraction I did not really want to marry him, but just when I was trying to disentangle myself from the whole affair, Mama's efforts to halt what she regarded as an appalling match goaded me into it. I had returned home very tired and went to my mother's bedroom to tell her that I had decided to finish with Paul. She was sitting at her dressing table in front of the Italian mirror around which romped carved golden cherubs. 'Ma,' I said, slumping into an armchair, 'I think it's off.'

She whirled round, throwing hairbrushes in the air. 'How could you be so cruel as to torture me about that man for nothing?'

I felt yet more weary. 'Could I travel around the world instead?'

'No,' she said angrily, 'you can't.'

Within two weeks I married Paul. But I so nearly didn't. On the day in question my two great friends, Rose and Winifred, took me out to lunch at a Piccadilly restaurant called the Coq d'Or. Rose pinned a huge camelia to my jacket and, after a delicious lunch and rather too much wine, we drove in Rose's car to the Harrow Road register office. Paul was due to meet us there on his return from Richmond Park where he was training horses. I felt tiddly, yet unhappy.

Rose said, 'Don't just get married because of my flower.' She had already left her husband and knew it was idiotic to marry merely to change a situation. Maybe, if we'd had less wine. . .? Or more wine. . . ? However, we got there, and Paul arrived in his car heaped with saddles due for repair. We entered a room with a wooden floor. A register book was produced. Rose and Winifred signed as witnesses and we came out. 'You must drive Anita home,' Rose said to Paul. 'Her mother has given in. It's accepted.'

'I cannot,' boomed the bridegroom. 'There is not room in the car with these saddles, and they must be mended. You take her. I will follow.'

My attendants flared up. '*Not drive your wife away! We'll take the saddles*.' My heart had turned to lead at the word 'wife', but I acquiesced. The saddles were heaped into Rose's car and that was that.

15
End of my Russian Phase

Looking back at the fever heat of those last years before the Second World War the bedlam of my personal life seems entangled in the political eruptions that were brewing. Paul Rodzianko, being a Russian in exile, was more sensitive to the mounting pulse of Europe than most Englishmen. He had escaped his country's Revolution in 1917 while on a mission to the Italian front. Then he had joined the British Army and accompanied General Sir Alfred Knox to Ekaterinberg in a fruitless effort to save the Czar and his family. They found only the bones thrown into a limepit, but Paul recognized one little body – that of their pet dog. After Paul returned to England King George V asked him to lunch at Buckingham Palace to describe the death of his cousin in detail. Paul arrived on a motor-cycle, his only means of transport, and had some difficulty getting past the sentries. Then he found himself lunching alone with King George and Queen Mary, who lowered her eyes each time her spouse used strong language. 'I'm sorry, my dear,' King George would say, 'but he *was* my cousin . . . the poor things, the poor, poor girls.'

Later Paul trained horses in England until the Irish Army invited him to improve their show-jumping team. For four years Paul had worked in Dublin, wearing the uniform of an Irish colonel, hung with medals from half a dozen countries and delighting in the natural ability of the Irish men in his jumping team, not to mention the Irish horses.

Paul had obtained his own training in the Italian Cavalry School at Turin where the great Caprilli taught what was called 'the forward seat'. Paul objected to this name which, he said, was inaccurate. There was only a *correct* seat which ensured the rider's centre of gravity remaining over the horse's centre of gravity when jumping. But, to the unenlightened, the way in which the Italian and French military teams rode appeared to be very forward indeed.

To Paul the entire world was divided between pupils and non-pupils – that is between people trying to do something well and the rest. Among non-pupils he tolerated pretty women. 'She is stupid but she is beautiful,' was a standard remark. I was not beautiful but I was a great trier. I did so want to do things well – dance, write, swim and ride well. I'd always loved riding but I was nervous. Paul made me keep my heels down and my knees in. He strove to make me sit up proudly and yet remain relaxed and 'go with the horse'.

'Coordination of the muscles,' he would roar – 'coordination' being his longest English word.

Sergei Rodzianko, Paul's younger brother, had been taught by him in Russia. When Sergei escaped, by a route that took him half around the world, he did not meet Paul for five years. Eventually, reaching England after many hair-raising adventures, he arrived at Paul's riding school to find a class in progress. When Sergei walked in, Paul's reaction was merely to draw a deep breath and continue his lecture. 'Here comes my brother – the best pupil I ever had – he can demonstrate what I was telling you.' Sergei found himself in the saddle before he had the chance to describe his escape from the Bolsheviks.

As the threat of another war loomed I took more interest in my brothers than in this curious lover whom I had married, as it were, by mistake. Having brought me up to be as impractical as possible, the family blithely turned me adrift without any allowance when I married a penniless man. I scarcely knew how to make a cup of tea. We were always driving around England to look at horses and when we had been married a couple of weeks Paul suggested a picnic. Someone had given us a luxurious wicker picnic basket. I peered into this and considered the thermoses might well be filled with healthy spinach soup. I then bought a bundle of spinach but did not realize that such vegetables need washing. After some boiling I poured a pretty green liquid into the flasks and cut sandwiches. When we got down to our open-air feast, Paul grimaced at the soup and boomed, 'What is this? Are we expected to swallow gravel?' Realizing I was no housekeeper, I felt dispirited but Paul's Slav temperament soared up and down whatever the soup was like. I suppose I was carried away by the glamour of that vanished Russian world which he managed to carry with him. London was full of emigrés and they were all musical and all had guts, but Paul won a unique respect for his knowledge of horses. Wherever he went Englishmen would ask him questions about bits, the art of inducing a horse to flex, the amount of pushing with the rider's legs that might be desirable. Without noticing it, Paul always sat astride a chair, leaning over the back to talk as if he were sitting on a horse. I could not keep up with his vitality. Whatever happened in our daily routine he always behaved as if leading a cavalry charge. But I had to admit there was one thing he never became – Paul was not dull.

We lived in a flat near his Richmond Park riding establishment but most of our meals continued to be taken in Westbourne Terrace. It was rather humiliating never to have noticed Mrs Young's delicious cooking until I left home, but the contrast between repasts at Mama's table and those in my flat stood out. Only the dogs ate well in our entourage. Paul's Dalmatian and my dear little Aberdeen terrier Gemma never pulled a face over their quota of raw mince.

Paul had a huge appetite. He could not have married me for money – perhaps he married me for Mama's food. Anyway, we regularly turned up in her dining room. If she was having a party and did not want us, there would be plenty of leftovers. And we were often invited out to dinner. Then we changed into evening dress. Paul always made a party go. He sang Russian songs in a deep bass voice and, if asked, would bring his old sword which had somehow survived from pre-revolutionary days in the Chevalier Guards (the Czar's Household Cavalry). With this sword he cut the necks off champagne bottles with one clean swipe. Such tricks kept him very popular. He was one of those rare Russians who drank little so his vitality remained unimpaired.

And Rose Vincent – that strange girl whose life had been bedevilled by a fortune – what was happening to her with her poetic streak and her cobwebby beauty? It is difficult to write about a person one has loved. No one who knew Rose could remain impartial, nor is it possible to describe the will-o'-the-wisp light she could switch on.

When we had first met as children, we had disliked each other. Then her mother died, leaving her and a younger brother to wander Europe in the care of their handsome, unpaternal Irish father. Rose came out as sulkily as I did. When Jack and I were sent to stay in Muckross House, the Vincents' glorious Killarney home, we still eyed each other coldly. Then Jack went out on the mountains to look for red deer and lost Mr Vincent's binoculars in the heather. Rose stood up for us against her father's grumbles. From that day we were friends.

After her marriage I visited Rose at Northcourt, the rambling sixteenth-century house in the Isle of Wight, abode of the Lords Burgh. She was twenty when her son was born, and twenty-one when she left Burgh and came to London with her baby. Nannies and Austrian maids filled her house. And she had an interesting man friend, an engineer studying aeroplane design. Mama, who had known Rose since she was 'a pale little ghost of a baby', was outraged by her behaviour and made us laugh with remarks such as, 'It's unnecessary to be piggy when you're so rich.'

Rose had everything – intellect, humour, wit, grace, a perfect figure, magnolia skin, long delicate hands and feet. She was the best company in the world and her face the most unusual in its beauty I have ever seen. Only one thing seemed to have been withheld by the fairies who came to her christening – happiness.

During this very difficult period of our lives – the months leading up to the war – we became emotionally bound together. Rose had married before I did and regretted it. Now she saw me struggling in the coils of a thoughtless matrimonial muddle and she sorrowed at my plight. We'd walked into marriage for different reasons. We had our eyes wide open, and of course we were to blame. But that did not make it easier.

Paul hated her. I remember a party in some studio where he was at his most Slav. His cousin, Prince Felix Yousoupoff (one of the group who had shot Rasputin), was singing to a balalaika – which he did extremely well – and Paul kept roaring, 'Blasted fellow – can't even shoot a man. Rasputin falls down and Felix faints – what's the good of him? If you shoot, you shoot properly.'

Rose, who loved Russian music, defended Yousoupoff. 'Blasted woman.' Paul bellowed his favourite adjective again. 'I never want to see her – but the food in her house is so good.'

On another occasion we went to the Hungaria, a restaurant near Piccadilly where the Russian orchestra always played the Rodzianko March when Paul entered. At 2 a.m. the restaurant closed. Rose, in terrific form, hired the orchestra – zither and all – to come on to Westbourne Terrace where the party could continue. Twenty of us, including the Irish show-jumping team, who happened to be in London for the horse show, piled into taxis with many magnums of champagne. I had the latch key and bolts were seldom drawn in case some member of our absent-minded family should return home late. Mama was away, but I think she would have enjoyed seeing her drawing room put to such good use. I remember Nadine MacDougall, who was to marry Prince Andrew of Russia, the Czar's nephew, being lifted onto a table where she danced to our clapping. The housemaids woke up and came down in their dressing-gowns and hair-curlers to see what the noise could be. They weren't frightened. We did not *sound* like burglars. Even Paul had to admit that this party extended by Rose into the dawn was about the best any of us would ever remember.

In that summer of 1938 we travelled to Italy to look at the cavalry school in Turin, where horses slid on their haunches down sandy slopes while the instructor cried, 'Keep forward – *avanti!*' On our way back we stayed in Berlin. Paul's pals were his former commanding officers – Mannerheim, who had become Finland's leader, after the Revolution, and Skoropadsky, who had less successfully taken on the hereditary title of Hetman of the Ukraine. Mannerheim was passing through Berlin and we saw him in an hotel, but Skoropadsky lived in his own Potsdam house and we spent several days with him talking about the possibility of the Ukraine regaining independence. Skoropadsky thought that Hitler's Germany might help.* I returned to England drugged with political issues I had never heard of before.

Meanwhile Desmond had grown to six feet four inches. Nanny remained with us and lived on the nursery floor still knitting his socks. Over the years these had increased in length from two to fourteen inches.

Having obtained his degree at Magdalen College, Cambridge, Jack had become an officer in the Irish Guards. There was a hold-up over his deaf ear for the ear drum had been completely destroyed by that early mastoid. At his medical examination the doctor argued that if a shell landed on his better side the other ear would be useless. It took a royal field-marshal to clinch the matter. 'It is my wish that this gentleman be given a second medical,' ordered the Duke of Connaught. 'A shell may fall on his left side but is equally likely to fall on his right side or indeed on his pate.'

So Jack became a second lieutenant with a red tunic and a bearskin and was stationed in Wellington Barracks beside Buckingham Palace. Sometimes he would be sent to guard the Tower of London where the hauntings worried his troopers. Jack loved the ghostliness of the Tower at night. He particularly enjoyed inspecting the sentries by moonlight. When snow had fallen, there would be absolute silence. His footsteps

---

* Hetman Skoropadsky was killed in 1945 when the Russians took Berlin.

made no sound, nor did the stamping feet of the soldiers. It was so eerie that even a Leslie bred to ghostlore could not stop looking over his shoulder.

When returning his soldiers to barracks Jack had to march them a couple of miles through streets of staring onlookers, and policemen on duty would see the red coats coming and hold up traffic at each crossing. One morning Jack found the usual route closed for repair. There was nothing for it but to march on by guesswork. Bearskin on head, sword at side, he strode along, realizing with horror that he did not know which way to go and that it was impossible to ask. The soldiers were trained to obey their officer's commands – theirs not to reason why, theirs but to do and die, etc. Jack tried to look up at the sun, but his fur bearskin hid the sky and he longed to question each policeman standing with arm outstretched to let them march by. On they went and Jack feared the Thames might open out before him, but luckily they reached Trafalgar Square and by the time they had made their way through St James's Park the nervous sweat was drying on Jack's brow.

Officers of the Guards Brigade were automatically invited to debutante balls. Mothers frantically sought to corral the right sort of young men as dancing partners and invitations would be issued to an entire officers' mess. Those off duty could go and quaff champagne at the bar, but it was imperative not to get drunk. If netted and introduced to a girl, the officer had to ask her to dance. The price for consuming the best bubbly was pushing a shy deb around the dance floor. If a young man did not behave properly the mothers, who got together to prepare 'lists', would strike out his name. Henceforth, a black sheep would never receive a personal invitation.

During that extraordinary fling, in the months between Munich and the outbreak of war, we attended the last balls ever given in Derby House, Dudley House, Norfolk House and the historic Elizabethan mansion lying in its own park, Holland House. In July 1939, just before Hitler marched into Poland, I went to the dance given in her Bryanston Square house by Lady Bailey, the sister of our Monaghan neighbour, Lord Rossmore. It was the last of its sort and I was to see this house demolished by a bomb just over a year later. I remember the tiaraed older women and, because royalty was present, the men wearing ribbons across their white waistcoats and rows of medals. Paul had plenty of these. If medals could have spawned rations he need never have gone hungry.

Soon after this dance an unusual accident befell Paul. Riding in Richmond Park with three pupils, he had halted to explain something, when one of the horses turned on its haunches and kicked out, breaking Paul's leg badly. I was resting at home – to tell the truth I was smugly reading some glowing reviews of my *Life of Rodin* which Prentice-Hall had published in America – when the phone rang to say Paul was being taken to hospital with a compound fracture. By the time I got there his boot had been cut off and the leg was in traction.

I spent three weeks returning to their owners the eight horses which Paul had been training. At the end of July I went to my grandmother's last London teaparty. She was in a highly nervous state for the only topic was the possibility of war. Her guests were Lady Astor, Lady Salisbury, Lady Londonderry, Lady d'Abernon and Priscilla Lady Annesley (the famed Edwardian beauty who still could not resist flirting with my grandfather and turning her Grecian profile against the light for all to see). The only man I can remember was Dr Axel Munthe, fascinating author of *The Story of San Michele*.

The hospital got Paul's leg into plaster remarkably quickly – in time for him to hobble with crutches to the Dublin Horse Show. He could not have borne to miss the sight of his 'pupils' of the Irish team soaring over those jumps, and if any officer made a mistake in timing Paul would be at the exit waiting to curse him with mighty Russian oaths.

It was a tremendously hot August, and his plaster began to hurt. We travelled back to London for a new cast, and my diary recorded: 'Paul very wild and Russian. Hobbling round on crutches singing the Volga Boat Song to bewildered porters.' When he went off to harangue the War Office, I joined Mama in the little Hertfordshire cottage which she had bought for weekends.

So there I was in August 1939, alone with Mama in her small green oasis, thirty miles from London. Pa had gone to Ireland with Desmond. Jack was in camp prior to an expected two-month leave in America which he had not visited since babyhood. The sun blazed down and the old gardener and our village cook trailed in to listen to the radio news every hour or so, and made comments about 'that there Hitler' in their blurred Hertfordshire accents.

The unbelievable happened. Mr Chamberlain declared war. Now one was going to see what human beings, who had invented the gin-trap for animals and the harpoon for whales, could do to each other. We were stunned. Was it unpatriotic to put sugar in one's tea? Mama, determined to *do something*, announced that one pat of butter and no more should be allotted to each breakfast tray. Next morning, the first of the war, her frightened voice woke me before dawn. 'Do you hear the rattles? It must be gas wardens. . . .'

This seemed strange, seven miles from any town, but I peered sleepily from my window. A tremendous din certainly seemed to be approaching down the lane. Several minutes later a clanking harvesting machine came into view. 'For heaven's sake, Mama – go back to bed.' That was the beginning of my war.

Within a month my mother retreated to Ireland to stay at Castle Leslie with my grandparents. Jack had to abandon his projected trip to America when all army leave was cancelled, and Desmond, who had just reached seventeen, entered Trinity College, Dublin. What should I do? I did not really care as long as these new circumstances took me away from Paul. My Russian phase was over.

16
War 1939

The nasty facets of war lie in discomfort, boredom and death. At the beginning none of these afflicted us. We stared at the sky but nothing fell out of it and we were certainly not bored. Even the hardships inherent in military training did not seem onerous while the good weather lasted.

How did our brains work during this extraordinary moment in history? We woke each morning wondering if the war could be true, and some knew fear or anger. I only felt that I was lucky to be free when jobs of every kind were suddenly materializing. For the first time in my lifetime girls were wanted everywhere. With feverish interest I read advertisements and my married friends groaned at commitments that held them chained. The lease of Mama's big London house had ended before the war and after much cogitation she had taken a sunny fifth-floor flat which could be run by a mere two servants. Hostilities caused cook and housemaid to retire, so Pa and I, servantless, moved into this new flat, and Paul, hobbling still and most indignant because the War Office had not immediately employed him, followed us muttering, 'Anita cannot cook but I don't know where else to go.' Pa and I possessed no housekeeping talents and we stuck to unrationed potatoes and cabbage. When Jack arrived from camp he only wanted to sleep, and when Desmond arrived from Trinity College, Dublin, he only wanted a telephone on which to ring girls. When any of us became really hungry we went to a restaurant and many outings turned into merry binges with Rose.

She was attracted by male courage and her intimates included test pilots from De Havillands. She rented Mama's Hertfordshire cottage which lay a few miles from the aircraft factory and when not entertaining heroes, she could leave her little son there with his pretty nurse (who was well able to do her fair share of De Havilland entertaining). There was always a bed for Rose in our London flat and when not discussing what armies we ought to join, we would sally forth with friends in the eerie blackout where night life had a special savour.

Our haunts varied from smart restaurants to discoveries in Soho. London quivered excitingly at night. Cars drove slowly with the tiny permitted sidelights called cats' eyes, and I will never forget the sound of dance music overheard in a darkened street and the thrill of pushing past blankets hung as blackout curtains in front of the entry to stumble into a delicious blue-lighted alcoholic haze where uniformed figures swayed on the dance floor.

Nor am I likely to forget the first time I left Pa in the flat on his own. He insisted he could look after himself. 'All I want is Ovaltine.' So I showed him how to light the gas cooker with matches and went off to the country. When I returned two days later the porter and two air-raid wardens wearing masks were stumbling around the flat looking for a gas leak. Eventually they discovered the cooker full on but unlit. It had been running for two days. Pa had indeed made himself Ovaltine according to my directions and then, with what must have been gargantuan puffs, he had blown out the gas as one blows out a candle, and departed. The smell had frightened tenants in other flats, who wondered if the Germans were attacking.

Each morning in London I would wake in Mama's bedroom with its sunny bow window, carved French bed and Italian-cherub dressing-table and try to organize entertainment for Jack when he was off duty, or for Pa after he had enrolled in the Home Guard headquarters in Sloane Street. My father enjoyed sleeping on a camp bed beside a telephone waiting for air raids. As for Paul, to our relief he left the flat and went away to argue with generals he had fought beside in the *last* war.

By day as at night London had a different look. Over squares and open spaces floated silver barrage balloons which dangled cables intended to entangle low-flying enemy aircraft. Pa's verses about them appeared in the press.

Ode to the Balloon Barrage

O globular-looking and gluttonous
Plumpy and muttonous!
  I watch you floating over Regent's Park

Each hanging like an Indiarubber Ark
Or floating like some dead and bloated Dove
  Headless, wingless,
  Like Larva, stingless, . . .

One day when my father was living in the flat he suddenly began to talk to me. He recalled the winter of 1907 when, as a free young man discovering the world for himself, he had stayed with Tolstoy in Russia. One day, as they walked down the snow-covered street in the village Yasnaya Polyana, the great writer suddenly turned to my father and said, 'They must choose between me and the bayonets.'

Pa leaned back in his chair while recounting this and for once his eyes did not close with boredom while speaking to a member of his family. 'That choice,' he said, 'was made after Tolstoy's death when Russia went to war with Germany. It is worth remembering,' he continued, 'that in the Napoleonic wars Russia, England and Germany fought France, then in the Crimean War England and France fought Russia, and then in 1914 England, France and Russia fought Germany. Now we are at it again. One wonders what the pattern will be this time!'

My friends with children were glued to their country homes, and nannies thought they were hard done by, never before having had to look after their charges without the help of nurse maids. At Christmas I went to stay in Somerset with Betsan and her husband, Jack Coats. The city children evacuated with helpers into her luxurious home had raised such cries of protest at being 'dumped in the back of beyond' that the authorities had removed them. The only guest when I arrived was the Biku, an enchanting Burmese monk clad in yellow robes, who had been sent to Europe by his monastery to 'study European education'. He landed in England as war was declared. Stepping off the boat, with all his worldly possessions in a bandanna handkerchief, he was ordered to a poison-gas course. The authorities then sent him to live with these well-known vegetarian Theosophists. He wore his yellow robes until he eventually joined an ARP unit in London and spent four years imperturbably lifting bodies out of bombed debris. It was easy for him to view physical death.

Betsan puzzled the fox-hunting gentry, who had once known her as a smart-set deb. She had built a chapel for leaders of different great religions and country squires wondered what on earth Christianity, Buddhism and Islam could have in common. It was instructive to watch Biku meditating in the little chapel. Never had I seen a being so immovable. Not an eyelid would flicker as he sat there with his legs folded into the lotus position. He made one feel so twitchy.

My married friends were spread over England. Cousin Kitty had retreated to her brother's home, Bowood, with three small boys, and our nanny was helping their nanny. Kitty planned to run Bowood for Charlie, who was unmarried and soon leaving for the Middle East. Her own husband and numerous relations could dash there on leave. The vast magnificent house, impregnated by successive Lord Lansdownes with England's history, would in this war be a refuge.

In London we met Charlie Lansdowne and other cousins descended from that dreamy old artist, Sir John Leslie. Three would be captured and two of these escape – one of them David James, so brilliantly that he was decorated for his exploit and sent to lecture military establishments on the techniques of disguise. (David crossed Europe in his naval uniform with a false passport, pretending to be a Rumanian Colonel Bugeroff – pronounced phonetically.) Edward Hope, who eventually married my friend Winifred, won a Military Cross with the Grenadier Guards, and William Crawshay – he who had been so dolefully instructed in the facts of life – would be dropped by parachute into France to organize Resistance fighters.

Of the lot Kitty's two brothers did not survive. Both were killed in the same week in 1945 – Charlie Lansdowne in Italy and young Ned in Normandy. Bowood, which Kitty ran during the bitter war years, would pass on to a cousin.

There was hardly a night of that strange first winter of war when Rose and I did not go out. Our escorts would be in khaki, navy blue or air-force blue. Rosa Lewis, who had run the Cavendish Hotel through the other war, kept going during this one too. One night I went there with Randolph Churchill and Ava. They were, as usual, arguing politics to the popping of champagne corks. Ava was an officer in the Royal Horse Guards – the Blues. Things had gone wrong for him and although his lucid mind still twanged with originality, he seemed obsessed by bitter disappointment with himself. Now he was gnawing his heart out because the colonel, perhaps reasonably, thought he would be more useful in some form of intelligence than in regimental duties. I found it hard to see him destroying himself – he who had talked to me with passion of the human brain as 'the only gadget in the universe capable of abstract thought'.

Rosa Lewis buzzed around and Ava asked for brandy. She gave him an old-fashioned look, for Rosa liked to keep her clients on the bubbly. 'Can make you silly, dear, but not drunk. You are never silly, Lord Dufferin, but you can be drunk.' He still was able to tease me. 'Don't you remember the first time I explained to you that only having a body prevents one being able to walk through walls? You couldn't take it in.' I had taken it in, and if one had to be stuck in a body – well, by this time mine was better than his. Dancing had kept me fit. I had noticed early on that the chorus line did not drink and the government front bench did.

In the dark night, in London of the blackout, we parted and I never saw him again before he was killed near the old Burmese capital from which he took his name.

17
War 1940

The phoney war as we called it held amusing moments for girls like myself stumbling around in the blackout wondering quite what to do. The variety of jobs offered exhilarated but we thought carefully before signing on 'for the duration'. Sarah Churchill had given up the stage to learn photographic identification in the Air Force. Diana bloomed as a recruiting officer in the Women's Navy and very smart she looked in uniform, sitting in Harrods enticing the right sort with those hints of excitement which Churchills were able to spread like jam over the most commonplace tasks. It was no longer a mistake to have been born a girl. We had become useful – and if the boys were going to be wiped out as in the last war we thought we could at least count on being killed in *lesser* numbers.

Margaret came back into our lives. She had spent two years in French Equatorial Africa with her officer husband and I think the end of the marriage was in sight. War precipitated the matter. As France fell, Margaret happened to be returning to visit her mother. She arrived in London, triumphantly wearing a smart hat. 'Look – the last *chapeau* to get out of Paris!' What joy it was to have her in our midst. Within a week she had joined the Mechanical Transport Corps and was in khaki, driving ambulances for first-aid posts.

'It's too ridiculous,' she said. 'I'm French now so only muscular jobs are permitted. Happily I've handled heavy trucks in the Sahara and this is more real than being an interpreter at the War Office.'

She seemed more mature, more beautiful, less tantalizingly intellectual. Her hours of duty were twenty-four hours on, twenty-four hours off. And the 'off' were packed with incident for her sparkle transformed a room. We had friends who were pilots in the Fleet Air Arm. One evening they phoned from Portsmouth – 'We are off.' We visualized their planes like bees flying after the aircraft carrier which had already sailed. They would follow her and land on the deck – silvery bees winging away from England towards death between sea and sky, but death wove a way into the tapestry very gradually. Everyone seemed to be preparing, no one actually getting killed except in the North Sea where our submarines were incessantly sunk.

Margaret fell in love with a young officer. Her husband remained in the French Army in North Africa and did not answer her letters begging for a divorce. She tried not to mind, but his refusal to communicate prevented her marrying the man she loved. 'Perhaps the war is a comfort,' she said. 'It gives one something to think about that isn't oneself and one's own stupidities.' *

A cold spell turned the land to iron. My only remaining horse, which I had kept with friends in the Grafton country so as to steal an occasional gallop, could not even walk the slippery roads. The Finnish–Russian war held world attention. As Paul had served under Field-Marshal Mannerheim in the old days in Russia, he wrote a book about the Finnish leader and leaped to help – leaped literally for the plaster had been cut off his leg and he could chase around London raising ski clothes and rifles. Even Mama remembered that she had a padded après-ski outfit packed away. Lorryloads of Lillywhite equipment bought for Alpine holidays were sorted and sent to Finland. Young bloods in every British regiment chaffed to join volunteer units. Having written his book, Paul made off towards some military liaison department and I heaved a sigh of relief. Meanwhile, Hitler's armies were preparing.

The killing started suddenly. Like a bolt from the blue the fiasco of the Norwegian campaign hit us. Finland was forgotten during our unsuccessful efforts to prevent Germany taking Norway. And Mama arrived in London eager to see Jack whenever he came off duty. She did not find her new flat spotless, but she accepted it as it was. My culinary efforts were a sad descent from the glories of Mrs Young's day.

---

* Over thirty years later I met this man at a London cocktail party. He told me, 'I am a romantic. I keep Margaret's letters tied up with blue ribbon. Maybe I will allow them to be published after my death.' I said, 'I bet they are good.' 'Yes,' he replied, 'very good.' And we stood there looking at each other in the crowded room while memories surged back.

April passed. May came. Blazing sun. Blue skies. Unbelievable hourly news. Chamberlain Out. Winston In. Mama decided she could only be a nuisance in London and we hurried her to the Dublin mail train. 'I don't care if I can't get a cabin,' she said. This was war indeed.

Rose and I drove on the last of her rationed petrol to the cottage for a weekend with Rose's small son, and we laughed to hear that Colonel Harrison, who owned 5000 acres of land in Hertfordshire, had ordered his twelve gamekeepers to watch out for disguised parachutists landing in his shooting coverts. Within a week we learned that German soldiers dressed as nuns and farm yokels were tumbling out of the Belgian skies and mockery froze on our lips. Dunkirk. Rose, whose steam yacht *Leprechaun* had been commandeered by the Navy, fretted that she could not personally rescue troops. We lived between radio and telephone. John Erne, our Irish neighbour, was killed – I thought of his baby son, now Lord Erne and heir to Crom Castle as John had been as a little boy when *his* father had disappeared in a shell burst in the other war. Pa's lawyer wrote a poignant account of his daughter who learned of her husband's death in action the day her first baby was born. 'One cannot expect her to ever get over it.' I thought of the young engaged couple before the war – joyful and unsuspecting of fate. How lucky I was to be husbandless, childless, unloving, unloved.

On 21 May came the hammerblow – expected but none the less gut-tearing. Jack phoned from a call box. 'We're off. It's a lovely moonlit night.' Next evening papers had it: 'Irish Guards in action around Boulogne'. Within a few days the regiment was back – at least some of it was back. Two officers had been killed in the docks and two young lieutenants sent to command forward posts were missing. These were Lord Dunboyne and Jack.

I walked across the park to Wellington Barracks. The regimental sergeant major could only say that advanced posts had been overrun but missing men kept trickling back after being picked up by ships along the French coast. Soldiers with extraordinary escape stories continually reported. For two weeks I sat by our London telephone nervously lifting the receiver each time it rang. Our grandparents had just installed their first telephone at Castle Leslie – the number was Glaslough 2 – and this innovation added to their strained nerves.

Now the fantasy of war took on a new aspect. Our addled minds reeled. Casualty lists filled the newspapers. So many friends had been killed in the fall of France that one did not know how to compose coherent letters. Then came a phone call from Wellington Barracks

saying that two Irish Guardsmen captured outside Boulogne had escaped and said they had seen their missing lieutenants alive. I hardly
dared to phone Glaslough but the regimental sergeant major himself
rang me. 'Look – I'm sending Sergeant Hayes to see you – he'll tell
you everything.'

On 27 June a stalwart soldier arrived with his sixteen-year-old wife
and we enjoyed a wonderful meal while he recounted the events of the
last two weeks. He had been captured with Jack – they were in a
dugout on the city outskirts and had looked up to see a line of Germans
with machine-guns. It happened so quickly they never had the chance
to fire a shot. Paddy Dunboyne commanded the adjoining post. Meanwhile Boulogne was being heavily shelled. The Guards Brigade, ordered
to re-embark, was suffering heavy casualties in the process. After capture men and officers were separated and Sergeant Hayes could only
say he had seen the two young officers put into a truck which rolled
away eastwards – 'but they were alive all right'. Hayes and a pal had
run for it, travelled down the coast and found a ship.

For six weeks we waited. Then came an official Red Cross postcard
signed by Jack. I thought how strange it looked lying on the carpet
with the other mail. We could not guess it would be five years before
we saw him again.

This was June 1940. We were wound up like watches. Some over-
wound, unable to tick. In a stupor we telephoned, ate, slept, listened
to the radio, glanced expectantly at the sky.

Raids started. A German bomber dropped the first lot on south
London. We exclaimed. Bombs were a novelty, though warning sirens
were not, for quite a few had gone off by mistake. I cut out and pasted
in my diary a newspaper advertisement for the Dorchester Hotel in
Park Lane:

> ONE OF THE SAFEST BUILDINGS IN THE WORLD
> With an air-raid shelter which is veritably bomb-proof.

Even then I thought it funny.

Lionel arrived back from France where he'd searched vainly for his
regiment. They had been killed or captured or evacuated in the sham-
bles. Rose gave a farewell dinner at Quaglino's for her young brother
Bill Vincent, now of the Royal Enniskillen Fusiliers. But farewell from
what to where?

Yet entertaining continued. I dined out every night. On 2 July I
wrote, 'Hugh Walpole was of the company, holding forth in a dazed

way about the young Hitler he had known well – they both used to frequent Cosima Wagner's villa and Walpole says that without external femininity Hitler aroused a kind of protective instinct in other men – you put out your arm to stop him falling just as you would for an hysterical woman. Walpole is the only person I know who met Hitler in the early days. He can't understand why he didn't get shot.'

At the end of July my diary records, 'Went to drink champagne with Rose's father and Derry, her step-mother, back from Cannes after dreadful 22 days in a small coal-boat – 4 days without food.' They were off to Ireland where Mr Vincent had presented magnificent Muckross House and its 6000-acre estate to the nation. Derry, listed by columnists as among the world's six best-dressed women, had lost all her clothes but no hardship could dint her fabulous beauty. Like Mama, she was going to face a tough war searching Dublin for real lace for her underwear.

With no brother to look after I studied carefully the jobs listed in newspapers. One evening I came in tired, picked up the *Evening Standard* and saw a half-page devoted to the Mechanized Transport Corps which wanted sixty ambulance drivers for Kenya. As I read the print my heart began to pound. I knew this was for me.

The Mechanized Transport Corps was a voluntary unit of considerable renown. Drivers like Margaret were already standing by with ambulances at air-raid posts, and some members used their own cars to drive Very Important Persons for the War Office. An MTC unit attached to the French Army had been captured by advancing Germans and its cool-headed leader, Penelope Otto, had won acclaim for leading a successful escape.

Penny's exploit proved good publicity for the MTC. American shops and firms were generously donating funds for new ambulances. No less a personage than General Smuts had requested an MTC unit to be based at Mombasa and Penny Otto had already sailed with twenty-six girls. Sixty more were to join her.

Trembling with excitement and fearful that all places might be already filled, I hurried to MTC headquarters in Ebury Street near Victoria Station. In and out of the building strode ladies in khaki uniforms which were given added chic by a polished Sam Browne belt and a jaunty cap based on the French kepi. A girl with red fingernails was taking particulars and asking at what we excelled. We learned that we had to pay for our own training but that thereafter we could change jobs within the corps. I signed on.

The sudden intrusion of war into peace began next day when I left London for a weekend at Charleston Manor, the lovely Sussex home of artist Oswald Birley and his wife Rhoda. The house lay only a mile from the sea, sheltered by a great tree-covered hill, and beside the manor stood the finest medieval tithe barn in England. Within its thatched precincts a troops' concert was to be held, followed by a dance. It was blazing hot and the Birleys had arranged an outdoor lunch for their guests. We sat about in the rose garden while the Birley children, Mark and Maxime, rushed around filling our plates with chicken salad and our glasses with white wine. Paper napkins were distributed and several gentlemen sat fanning themselves in the shade.

Suddenly a roaring sounded overhead and a wounded German bomber with smoke pouring from the fuselage passed over our heads. We thought it was going to hit the trees. It flew so low that we could see faces in the perspex window ... and then suddenly it was gone ... over the Channel in one minute, over France in ten.

'Why didn't anyone take cover?' asked Oswald Birley angrily.

We stared at him open-mouthed, plates in one hand, forks in the other. Why? Because the incident was over before we realized anything weird had happened. Only when the silence came surging back and the blue sky was empty did we take it in. The injured enemy had been only a few feet above us. We would never know if it reached base or was among the planes which fell into the sea that day.

During the rest of August I continued to make my way daily to MTC headquarters, and we started to talk a new jargon. Instead of merely turning up we 'reported for duty' and a drawing-room lecture on petrol filters had to be called 'Maintenance'. Members of the MTC purchased their uniforms at the top tailors of Savile Row. Other ranks in the ATS had to wear bulgy outfits from the quartermaster's store, whereas we trooped to Hardy Amies for fittings – and the broad-shouldered, slim-waisted look of the thirties suited young women.

However, the MTC did want to make certain its drivers *could* drive, so a very ancient car, with brake and accelerator in opposite-to-usual places, was used for tests. Round Hyde Park Corner I bumped, trying madly to concentrate on the pedals and hoping no friends would see me in my smart new khaki on this ignoble jaunt.

Final selection of members for the Kenya Unit was scheduled to take place during a ten-day camp where the dedicated could learn to remove wheels and mend punctures with a stiff upper lip. Tin basins and sleeping bags could be begged or borrowed and 'rheumatic drivers' were allowed to bring camp beds! Hilariously we dragged our equipment to headquarters and were lined up along Ebury Street to be photographed by the press. Tin hats were issued and added to the tiresome gas-masks which everyone had to carry. It was 28 August 1940 – a hot day, almost ominously still and expectant. There seemed to be few people in the streets. Occasional ack-ack fire sounded and a few high German raiders sailed across the sky. I noticed the trees of London squares were just touched with gold.

At Euston Station we debussed and made our way with much saluting and laughter to our train. Amused porters carried our heavy bed-rolls, and our officers, whom we now addressed as 'Madam', did the tipping. An hour away in Hertfordshire a fine beech grove had been made available by its lady owner. The big house, Gaddeston Place, from which civilian faces peered at us admiringly, was out of bounds but tents awaited and a water supply had been laid on by means of long hoses.

An advance party of MTC stalwarts was already cooking our evening meal. It smelt delicious. We were three or four to a tent and having arranged our belongings and been implored not to incapacitate ourselves by tripping over guyropes, we fell happily into sleeping bags on the crackly dry beech leaves.

Next morning in the rosy light of dawn a bugle awoke us. I realized the MTC could even produce a girl with puffing cherub cheeks to blow Reveille. Most of the next ten days was solemnly devoted to jungle lore. Divided into 'troops', we also lurched off into the shimmering woods for lectures on engines. We tugged at wheels, twisted spanners, mended punctures and made friends. Above all we made friends.

A zealous lady wearing captain's pips instructed us in woodcraft – there was a competition for the best twig soap-holders – and we learned that almost every object on which civilization depends can be made of twigs and twine. But of the eighty who had boarded the train for this selection camp quite a number sneaked away. The initial cry about picking the Kenya Unit with a toothcomb faded as members of the MTC slid back to London, having decided they were better fitted to other jobs. In 1940 you could still *choose*.

A telegram arrived for me. My corporal, a pale-faced girl with charming manners, waited anxiously while I tore open the envelope. It was not bad news. It was Rose asking if she could join the camp three days late. I hurried to an officer. 'A new recruit, Madam. May she. . . ?' 'Certainly.' So Rose arrived from Mama's cottage, which was only ten miles away. She had hired a limousine for the journey and wore what she imagined would approximate to our uniform – brown tweeds and a round felt hat with turned-up brim which made her look about twelve years old. Rose had decided that Kenya needed her. The little son Peter could be left with his pretty nurse safe in the country with a variety of test pilots and fighter pilots to guard him.

Rose had brought plenty of gear but she didn't get on with it too well – and found that the beechnuts which got into her blankets tickled. However, she ran like mad when the bugle blew and gallantly tried to drill. I'd got the hang of it by now, but Rosie, who stood next to me, would stand at ease by stamping her right foot instead of her left foot so it always came down on my toes. A route march proved too much. This was a full-dress affair, in which we wore tin hats and carried gas masks. 'In twos. In threes,' shouted our exuberant sergeant major and away we strode *singing*. Farm workers stared agog while far up in the pale blue sky enemy bombers hummed.

Next day Rose whispered, 'I don't think this is for me. I must get to a telephone.' I remonstrated. 'We aren't allowed to phone.' But she managed it. A limousine reappeared and the Lady Burgh drove away, still in her round felt hat with up-turned brim, looking not twelve but ten years old, and rather guilty.

I finished the course with inordinate enjoyment, and on 7 September we travelled back to London. While we were marching in tin hats and making twig furniture, the Battle of Britain was being fought over our heads. As the bus returned us from Euston to Ebury Street we noticed houses that had been standing ten days before lying in rubble. The bus driver dropped us off at corners near our various homes. Strangely enough there *were* taxis around on this the date on which Hitler's terror raids began. On that very afternoon Göring and Kesselring were standing on the Cap Blanc Nez cliffs watching 1000 aircraft make for London. Göring had announced over the radio, 'I myself have taken command of the Luftwaffe's battle for Britain,' and while we waved for taxis the sky overhead became streaked with condensation trails from fighting aircraft. I found myself alone in the flat and that evening was very noisy indeed. In fact I thought wistfully of our tents in the quiet beech grove.

While London absorbed its first air raids we never ceased to wonder at craters in familiar streets and to stare bemusedly at Spitfires and Messerschmitts engaging in dog fights – silver flies weaving white trails of vapour. And none of us – literally none – not the air marshals, nor the Cabinet, nor Göring sitting in his special train in France – realized that during these few days Germany lost the war. She lost the Battle of Britain because Hitler was diverting his bombers from our fighter airfields to attack London. And while the Führer switched from vital targets, England had the luck to have Air Marshal Dowding at the head of Fighter Command. He had no publicity and few of us had heard of the man who was winning the Battle of Britain over our heads.

We ourselves felt no sense of catastrophe for London under bombardment presented terrific theatre. Pa would arrive tired after a night of 'sweeping up fire bombs' as he called it and he seemed content as never before. Although he was so highly strung, danger meant nothing to Pa, nor could the crash of bombs ruffle this man who became hysterical if a housemaid zoomed around with a carpet sweeper while he was writing! Now he had found his niche for the duration of this war. He *liked* sleeping on a camp bed, and he *liked* eating at the Home Guard canteen. Carrying the obligatory gas-mask jammed with books, and permitted to devise a peculiar uniform of his own, Pa could, when off duty, trot around London to cheer up nervy lady friends. The mixture of danger, discipline and freedom suited him. Watching the docks on fire from a rooftop stimulated him into writing sonnets. And when we stood together in Hyde Park watching the Dornier that had just bombed Buckingham Palace being shot down, we both hurried home to scribble accounts of its wings floating like teatrays in the sky while the crew descended by parachute to Victoria Station!

Every now and again Lionel would turn up from the Cameron Highlanders. Once Pa said, 'We three must be photographed together in uniform.' So we walked out to find a professional photographer, but just around the corner we came on an enormous new crater – and there we asked a passer-by to snap us with my camera.

I could see exactly how my father and uncles were going to spend the war – Pa in that old-style tin hat, Lionel in kilt and sporran, and Uncle Seymour, whose lameness had prevented him ever getting into uniform, announced that he was settling down in London for the duration because without his organizing power no fresh food would reach Queen Charlotte's Maternity Hospital. 'And I shall continue with the debutante's ball – Mary Churchill has *got* to come out next year and where else can Winston and Clemmie give her a proper party? Queen Charlotte's Annual Ball in Grosvenor House must go right on. Devil take the bombs.'

Curiously enough, Pa could from his camp bed at Home Guard headquarters reach out a hand and telephone the Prime Minister. One night Winston, who slept in a concrete shelter built near Downing Street, rang him up with a sudden idea. 'What do you remember about our American grandfather, Leonard Jerome? We want to bring America into the war. . . . Hasn't our grandfather's story got some appeal?'

Pa knew little about Leonard Jerome – he had been only six when he died and although he could remember seeing old Grandpa Jerome sitting in a red velvet chair, Winston, who had been sixteen, certainly had clearer memories. Pa started to collect anecdotes about him in the midst of the London Blitz, but he was really more interested in chasing fire bombs with what he called his 'broom'! And eventually he would hand all the Jerome material to me.

Meanwhile MTC training continued. When the day came for 'Convoy Practice' we drove forth in cars of every description, instructed to watch the leader signalling turns and stops with painted paddles. We reached Hyde Park and started to crawl around in caterpillar formation. This activity came to a halt when air-raid sirens wailed. Normally we did not pay attention, but as we were in uniform it was considered right and proper that we should obey official instructions. So we climbed out of our vehicles and retired into the big park shelters. Distant bombs fell. An hour passed. We grew restless. Then an MTC officer arrived with a tape measure which she wrapped around our waists and busts in the half-light, pencilling the results in a notebook marked 'Tropical Kit'.

Next day, the MTC issued kit bags. 'No civilian clothes allowed. You have got to be able to carry your own luggage.' All the Kenya Unit now needed was to get off. But this did not seem easy. The original eighty girls who had gone to camp had melted to sixty and now many of these felt they ought to remain in England driving for the MTC in case of invasion.

Mrs Newall, who was to be our commanding officer, appeared on the scene wearing the best-cut uniform of all, with a real revolver at her waist. With this chic appendage she had been away raising funds for new ambulances. The response to Penny Otto's escape had been electric. A dozen Dodge vans donated by New York department stores were to travel from the USA to Africa direct.

A list appeared on the MTC notice board naming the Kenya Unit. I was among the forty-three privates; there were also eight corporals, two sergeants, and one unfortunate girl found herself nominated sergeant major. The day after she read of her new status, Patricia Woodhouse was ordered to officiate at a parade for the High Commissioner of South Africa, which would be watched by the press. Mrs Newall explained that all Patricia had to do was march us down Whitehall to the High Commissioner's office in Downing Street. We all knew how to march didn't we? Left-right, left-right? Then just before we lined up Mrs Newall announced that we must salute the Cenotaph in passing. This was really too much. We hadn't reached 'Eyes right', but we started off and an air raid came to our rescue. The streets emptied. Ack-ack made it impossible for Pat's impassioned commands to be heard (or overheard by fleeing journalists). Fifty girls of the Kenya Unit turned their heads as one – or almost as one – but our audience had gone underground.

As air raids intensified the MTC began asking us *not* to report daily! Ebury Street had become a particularly unsalubrious zone. Occasionally when wending my way home I had been frightened. It was lonely when the sirens went and suddenly the streets became empty. Once when a V of German bombers was sailing overhead I stood to watch the glint of our attacking Spitfires. Then, as bombs landed, I scuttled down the nearest area steps. An old servant opened the door and drew me into the basement. After ten minutes' silence I left. 'Thank you,' I said. 'Oh, that Hitler!' she replied, angrily staring upward.

It was about three in the afternoon. At Hyde Park Corner there was not a soul in sight. Not a car. Nothing. I glanced apprehensively across the wide open spaces to be crossed before I reached Park Lane where, even if one had not read its advertisements, the Dorchester Hotel always looked so safe. Pa often went there to see Lady Cunard, who had moved to a suite. One felt death so unlikely at the Dorchester – especially at Lady Cunard's table while launching a *bon mot*.

The nights became extraordinary. I was now sleeping alone in Mama's flat and seldom looked in on the basement which had been turned into a local air-raid shelter, but one night bomb crashes or our own ack-ack kept lifting the bedclothes off my legs. So I reversed previous decisions. One glance at the families lying on mattresses drove me out into the cool night air. I stood gazing up into the night sky which hummed with enemy planes flying in V formation like wild geese. The incredibility of German bombers right there overhead – over Mama's flat with its Chippendale chairs and Chinese panels! Odd things amaze. It was after all perfectly logical for enemy bombers to keep formation, but I never ceased to be surprised at the neat arrow shape in which bombers flew. For some strange reason this V-shape made them seem part of a dream.

Towards dawn there usually came a quiet spell. Then one crept back to bed and slept. Meanwhile those German crews who had returned safely were, I suppose, being given breakfast in the mess.

18
Farewell

During that month of September 1940 London changed. My mind centred on how to get to MTC headquarters in Ebury Street each morning and the staff there – all volunteer clerks and typists – began to look haggard as drivers debated if they should remain in the Kenya Unit or serve at home during the expected invasion.

September was entirely different to August. London's docks went up in flames and bombs crashed in the streets one knew. The city's aspect altered – she was like a beautiful woman having teeth knocked out. People who left London even for a few days could not imagine the routine of those who remained. One minded such curious things. It was painful to see that historic Elizabethan mansion, Holland House, go up in flames. It also caused us indignation when Hardy Amies' button-holing machine in Savile Row received a hit and tunics were returned to the MTC with no possible method of fastening!

Within a fortnight of the Vincents' escape from France, Rose had received a Dublin phonecall. She cried with laughter. 'Darling, Derry has telephoned from Ireland that I have got to procure for her twelve chiffon handkerchiefs only made by Fortnum and Mason.'

By then shopping in Piccadilly was none too easy, but we walked across Regent's Park to Oxford Circus where we noticed with dismay that several big department stores had been hit by bombs. Smoke was pouring out of John Lewis and Peter Robinson's. But the quest for chiffon handkerchiefs had filled us with demonic determination and we marched on.

When we returned with what the salesgirl called 'the last *two* chiffon handkerchiefs in Europe', it was to discover that several elegant Nash houses in Park Crescent had been demolished by a bomb and my great-aunt Consie, now eighty-two, who lived a few doors away, had somewhat indignantly decided to retreat to Bowood in Wiltshire. Exhausted maids were packing and they were all about to join Kitty and the great-grandchildren. Trains still ran from Paddington Station.

A day or so later Paul's cousin, Princess Katia Galitzine, was on her way to work when a bomb fell on her bus in Regent Street. She and two others were carried out of the wrecked vehicle while a call went to other buses held up by the crater for a doctor. 'No doctor. Fetch an Orthodox priest,' Katia said as she died.

Amidst the tragedies, the sorrows and bewilderment of soldiers who returned on leave to find homes in rubble and families killed, we continued to ask our headquarters what we should do. The MTC had always distinguished itself in action and one or two girls were released from the Women's Army to join us and so was a lady in air-force blue. They knew how to march rather well, but now as a mark of favour the Grenadier Guards loaned its drill sergeant to the MTC for the day. Amidst incessant crashes and with enemy planes fighting overhead we solemnly tried to learn a new kind of turn in Chester Square. Round and round we marched. My diary records: 'The sergeant major had a huge moustache. Unfortunately we could not understand his cries of "Squad – Hup – Hup" but it was less terrifying than being marched under the wheels of cars by our own girl.'

One morning an MTC dispatch rider reached the flat on a motorcycle. She wore leggings, goggles, helmet – the lot. 'Look here,' she said standing in the door, 'if you are determined to go the unit will be sailing in two weeks. The MTC suggests you clear off on embarkation leave. Here is your travel permit for Ireland. When you get back report to HQ – if the house is still standing – and get further instructions.'

She was one of those jolly apple-cheeked English country girls – generally seen in jodhpurs holding their hunters at horse shows. 'Tell them I'll be back before 15 October,' I said, snatching the permit. She grinned, waved and drove off on her motor-cycle which responded to a workmanlike kick of her gaitered leg.

When in uniform travel was free. Papers in hand, I boarded the train for Liverpool. There was no problem getting on the boat and I had learned from others the etiquette for entering neutral Ireland. Sitting in the morning train out of Belfast I waited for the Border. Armagh, Killylea, Tynan – the next station would be Glaslough in the Irish Republic. Off came my cap and over my tunic went a mackintosh.

Dawson our old groom was waiting with my great-grandparents' brougham pulled by a fine new horse named Diamond, Mama's present to Granny Leonie and Papa Jack for their diamond wedding. She could hardly guess that Diamond would be their sole means of transport for the next five years!

The difference between England and Ireland in 1940 was very extraordinary but the thousands of Irishmen who joined the British forces found it perfectly normal to travel back on leave, disguise their uniforms as they entered their own country, and then bring back butter and whiskey for their chums.

So there I was – two miles over the Border in neutral Eire – back on the doorstep of Castle Leslie, welcomed for what was called 'leave before proceeding overseas'. The servants rejoiced and the family took my going pretty well. Considering that Jack was a prisoner of war and Desmond about to join the RAF, someone might have demurred. But although Mama suggested wistfully that I should remain at home for a bit, 'to fatten up' as she put it, neither she nor my grandmother tried to hold me back.

I knew it would not be easy for them to endure this second world war in an Irish backwater while their sons – Granny's remaining three sons and Mama's two – lived in danger. But philosophically they faced the fact that I, the only girl in two generations, was off to the ends of the earth. Granny was intrigued by my uniform, but the Kenya Unit flash sewn to my tunic worried her. 'Isn't your destination a secret?' she asked. She had been taught to be so discreet.

In my diary for 8 October 1940 I wrote: 'Walked through the brilliant woods and had discussions with Gran by her fire. She was wrapped in pink tulle held by diamond butterflies and reading over old letters. On the mantel stood an old-fashioned photo of her in tight black velvet with a naughty-faced little boy in high boots – it is Winston aged six, tie askew. Near it lies last week's letter from Clemmie saying, "Pray for us." '

In my bones I knew this was the last time I would see my grandparents for they were over eighty. My grandmother sensed the fragility of every moment. I spent hours sitting with her in the mauve bedroom discussing that world she had seen destroyed in 1914 and then hurrying to the red bedroom for a tête-à-tête with my mother who was frightened not only of U-boats that might sink our ship but also of freckles which could mar my complexion. She still produced wonderful remarks such as, 'Don't get sunburnt in Africa – men hate it.'

Bill Vincent, whose farewell dinner in London had only got him as far as Omagh – twenty-five miles away in Northern Ireland – came over from his regiment to see my grandmother. Bill was twenty-three and I heard him laughing with her. 'I've been brought up in the Ritz Hotels of Europe but now I've found home – it's the mess of the Enniskillen Fusiliers and I love it.' When he left he murmured, 'Scent, tulle and – and all for me – ' There lay the magic of her generation. She made him feel how important he was to her.

Outside I visited the estate workers – just as I used to as a child. And there was wishing of good luck. Eight men worked on the farm and four in the garden. The foresters, whose thinning and felling of trees was to be diverted during summer seasons into cutting turf, would never see a bomber cross the sky or know the sounds of battle. When soldiers came home on leave there might be great fireside tales but Ireland would suffer no hardship, except that the trains – always slow – went slower and cars disappeared entirely from the roads. The whole place seemed unchangeable. Wells, our very English butler, humiliated at finding himself in a neutral country, had painted the top-floor window-panes dark blue to show sympathy with the North. It galled him that houses only two miles away should have full blackout regulations while Glaslough village could blaze with light.

Mama's health was deteriorating. She no longer played tennis or golf – only bridge. As petrol in Ireland had become non-existent the bank-manager's wife and the doctor's daughter travelled twice a week by train from Monaghan town for afternoons of rubbers accompanied by huge teas of cake and hot scones.

No blackout. No food rationing. No petrol. Masses of butter and cream, meat and whiskey. Trains chugged along powered by turf, horses were harnessed to old carriages. Later, when our home-made electric light ceased, Victorian paraffin lamps would be pulled from cupboards. Then no paraffin, only candles. Then even these would be in short supply. But the flickering wood fires never went out in the big icy bedrooms of Castle Leslie, and my mother and grandparents never ceased to dress for dinner, even when they carried hot-water bottles and fur rugs to the dining room. Six servants and two personal maids continued to look after the family. Mr Wells, who was devoted to my grandfather, had condescended to become his valet as well as waiting at table. Castle Leslie would carry on throughout the war like all the big houses of Ireland. The inmates might freeze but huge meals appeared. If you can't export butter and meat you have to eat it!

The day came which was my last. I divided the hours between

mother and grandmother. They wanted to talk about different things. The train to Belfast left at 5 p.m. Mama was set on driving to the station so that she could steal a few more minutes of me. I went to the mauve room to say goodbye to Granny Leonie. She was sitting by the fire – rather quiet for her – all ribbons and lace. I kissed her goodbye. There was a sprig of heliotrope, her favourite flower, in a vase on the table. At the door I turned and she waved, a tiny figure in the big armchair. I waved back and slipped out. For a moment I stood reeling by the closed door while her charm hit me afresh. No wonder all those men had been in love with her in the long ago.

My grandfather came to the front door to see me drive away in the ancient brougham with its frayed blue upholstery and ivory fittings. The old gentleman was getting a little vague. My departure must have reminded him of times he had seen me off to school, for he pressed a tip into my hand. 'Take this my dear and be careful of yourself.' I put the pound note in my pocket and heard my voice saying as so often before, 'Thank you very much. I will do as you say.'

Then I climbed into the carriage beside Mama. Dawson, who had taught me to ride, was crying, 'Whoa. Stand boy,' to the horse. Wells stood on the doorstep and bowed his farewell approvingly.

As we trotted down the drive and out through the Gothic lodge gates the sky had turned yellow and fleets of black rooks were cawing over the woods. October was their noisiest month.

Index